THE COMPLETE IDIOT'S GUIDE® TO

Risk Management

by Annetta Cortez

ALPHA

A member of Penguin Group (USA) Inc.

To my family, who put up with me.

ALPHA BOOKS

Published by the Penguin Group

Penguin Group (USA) Inc., 375 Hudson Street, New York, New York 10014, USA

Penguin Group (Canada), 90 Eglinton Avenue East, Suite 700, Toronto, Ontario M4P 2Y3, Canada (a division of Pearson Penguin Canada Inc.)

Penguin Books Ltd., 80 Strand, London WC2R 0RL, England

Penguin Ireland, 25 St. Stephen's Green, Dublin 2, Ireland (a division of Penguin Books Ltd.)

Penguin Group (Australia), 250 Camberwell Road, Camberwell, Victoria 3124, Australia (a division of Pearson Australia Group Pty. Ltd.)

Penguin Books India Pvt. Ltd., 11 Community Centre, Panchsheel Park, New Delhi—110 017, India

Penguin Group (NZ), 67 Apollo Drive, Rosedale, North Shore, Auckland 1311, New Zealand (a division of Pearson New Zealand Ltd.)

Penguin Books (South Africa) (Pty.) Ltd., 24 Sturdee Avenue, Rosebank, Johannesburg 2196, South Africa

Penguin Books Ltd., Registered Offices: 80 Strand, London WC2R 0RL, England

International Standard Book Number: 978-1-59257-958-7
Library of Congress Catalog Card Number: 2009932959

12   11   10   8   7   6   5   4   3   2   1

Interpretation of the printing code: The rightmost number of the first series of numbers is the year of the book's printing; the rightmost number of the second series of numbers is the number of the book's printing. For example, a printing code of 10-1 shows that the first printing occurred in 2010.

Printed in the United States of America

Note: This publication contains the opinions and ideas of its author. It is intended to provide helpful and informative material on the subject matter covered. It is sold with the understanding that the author and publisher are not engaged in rendering professional services in the book. If the reader requires personal assistance or advice, a competent professional should be consulted.

The author and publisher specifically disclaim any responsibility for any liability, loss, or risk, personal or otherwise, which is incurred as a consequence, directly or indirectly, of the use and application of any of the contents of this book.

Most Alpha books are available at special quantity discounts for bulk purchases for sales promotions, premiums, fundraising, or educational use. Special books, or book excerpts, can also be created to fit specific needs.

For details, write: Special Markets, Alpha Books, 375 Hudson Street, New York, NY 10014.

Publisher: *Marie Butler-Knight*
Editorial Director: *Mike Sanders*
Senior Managing Editor: *Billy Fields*
Senior Acquisitions Editor: *Paul Dinas*
Development Editor: *Jennifer Moore*
Senior Production Editor: *Janette Lynn*

Copy Editor: *Teresa Elsey*
Cartoonist: *Steve Barr*
Cover Designer: *Kurt Owens*
Book Designer: *Trina Wurst*
Indexer: *Angie Bess*
Layout: *Chad Dressler*
Proofreader: *John Etchison*

Contents at a Glance

Part 1:   **What Is Risk Management?**   1

1   What Is Risk?   3
Types of risk, pitfalls companies face, and the whole business of uncertain outcomes.

2   Why Manage Risk?   15
How risk helps you protect the downside and grow the upside of your business.

3   Why Is Risk Management So Hard to Implement?   27
How to overcome in-house resistance to implementing risk management processes.

4   Risk Management Guidelines   37
Rules of thumb for successfully establishing an enduring risk management capability

5   Introducing the Risk Management Process   49
The four key steps of the process: identify, measure and assess, manage, monitor.

Part 2:   **What Causes Risk?**   59

6   Categorizing Risk   61
Risk's main categories and subcategories.

7   Which Risks Are Lurking in Your Shop?   75
Get to know your risks by understanding your organization and the type of business you are in.

Part 3:   **Assessing Risk**   89

8   How Do You Measure Up?   91
All the reasons for building and using risk measures and models.

9   Forecasting Risks   103
How to compare risks, use leading and lagging indicators, and analyze events that led to losses.

10   Impact!   121
The differences between expected loss and unexpected loss—and how to measure them.

Part 4:   Managing and Mitigating Risk   **137**

    11   Treating Risk   139
         *The four methods of treating risk and how to choose the
         best methods for your company.*

    12   Reducing the Likelihood of Risk Events   149
         *The use of risk limits, triggers, controls, and outsourcing
         to reduce the chances of a risk event occurring.*

    13   Reducing the Impact   161
         *What happens when a risk event has already occurred?
         Techniques for reducing the impact on your business.*

Part 5:   Deep Dive: Focused Solutions   **175**

    14   Measuring and Managing Strategic Risks   177
         *The special challenges and specific ways of addressing
         your strategic risk.*

    15   Measuring and Managing Financial Risks   187
         *How to size up financial roadblocks—and
         opportunities—to best utilize your cash and reserves.*

    16   Measuring and Managing Operational Risks   199
         Ways to use your own resources to secure your operations.

Part 6:   Integration   **209**

    17   Inviting and Integrating Risk   211
         *How to introduce the risk management process to your
         business.*

    18   Integrating Risk into Business Governance   221
         *The myriad ways to create the framework for effective
         oversight of risk management.*

    19   Integrating Risk into Your Organization   233
         *The four lines of defense that make risk management
         everyone's business.*

    20   Building Risk into the Business Process   247
         *Ways to develop a new business rhythm that weaves
         together daily operations and risk management.*

    21   Your Risk Appetite   263
         *How hungry are you for risk? What is the right amount
         for your business?*

22 Profiting from Risk   277
    You, too, can make money from risk measures!

23 Lessons Learned   293
    Three case studies sum up the pitfalls, processes, and
    many benefits of effective risk management.

Appendixes

    A Glossary   307

    B Risk Categories Cheat Sheet   319

    C Simple Risk Equations   323

    D Risk Management Resources   327

       Index   333

Contents

Part 1: What Is Risk Management?   1

1 What Is Risk?   3

Uncertain Outcomes 4

How Do You Define Risk? 4

   Possibility of Loss or Injury......................................5

   Volatility...6

Types of Risk 6

Risk and Reward..7

   Modern Portfolio Theory...8

   Measuring and Comparing Risk and Return 8

Company Pitfalls 10

   Higher Return, Higher Risk 10

   Overdiversification..10

   Too Many Little Risks 11

   "It Can't Happen to Us"..11

   "It's Never Happened Before"..................................12

2 Why Manage Risk?   15

What Kills Companies? 16

Protect That Downside! 17

   Fewer Fires to Fight 18

   Fewer Management Surprises..................................18

   Reduced Earnings Volatility....................................19

   Reduced Budget Blowouts 19

   Protection of Assets..20

   More Efficient Issues Resolution 21

Grow the Upside 21

   Improved Competitiveness 21

   Improved Returns Relative to Risk 22

   Improved Efficiencies and Quality 22

   Improved Communication 23

   Increased Employee Confidence 23

Manage Obligations 24

   Reduced Fines and Compliance Costs 24

   Reduced Consequences..24

   Reduced Litigation 25

   Reduced Insurance Costs 25

   Reduced Business Interruptions.............................25

3 Why Is Risk Management So Hard to Implement?   **27**

Resistance to Change 28
Not Invented Here..29
Transparency Is Scary...30
Do We Have to Do It? 31
Finding and Managing the Right Data 31
How Do We Know It's Right?..32
Other Tough Questions 33
Stalling the Process 34
Achieving a Balance..34
Upper-Level Support 35

4 Risk Management Guidelines   **37**

Know Your Risks 38
Know Your Appetite for Risk..40
Use a Common Language 40
Develop Capabilities Right for You...41
Implement Simple Measures and Approaches 41
    Fit Capabilities into Existing Processes....................................*42*
    Don't Overdo It *43*
Provide Clear Direction..43
Expect the Unexpected 44
    Don't Be Afraid to Forecast..*45*
    Pay Attention *45*
Continuously Make Improvements 46

5 Introducing the Risk Management Process   **49**

What Are the Key Steps?...50
    Step 1: Identify Risks *51*
    Step 2: Measure and Assess Risks..*52*
    Step 3: Manage Risks *52*
    Step 4: Monitor Risks *53*
Establishing the Context...54
Dealing with Stakeholders 55
Communicating with Stakeholders...55
    The Process..*56*
    The Form..*56*
Things to Remember 57

Part 2:   What Causes Risk?   **59**

6   Categorizing Risk   **61**

Why Categorize Risk? 62
Rules of Thumb 62
   Mutually Exclusive, Collectively Exhaustive 62
   Industry-Specific Risks 62
Risk Categories and Subcategories................................63
   Strategic/Business Risks...64
   Strategic Risk at Work 65
   Financial Risks 66
   Financial Risk at Work 68
   Operational Risks...69
   Operational Risks at Work 71
Who Holds These Risks? 72

7   Which Risks Are Lurking in Your Shop?   **75**

Know Your Business...76
   Industry Risks...77
   Size and Growth Projection......................................77
   How Established Are You?..78
   Competitive Landscape 79
   Suppliers..80
   Customers...80
Know Your Organization 81
   Company Mission and Product 82
   The Workforce 83
   Governance and Decision-Making.............................84
   Processes and Controls 84
   Systems and Technology..84
Rolling Up Your Sleeves 85
   Strengths, Weaknesses, Opportunities, and Threats......85
   Use Your Organization 86
   What Keeps You Up at Night?...................................86
   War-Gaming..87
   Call the Experts...87

Part 3:   Assessing Risk   **89**

8   How Do You Measure Up?   **91**

Why Measure Risk? 92
   How Much Mitigation Do You Need? 92

Using Risk Measures 93
  Some Basic Rules 94
  Keeping It Simple 95
Key Measurement Concepts 96
  Likelihood and Probability 96
  How Will They Impact Me? 96
  Estimating Severity 97
  How Do They Relate to Each Other? 98
  How Will They Look over Time? 99
What to Measure 99
  How Risks Are Distributed 100
  Risk vs. Return 101

9 Forecasting Risks   103

Comparing Risks 104
  The Risk Matrix 104
  Consequence and Likelihood Tables 105
Working the Comparisons 107
Implementation 109
What Are the Odds? 109
  How to Establish Likelihood 110
  Working with the Odds 111
  Rank Ordering Risks 111
  A Simpler Approach 112
Analyzing What Happened 112
  Events That Lead to Losses 113
  How Did Events Occur? 114
  How Much Did It Hurt? 114
  Dealing with Recurring Events 115
  Focusing on the Aftermath 116
Leading and Lagging Indicators 117
  What Are They Good For? 118
  Applying Indicators 118

10 Impact!   121

Expected Loss 121
  Measure It Up 122
  Figuring in Expected Loss 122
Unexpected Loss 123
  Measure It Up 123
  Figuring in Unexpected Loss 124

Measuring Groups of Risks...126
   Bottom-Up Approaches.......................................*127*
   A Top-Down Approach.......................................*129*
   Putting Them to Use *129*
Conducting Stress Tests...130
   Key Approaches..*130*
   Putting Them to Use *131*
Converting Measures to Money 132
Analyzing Risk and Reward 134
   Key Approaches..*134*
   Putting Them to Use *136*

Part 4: Managing and Mitigating Risk   137

11   Treating Risk   139

Initial Considerations...140
Methods for Treating Risk...140
   Avoid It..*141*
   Transfer It..*142*
   Reduce the Likelihood......................................*143*
   Reduce the Impact...*144*
Choosing the Right Methods for Your Risks.....................144
   Evaluating Options...*145*
   Residual Risk..*145*
   Cost-Benefit Analysis *146*
   Choosing a Cost-Benefit Option *147*
   Putting the Plan in Place....................................*147*

12   Reducing the Likelihood of Risk Events   149

Limiting Your Exposure to Risks..................................150
   Understanding Risk Limits *151*
   Building Risk Exposure Limits...............................*152*
Triggers and Controls 153
   Types of Triggers and Controls...............................*154*
   Using Triggers and Controls *154*
"Outsourcing" Your Risks 155
   Thinking About Outsourcing *155*
   Risks That Can Be Outsourced...............................*156*
Working with Your People 157
   Workplace Culture and Environment *157*
   Training and Education......................................*158*

     People-Based Controls *158*
     Incentives...*158*
     Checklists...*159*

13 Reducing the Impact   **161**

    Contingency Plans...162
     Cash Crisis Liquidity Plan *162*
     Business Continuity Plan..*163*
     Disaster Recovery Plan...*163*
     Key Considerations *164*
     Putting Them to Use *165*
    Buffers and Reserves 166
     How They Work *166*
     Implementing Buffers and Reserves *167*
    Hedging 168
     Natural Hedges *169*
     How Hedging Works...*170*
    Diversification 171
    Insurance...172
     Key Considerations...*173*
     What Should You Insure? *173*

Part 5: Deep Dive: Focused Solutions   **175**

14 Measuring and Managing Strategic Risk   **177**

    Measuring and Analyzing Strategic Risk...................................178
     Watch the Signals *178*
     Build Awareness *178*
     Know Who's Watching...*179*
     Consider Stakeholders *180*
     When All Else Fails *180*
    Managing and Mitigating Strategic Risk..................................181
     What's in the Plan? *181*
     Range of Outcomes...*182*
     How to Buffer for Strategic Risk *183*
    Pitfalls in Managing Strategic Risks 184
     Don't Ignore It *184*
     Get Out of the Past..*184*
     Be Aware of Changes in Complexity..*184*

15 Measuring and Managing Financial Risks **187**

Measuring and Analyzing Financial Risk 188
    What to Do About Credit Risk..................................*188*
    What to Do About Market Risk.................................*189*
Managing and Mitigating Financial Risks..............................191
    Using Reserves..*192*
    Using Buffers *192*
    Combining Buffers and Reserves.............................*193*
    Financial Hedging *194*
    Real Live Diversification..................................*195*
Pitfalls in Managing Financial Risk....................................196

16 Measuring and Managing Operational Risks **199**

Measuring and Analyzing Operational Risk...........................200
    What's the Score? *200*
    Take It to the Team......................................*201*
    Using Loss Event Capture.................................*202*
    Root Cause Analysis *203*
Managing and Mitigating Operational Risks 205
    Be Prepared *205*
    Back to the Team Again *207*
Building Buffers..207

Part 6: Integration **209**

17 Inviting and Integrating Risk **211**

Where to Build In Risk Approaches....................................212
    Governance..*212*
    Organization..*213*
    Culture..*213*
    Business Processes *215*
    New Projects..*215*
Choosing What's Right for Your Business 216
    Striking the Balance *216*
    Things to Consider......................................*217*

18 Integrating Risk into Business Governance **221**

Role of Management..222
    Committees..*223*
    Independence..*223*

Stakeholder Management 225
   Customer Management..225
   Employee Management 226
   Board and Advisory Group Management 226
Your Policy Framework..227
   Reviewing Company Policies..228
   Building Risk into Policies...228
   Managing Policy Implementation...229
Meshing Risk Culture and Your Business Values....................229
   What Sets Great Apart from Good?...230
   Culture vs. Investment...231
   Business Blow-Ups: Case Studies 231

19 Integrating Risk into Your Organization   233

Building the Framework 234
Risk Management Is Everyone's Business 234
Four Lines of Defense..235
   The Front Line: Business Management and Risk.......................235
   Running Alongside: Compliance Management...........................236
   The Backstop: Audit..238
   Setting the Tone: Senior Management and Board.....................239
Who Are Your Risk Managers? 240
   Human Resources..241
   Legal..241
   Strategic Planning...241
   Finance/Accounting...242
Managing Risk Through Employee Compensation 243
   Using Incentives..244
   Linking Performance to Incentives 245

20 Building Risk into the Business Process   247

Three Keys to Integration 248
Develop a Business Rhythm...248
   Including Risk in Your Business Plans....................................249
   Incorporating the Risk Appetite Statement.............................250
   Budgeting Risk 250
   Driving Business Through Risk and Reward 251
   Allocating Economic Capital...252
   Using RAROC vs. Economic Profit 253
   Forecasting Risks...253

Setting Performance Targets 254
Benefits of Risk vs. Reward 254
Keep Your Finger on the Pulse 255
Building Risk Controls into Business Processes 255
A Builder's Approach 256
Monitoring Exposures 257
Monitoring Groups of Risk 257
Reporting 258
The Key Elements of a Report 259
Identify Your Audience 259
Create an Impact 260
Set a Schedule 261

21 Your Risk Appetite   **263**

The Broad Concepts 264
The Risk Appetite Statement 264
How Hungry Are You for Risk? 265
What Is the Right Amount of Risk? 266
More on Credit Ratings 267
Target Risk and Return 268
How Do I Take Control? 268
Key Questions to Ask 269
Building Your Risk Appetite Statement 270
Navigating Through Risk Appetite 270
Setting Boundaries 272
Determining the Framework 272
Putting It to Work 274

22 Profiting from Risk   **277**

Risk and Reward Day to Day 278
Where to Look 278
Three Opportunity Areas 279
Developing and Targeting Products 280
Using Risk Information to Target Customers 281
Categorizing Customers 282
Customer Scorecards and Risk Profiles 283
Considering Risk in Pricing 284
A Risk Pricing Equation 284
Customer Considerations 285

Managing Customers 286
  Customer Profitability *286*
  Managing the Downside *288*
  Collecting from Customers *288*
Creating Better Processes 289
  Staging Process Decisions *289*
  Process Streamlining *290*

23 Lessons Learned   **293**

Case Study: Know Your Business 294
  Introducing Extensive Enterprise, Inc. *294*
  What's the Case? *295*
  What Went Wrong? *296*
  Mopping It Up *297*
Case Study: Keep It Simple 298
  Introducing HiTechUS *298*
  What's the Case? *299*
  What Went Wrong? *301*
  Mopping It Up *302*
Case Study: Using the Right Yardstick 302
  Introducing the GoGrow Company *303*
  What's the Case? *303*
  What Went Wrong? *304*
  Mopping It Up *305*
It's a Wrap 305

Appendixes

A Glossary   **307**

B Risk Categories Cheat Sheet   **319**

C Simple Risk Equations   **323**

D Risk Management Resources   **327**

   Index   **333**

Introduction

Risk management is one of those specialized business practices that can make anyone feel like an idiot. Which is to say, you're not an idiot. You can't possibly be: you picked up this book and are willing to take a brand-new approach to managing your business!

Risk management takes you through a parallel world of threats, risks, and processes. You may have been in business for 5 years, or 10, or 20. Maybe you are just starting a business. Perhaps you're a manager or employee of a company.

Whatever the case, this journey differs from any you have taken before. It will teach you things about your business and industry that you never knew.

I have worked at all levels of business with all forms of risk management. I have helped small businesses troubleshoot their systems and operations and build simple solutions that reduce or eliminate their risk. I have helped some of our nation's biggest financial institutions—Citigroup, the Federal Reserve—and the governments of other nations work out far more complex risk problems.

I love the challenge of identifying a risk, figuring out what to do about it, building the right measure or model, analyzing it, and resolving the problem. I hope you'll take up the challenge and find it both important and exciting. This book is yours to help you uncover what might ail your business—and then to make your business better.

Let's start our journey.

How to Use This Book

Risk management breaks down into simple steps and processes, all of which you can use in your business.

Part 1, "What Is Risk Management?," introduces the core concepts of risk management. It also helps you develop the rationale for developing risk management capabilities in your business, as well as some of the basics to help you get started.

Part 2, "What Causes Risk?," sets you up with the basic language of risk and allows you to start referring to your risks in the same way as risk professionals.

Part 3, "Assessing Risk," provides you with the core tools and techniques for measuring and assessing the risks that you have identified.

Part 4, "Managing and Mitigating Risk," establishes the range of methods used for managing and mitigating risk—and how to deploy these methods in your business.

Part 5, "Deep Dive: Focused Solutions," provides you with a close-up view of each key risk type and the core methods for measuring and managing each of those risks. You'll also receive helpful hints to avoid the classic pitfalls.

Part 6, "Integration," helps you build risk management into your day-to-day operations and develop a seamless operating environment. You'll also discover ways to make real money out of risk—not just prevent and manage it.

Extras

If nothing else, risk management is about information and awareness. I have a ton of information to share with you, so much that I've spiced up each chapter with some extras, which you'll find under these headings:

def•i•ni•tion

Learn particular terms and phrases that are spoken in the world of risk management.

Best Bets

There are countless ways to solve a risk problem—and these valuable tips make it a lot easier for you.

Red Flags

Since the red flag might as well be the "unofficial" symbol of risk management, these boxes highlight warning signs to be aware of.

Risk Factors

These tidbits of information can help further your understanding of risk—and give you some good little stories to tell your colleagues!

Acknowledgments

Above all, I'd like to thank my loving and patient husband who surprisingly still speaks to me. I'd also like to thank my daughter, Alex, for just being there for Mommy. Your sweet smiles and sense of humor get me through all of this. To the rest of my family, who pitched in to help when it was needed. To Cassie, for being my prototype and listening at every turn. To Kay, who gave me the impetus to do this project. You're still my best student! To my brother, Joe, who thinks I'm the biggest idiot of the lot—only a brother's prerogative. To Bob, the unsung hero. You are the one who made this possible. Finally, to all of my friends, colleagues, and clients through the years, who have helped teach me what I know today.

Trademarks

All terms mentioned in this book that are known to be or are suspected of being trademarks or service marks have been appropriately capitalized. Alpha Books and Penguin Group (USA) Inc. cannot attest to the accuracy of this information. Use of a term in this book should not be regarded as affecting the validity of any trademark or service mark.

Part 1

What Is Risk Management?

You and your business face risks every day. And the more adventurous you are, the more risks you will encounter. Many of those risks are recognizable and obvious, others are subtler, and some haven't developed yet. But even if you can't see the risks, they are there, lurking in the shadows, waiting for something—a decision, a mistake, a change of plans or direction—to materialize.

Every time the doors to your business swing open and the lights switch on, many actual or potential risks await you. Some are well worth taking; after all, success itself is built on taking calculated risks. Other risks need to be kept in check at all costs, so disruptive or damaging is their potential. Still others remain either ever-present or just out of sight, requiring close observation.

What are the differences among the various types of risk? And how do you manage them? Turn the page to find out.

Chapter 1

What Is Risk?

In This Chapter

- ◆ Risk leads to uncertain outcomes
- ◆ Risk appears in different forms
- ◆ Greater risk equals greater reward?
- ◆ The pitfalls of risk

It creeps up in business life, sometimes with plenty of warning—and sometimes without any advance notice whatsoever. It rides the waves of volatile financial markets or rumbles up from something completely out of your control, like a natural disaster. Whether your business planning and performance are poor or exceptional, you can be assured of one thing: risk is the shadow side of your business, waiting for the right conditions to surface and cause problems.

It's how you acknowledge, plan for, manage, and mitigate this risk that defines your risk management approach.

Uncertain Outcomes

Risk is any activity, occurrence, or decision in business or personal life that involves uncertainty. It can accompany even those decisions considered sure bets. Whether the uncertainty leads to negative or positive outcomes depends on the situation, the type of risk, and how the problem or solution affects the business or your life. You can usually feel the uncertainty of a risk in your gut. It's that feeling you get when attempting to dash across a busy street without the assistance of a stoplight or crosswalk.

Different folks handle uncertain outcomes in different ways. Some thrive on them, even becoming addicted to the thrill of living on the edge. They grow visibly excited and measure themselves by their poise while risking everything—from a few dollars to an entire business—on their decisions. Others try to avoid uncertainty whenever possible. Either way, people tend to respond to risk as if it were a drug. This goes particularly for company leaders, who display very specific strengths or weaknesses when they deal with uncertain outcomes.

Observant leaders tend to know when a risk is about to present itself. They plan ahead, read the warning signs, and recognize the weaknesses the upcoming situation could cause in their businesses. Larger companies can hire experts to handle major situations that have uncertain outcomes—often referred to as risk management situations. However, most smaller companies must equip themselves to deal with these situations on their own. Doing so begins with an understanding of how risk is defined in business.

How Do You Define Risk?

In business, risk refers to an event that, whether predictable or not, has an uncertain outcome. Beyond that very general definition, risk is subjective: what one businessperson considers risky, another businessperson might consider safe. Risk has a slightly different meaning for everyone, relative to each person's "risk appetite" and the level of danger or uncertainty in his or her situation.

Businesses try hard to discern future risks. They use a lot of complex measurement science to calculate the level of risk involved in any project. Ultimately, most businesses have the same goals when trying to identify and plan for risk: they seek to incorporate the following predictions into their short- and long-term planning:

◆ **Predictions of loss.** For instance, how to plan for situations when credit that is extended is not paid back.

- ◆ **Predictions of future volatility.** This can either be future volatility of earnings or any of the cash flows. Volatility is the result of changes in the business environment, changes in customer behavior, changes in competition, or even changes in capital markets.

- ◆ **Predictions of cash flows.** For example, how to plan for swings in cash flows due to seasonal cycles in the business or debt load requirements

- ◆ **Predictions of operational events**. How to plan for things like supplier failure, receipt of inferior material, or equipment failure.

Best Bets

Make sure everyone in your company shares the same definition of risk, and be sure to use the same definition when measuring, assessing, and managing risk.

All of these predictions involve trying to address the downside events and manage the upside events.

As it pertains to business, risk involves two important components: the possibility of loss or injury and volatility. Let's look more closely at each of these facets of risk.

Possibility of Loss or Injury

Risk is the possibility of injury, damage, or loss. In business and media reports, this facet of risk—its downside—is the major focus, as losses are most immediately apparent. However, the first half of the definition—"possibility"—is the more important part of this definition of risk. It describes the uncertainty associated with a potential future event. When evaluating risk and creating risk management measures and strategies, businesses try to look into the future. They use measurement approaches such as those described by *actuarial theory*.

def•i•ni•tion

Actuarial theory considers risk as the possibility of loss. It takes that possibility and multiplies it by the severity of loss to arrive at an actual dollar amount. This is the "science" used by actuaries, the people who develop and manage insurance pricing and predictions.

Volatility

Risk is the roller-coaster ride within business activity, an up-and-down journey with plenty of twists and turns along the way—many positive, some negative. *Finance theory* uses this volatility (usually when it comes to earnings) to capture uncertainty in a formal way. The key when evaluating risk is to plan for both positive and negative swings in returns.

def•i•ni•tion

Finance theory deals with investment decisions and the concept of the time value of money. It is derived from the field of economics.

Types of Risk

Once owners and risk managers understand the way risk manifests itself, they can define and measure it. As they become more familiar with risk, owners can often recognize and define a type of risk by analyzing how it germinated and evolved. Managers are then better equipped to develop techniques for managing such risks in the future.

Risk Factors

Risk management theory treats the source of volatility as the core feature of risk and uses the probability and severity of loss to determine the level of volatility. Volatility is synonymous with risk. It affects supply, sales, and cash flow, which are the lifeblood of any business.

This approach helps owners become more aware of hidden or subtle risks, which are at least as potentially dangerous as obvious risks to the business. Once people are aware of risks, they can more easily spot and act upon them.

The types of risk include:

◆ *New risks,* which are associated with new business activities.

◆ *Ever-present risks,* which are always around and constitute the majority of risks a business must face.

◆ *Concentrated risks,* in which several or many smaller, individual risks interact with each other and coalesce into a potential "perfect storm."

◆ *Contagious risks,* in which a small risk triggers an event that creates other risks and other damaging events.

◆ *Sudden risks,* which appear without warning; these include accidents, fires, devastating storms, floods, and sudden political shifts, licensing changes, or governmental actions.

Red Flags _____

Concentration and contagion are two of the biggest threats to your business. They have similar properties, but it is important to distinguish between the two because they require different mitigation approaches. A concentration is a number of small risks that seem to merge into one big event. Contagion is when one event sets off other events and afflicts other parts of the business.

Risk and Reward

Risk is about far more than fearing loss and planning for it. The other side of the "uncertain outcome" of risk is the upside—the reward. After all, risk can have both positive and negative outcomes.

Every time you invest in a stock, you're taking a chance that it could decline markedly or fail. That is a risk. The safer bet would be to put your money in a savings account, CD, or a bank money market, because your deposits are insured by the FDIC. However, the annual return is tiny, less than the rate of inflation. Compare the paltry, albeit very safe, reward of savings accounts to the potential reward of buying stocks: if the company in which you purchase stock takes off or grows handsomely, you could be looking at a 10 percent to 100 percent return—or more—in a single year. Over the course of time, that stock could yield even greater returns. In that case, you would be taking a positive risk and receiving a handsome reward. However, investing in stocks is still a risk: if your stock's value goes to zero, you lose your investment.

Red Flags _____

You've heard the sayings: "No guts, no glory" and "The greater the risk, the greater the reward." The more risk your business takes, the greater its potential reward—but also the greater its potential loss. How much risk do you take? How do you know when you're playing it safe and when you're playing with fire? To save yourself many sleepless nights, find answers to these questions through your risk management process, and then carefully shoot for the stars.

To get ahead of the competition and make a statement in the marketplace, owners must take risks. If you play it safe all the time, you are unlikely to keep up with a highly competitive market. Even the most conservative businessmen and women take risks they feel are necessary to grow their companies or to increase market share. The key is to determine which risks are potentially positive and which are potentially negative.

Modern Portfolio Theory

Risk management professionals often look to *modern portfolio theory (MPT)* to gain a better understanding of how risky a company's holdings and investments might be. When developing this theory, economist Harry Markowitz demonstrated that higher returns were consistently associated with higher volatility. With higher volatility comes higher risk. He also showed that the more a company diversifies its holdings, products, and marketplace, the more its risk can be reduced—to a point. (More on that point later in this chapter.)

def•i•ni•tion

Modern portfolio theory (MPT) proposes how rational investors will use diversification to optimize their portfolios, and how a risky asset should be priced. It compares the expected return of an asset to its expected volatility or standard deviation. The volatility is also viewed as the asset's "risk."

Risk management professionals measure the standard deviation and volatility in the normal course of business. This includes the volatility in the value of all of a company's holdings, investments, and cash flows. They compare this number to actual returns. The differences in amount and timing of volatility associated with each asset, cash flow, or holding means that by holding a variety of different assets, sources of cash flow, or other holdings, they can achieve diversification; and risk can be reduced proportionally. Understanding this diversification is also a key tool in risk management.

Measuring and Comparing Risk and Return

Harry Markowitz's modern portfolio theory helped the risk management industry develop tools and measures that every business owner can use to compare risk and return in a number of meaningful ways, including the following:

◆ Companies can compare the return on their investments to the risk level of the investments.

◆ Businesses can gauge acceptable levels of risk and compare relative returns, adjusted for risk, across different (competing) businesses and activities.

◆ Owners can then determine which products, investments, and activities are risky and which are creating better returns relative to the risk involved, known as a *risk-adjusted return.*

def•i•ni•tion

A **risk-adjusted return** is a simple return (earnings) that is adjusted for losses or costs associated with risk management. That adjusted return is then divided by the amount of risk (measured in dollars) that was associated with the activity. It is an extremely powerful measure because businesses can understand the source of their profitability and risks, then determine if they are achieving adequate returns for the risk they are assuming.

Imagine two small public relations firms that are providing the same service—let's say promoting recreational sports—to the same marketplace. One firm has decided to spend a lot of money on visible advertising, such as signage at Little League fields, banners at running events, and logo-studded bunting at swim meets. Every time a new prospect comes along, the company spends time and money preparing presentations that show that client's visibility months or years down the road. These moves are all risks: if prospective clients don't turn to the company for business or act upon the signage advertising, the company has spent a lot of money for nothing. The company has also decided to bill its clients at industry rates, adjusting nominally for the local market. The company evaluated the potential rewards to the business before taking these actions and concluded that the risk was worth it.

The other company, whose account representatives are just as skilled and qualified, decides to play it safe. The company counts on its community standing, having been around 10 years longer than the other company. It relies on word-of-mouth advertising; after all, the bottom line is tight. In order to appeal to the local market, it always underbids its competitor, securing accounts but operating at a tiny profit margin. This low-risk strategy has kept the company in business, but now the other company is making more money and beginning to win over some of this company's accounts. Local businesses are starting to understand that sometimes they have to spend more money to make more money. Because the older company has lowballed its billing, it cannot respond in kind.

Comparing actual risks to potential rewards is a crucial exercise in business and in risk management. Ask these questions:

How much extra risk does the company take?

Will it be worth it?

Company Pitfalls

Companies face a number of pitfalls when deciding how much risk to bring into their day-to-day operations.

Higher Return, Higher Risk

Many companies forget about volatility as a key factor in risk management. They figure that if they are doing well, they are in good shape and don't need to adjust their plans. Even if they track various losses within the company—from a single product to the whole bottom line—and work to manage loss, they fail to account for the fact that loss levels can rise or drop unexpectedly.

Best Bets

It is important to consider the inevitable ups and downs in any business environment. Project how the business will look in six months, one year, two years, and even five years. Consider what could go wrong and test for risks that other companies in your area or industry have experienced but that haven't afflicted your company yet.

Think of risk as a barge and volatility as a river. That river can rise or fall significantly, depending on how much water is entering or exiting the river. Although a company might identify risk and understand how it works in a stable economy and market—the barge floating on a placid river—it might not be ready for the fluctuations that volatility presents—those times when water levels rise or fall unexpectedly, leaving the barge in danger of floating off course or even hitting bottom.

Ultimately, although managing to an anticipated loss level is good practice, it is not the core of risk management. The core of risk management is being able to plan for unanticipated rises and falls.

Overdiversification

An alternative title for this section might be "Too Much of a Good Thing." Some companies think that diversifying into many different product or service lines—some even serving customers of wide-ranging income levels—is the way to go. "It minimizes risk," they say. "It guarantees that something will sell—no matter how bad the economy is," others add. They are right: diversification does lower risk, up to a point.

Diversification is a double-edged sword. The risk shoots the wrong way—higher—when the areas of diversification do not match the business plan. Diversification can create more risk by forcing a company to adopt techniques or use materials that are new and unfamiliar. This increases the risk of creating services or products that do not meet the high quality standards that the company is known for.

And even if the diversification is consistent with the business plan and up to company standards, it can create more strain on management and resources by setting up operational and financial risks. Diversification works best when it is rolled out slowly and managed carefully.

Too Many Little Risks

Every time a company grows or diversifies, the number of potential risks increases. These can add up to become overwhelming for owners, managers, and others tasked with managing risk.

Many companies are only outwardly focused, worried about competitors, customers, and the bottom line and unaware that they are creating risks each time they offer a new product or service. They may attempt too many strategies or projects at once. Or they may think that they have tackled all of the big issues—and they probably have— and that everything else is solid. However, they may have failed to notice little issues that have snuck between the cracks, issues that can add up and create a messy situation; in fact, they can lead to risk concentration.

Sometimes, owners and managers make the mistake of thinking that their risks are so highly diversified across the broad spectrum of the business that they will never converge with one another. Managers might also assume these risks' potential to cause problems is diluted by the strength of the rest of the company.

Unfortunately, no matter how far such risks are spread across the company, they can become too numerous to handle. Too many is too many, and then owners can't get their arms around them. This also increases the risk of contagion, which will certainly affect every aspect of the company.

"It Can't Happen to Us"

Everyone wants to be Superman. Every business owner wants to feel invincible, on top of the market, their customers' needs, the bottom line, … the world. It's especially easy for business owners to begin to feel invincible when they've racked up one great quarter after another of profitable sales. The banter is painfully common: "What? What risk? We've got it covered. It can't happen to us!"

Red Flags _____

Beware of that which makes you great! Often, the skill, product, or strategy that makes a company innovative or great can contribute to its eventual downfall. This is especially true when an even hungrier competitor rolls out an improved version of a product or service while the company rests on its successes. Watch out for one of the greatest risks of all: complacency.

This attitude is very common, particularly with successful companies. They might be more strategic and timely than their competitors. Because of their astute business planning, they might have studied and learned from the mistakes of current and past competitors and improved accordingly.

However, no one in business is invincible. Every company has strengths and weaknesses, and every company overlooks something that can become a risk. When this happens, even the mighty can fall.

"It's Never Happened Before"

History has a funny way of tricking people. It is simple (but not always easy) to improve upon past mistakes, because they have happened and have been evaluated. We have experienced the mistake; we know what to look for. However, it is much more difficult to plan for something that has never happened before. That's because you don't know what to plan for and you might not have any reason to anticipate your company would encounter such a problem.

The "it's never happened before" mistake could easily serve as the introduction to a talk about the subprime mortgage crisis, the simultaneous bailout and eventual bankruptcy of two automakers, or any number of economic events of the last few years. Try not to let it become the epitaph to your company, the company you spent years building only to have it come crashing down because of potential risks you ignored.

It is very important to plan for a variety of these unexpected occurrences. When you get right down to it, that's really what risk management is all about. If risk was routine and predictable, it wouldn't be risk!

The Least You Need to Know

- Your risk management approach will be defined by how you acknowledge, plan for, manage, and mitigate risk.

- In all businesses, risk has two common features: the possibility of loss, damage, or injury; and the degree of volatility.

- Taking risks entails both negative and positive outcomes.

- Businesses face countless "little" risks every day. Identify those risks that could become a threat.

Chapter 2

Why Manage Risk?

In This Chapter

- ◆ Promoting company strengths and profits
- ◆ Understanding why businesses fail
- ◆ Protecting business assets
- ◆ Growing the upside and protecting the downside

If risk is as much a part of daily business life as, say, breathing, then why manage it? The quick answer: by managing risk, we can either avoid the events that lead to loss or reduce the amount of loss when those events occur. Owners can bring principles and systematic processes into their businesses that help them make the decisions necessary to ensure the best possible outcome—no matter the situation. These risk management processes also help owners make critical decisions in day-to-day operations. They can assess uncertainty and implement the most efficient solutions to manage particular strategic options, projects, and operational issues.

You can't argue with the benefits. Good risk management can reduce earnings volatility and support successful growth opportunities by preventing the leakage of critical investment capital. This increases the firm's overall value, known as *shareholder value*. Risk management also promotes job and financial security. Firms that manage risk better perform better in good

def•i•ni•tion

Shareholder value provides a gauge of a company's value—based on total profit, stability of cash flow, and growth of profit from the present into the short- and long-term future—to investors, shareholders, officers, board members, and other interested parties.

and bad economic times. Also, managers employed by companies that manage risk well tend to survive tough times and thrive in recoveries and economic upturns. This, as you might expect, helps to improve the health of management and employees and reduce stress.

Finally, good risk management helps protect management and directors within companies. Should something go wrong, companies with good risk management procedures in place can provide auditors, regulators, insurance companies, the IRS, and other authorities with documentation showing the steps they took to avoid or remediate the situation.

What Kills Companies?

Bookshelves from here to the nearest business school are filled with well-crafted books on how to succeed in business. But despite the combined knowledge of centuries of business savvy, 33 percent of all business start-ups fail within two years and 56 percent fail within four years. How can well-conceived dreams, "can't miss" market strategies, and visions of endless revenue streams wither so quickly after the grand opening?

In this hypercompetitive, change-is-everything economy, few companies last even 30 years. Thanks to progress, mergers and acquisitions, and attrition, very few financial institutions exist in the same form they did 50 years ago. The economic and strategic risks in today's business climate are so prevalent that the old paradigm of creating a brick-and-mortar business and holding it for two, three, or four generations is out of date.

Red Flags

It is easy to pin today's business failures on shrinking marketplaces, industry consolidation or acquisition, the appetite of bigger companies, more sophisticated (and deceitful) customers, bad suppliers, or rising and falling economic fortunes. Yet the reasons why the store down the street didn't make it may come down to more familiar factors: poor operational decision-making, poor strategic response, lack of attention to outside threats, or lack of knowledge of the principal risks to the company's success.

Why do businesses fail? There are seven primary reasons:

- **Financial failure.** There are several types of financial failure, but for most businesses, it usually amounts to the inability to manage cash flow. This may be due to a variety of issues straining your cash, a specific obligation that can't be covered, or simply poor accounting or fiscal management practices.

- **Strategic inability to compete.** Competitors with better products and greater ability to reach the customer often force out longer-standing, less aggressive, companies.

- **Merger or takeover.** Competitors often swallow up companies by buying the business or top product lines or merging the company into their own.

- **Force majeure.** This is the "God forbid" reason. Many businesses fail because of natural disasters such as tornadoes, hurricanes, floods, and fires. In some countries, war is also a major business risk.

- **Fraud.** Roughly one third of businesses that fail do so because of fraud—embezzlement by employees, "cooking the books" to suit auditors and shareholders, and other misuses of money.

- **Loss of key supplier.** Businesses that lose key suppliers risk losing quality control—and customer satisfaction.

- **Loss of key customer.** Businesses that rely on a few large customers for most of their income face major risk of failure if a customer, or key channel for acquiring customers, moves on.

Ultimately, many businesses close because of financial failure. However, this happens only after other issues have severely taxed their reserves. This is why risk management is so concerned with understanding the financial impacts of the risks that businesses face.

Protect That Downside!

The promotional side of business focuses on the upside—that lofty place where your dreams, projections, revenue indicators, and future business plans meet with a receptive marketplace. It is easy to feed energy into the upside, to keep investing and planning for a successful future.

Risk Factors
Many of the reasons for installing a risk management program are present simultaneously. In fact, these reasons are often byproducts of one another. While you might begin with one objective, many other risks will invariably be addressed by your risk management plan.

However, many businesses fail to spend enough time protecting their downside—that often gray area fraught with peril, risk, unpredictable outcomes, and situations that can damage or take down a business. When you fail to manage downside of your business, the upside becomes nothing more than an impossible dream. While protecting the downside is not as interesting as working out the upside, it is more important in building a business that will succeed through any risk scenario and survive (and even thrive!) through economic upturns and downturns.

Fewer Fires to Fight

Something comes up: an emergency fill-in order, a sudden visit from a quality control inspector, an unplanned machine maintenance, an unanticipated drop in crucial inventory. These situations are fires that require everyone's immediate attention and resources. They create strain within your company and with suppliers and paralyze the flow of your business.

Every time you drop everything to douse the raging flames of a fire, it draws on precious resources. It creates bad blood between the business and key vendors and suppliers, among employees, and even with customers. Because of the widespread negative impact of these emergencies, businesses should take measures to prevent them through better planning, maintenance, or redundancy.

Fewer Management Surprises

Nothing quite sucks the wind out of a satisfied manager or owner's sails faster than discovering a major operations problem, a cash flow problem—or, worst yet, a pure loss of money. Surprise! Unfortunately, these types of surprises not only ruin decision-makers' days but are often caused by major systemic breakdowns that can set a business back days, weeks, or months.

Take America's subprime loan program. It raced along, blindly and aggressively—at highest risk—until the summer of 2008. And then, wham! All of the major banks found themselves at the forefront of a global recession, exposed to the lowest rungs of their downsides because no one stopped the subprime program when its danger first became apparent. Why? Because the short-term profits were so strong.

Unfortunately, surprises like this are difficult to explain to stakeholders such as investors, regulators, and officers. When a business is gutted by a serious problem that has been allowed to fester for weeks, months, or even years, it destroys faith in the firm and makes it harder to gain the confidence of customers, bankers, and suppliers. Case in point: Chrysler's public relations struggles with customers while it sat in bankruptcy in spring 2009.

Prudent risk and strategic planning enable owners to forecast external or internal events that could cause gradual or sudden changes in their business plans.

Reduced Earnings Volatility

Investors might not own businesses outright, but they have the right idea when it comes to profit flows. They seek stability and predictability. They steer away from the sharp ups and downs of high *earnings volatility*, a key signal of a risky company.

Stability is critical to investors and employees, who want to know their jobs, salaries, and futures are safe. Thus, business managers protect their downside by minimizing (as much as possible) the sharp highs and lows of their cash flow. A consistent flow supports salaries and benefits plans, increases investment capital, and grows profits.

def•i•ni•tion

Earnings volatility is the ebb and flow of a business's earnings over weeks, quarters, or years. A high earnings volatility can put your business at risk in a number of ways. A low earnings volatility suggests stability and long-term strength.

Reduced Budget Blowouts

It happens to virtually all budgets in all businesses at one time or another. The most well-crafted budget goes into a tailspin when the cost to complete a specific project soars. Lofty projected quarterly revenues tank when the economy turns, putting those big-ticket sales on which you built your budget on hold. It can even happen to entire states: Alaska's 2009 budget was based on oil selling for $70 per barrel. Prices far

Best Bets

Schedule the time and expense elements of your projects as precisely as possible. Know when the projects will finish and calculate the daily costs of any delays. A project might not be as attractive to a business if delays prove costly and negatively affect return on investment.

below $70 per barrel forced the state to cut programs, because no one had planned for the downside risk.

Budget blowouts are particularly troublesome because they seize up entire departments or operations. Risk management helps companies understand where weaknesses lurk, enabling them to take steps to prevent them. Should a blowout occur, risk management plans help a company isolate it to its budgetary department and to prevent its cost from eating at other projects or, worse, the operating cash flow.

Protection of Assets

Business assets consist of key physical items that drive any business forward. The three most critical asset categories are as follows:

- Financial
- Equipment
- Personnel

When any of these assets falter, the business falters. Consequently, business owners must protect the downside of all three assets, and they must do so in two ways: as they pertain to the bottom line and as a matter of safety.

Good financial risk management means understanding where the company is likely to take immediate financial loss, as well as ensuring that swings in cash flow do not lead to the inability to cover obligations. Often companies miss this point and do not develop appropriate buffers or reserves and then cannot cover payroll or other financial obligations.

Red Flags

Losing employees due to safety issues is *extremely* expensive. Loss of personnel due to downtime and loss of key information or skills can result in less efficient operations, fines, lawsuits, and increased insurance premiums.

With equipment, it is vital to keep up with repairs, upgrades, employee training, and general maintenance so that there is no unscheduled downtime or obsolete equipment. Maintaining equipment also helps keep the workplace safe.

Personnel remain any business's most vital asset. Without employees, the business will not run. Employees also hold many of the intellectual assets of the company. Good risk management includes determining which employees are key and which can become more valuable to the company through continued training.

More Efficient Issues Resolution

When something happens to your business, good risk management speeds up the process of finding efficient and specific approaches for identifying and resolving key issues. It also provides the means of evaluating the best options for mitigating the situation. When something happens, it is vital to find the best solution quickly and to implement it without delay.

Grow the Upside

No one enters business to focus on the downside. Business is all about growing the upside, winning new projects, landing new customers, expanding skills and operations, hitting profit and revenue projections, and building an even greater upside. How does something like risk fit into this scenario?

 Red Flags

When businesses consider their next moves, they always have plenty of projects and plans from which to choose. The challenge is selecting the right one. A simple analysis of risk and return can help prioritize projects and strategies. It can identify which projects are real winners and which ones need to be passed on. Risk management helps you choose your new projects wisely and helps you avoid taking on too many new projects at once.

Improved Competitiveness

One of risk management's greatest unsung benefits is the increased competitive edge it gives businesses. With risks identified, and either avoided or mitigated, companies can focus more resources, time, and decision-making manpower on identifying and assessing opportunities in the marketplace. The business can be more responsive to requests for proposals or the opening of new accounts. With added time and the security of knowing risks have been handled, owners and salespeople can focus on better understanding how to respond to specific opportunities. This enables the business to grow and thrive.

One of the ways in which risk can aid competitiveness is through improved pricing. How? Companies can create different price categories for different types of customers or products, based upon the level of risk they entail. This can ensure that the company is adequately compensated for higher risk (which will cost more to manage and mitigate) and can select or target customers with profiles aligned with the company's risk appetite. Banks, finance agencies, and insurance companies that target high-risk customers use this approach.

Improved Returns Relative to Risk

By being able to assess risk more formally on the upside, as well as the downside, companies can better understand where and how they are achieving returns. They can accurately project how much return is needed to support the risk they are taking as part of a business growth operation. Potentially, it is far better to spend money mitigating the effect of a known risk than paying to clean up the damage of an unknown risk after it hits!

A very successful money-making product might seem attractive. However, when you compare its profit-making potential to the risk it entails, the product is often less attractive. For instance, you might have a great idea for a new product, but if the materials are difficult to source or the manufacturing is very complex and requires specialized personnel, the product may become less financially attractive.

Improved Efficiencies and Quality

When risk is factored into business planning and operation, the business tends to becomes more efficient and provide higher-quality products and services. Resources, time, and better process monitoring techniques can be applied to making better products or improving customer interactions—all part of the risk associated with growing the business. The company can use its resources more widely, thanks to research it has done on the risks associated with each candidate. Most of all, in a stable business environment with few sudden interruptions caused by unforeseen problems, the company can focus on quality. In business, quality products are synonymous with stable operations.

Best Bets

Companies can optimize their efficiency when they work with quantitative approaches for measuring risk, return, and risk versus return. These include factoring in investment in new equipment, new processes, and new products. Analyze investment decisions by taking into consideration the risk associated with the project blowing out entirely or the aftermath of an unsuccessful market launch.

Improved Communication

One of the greatest upsides of risk management is its ability to increase quality communication in the workplace. Company-wide knowledge of the business's risk management strategy generates company-wide communication. This communication helps everyone understand the issues in the same way and enhances further insight through informed problem-solving.

Here's an example. A new accounting program has identified cost "leaks" from invoicing overcharges that have been hampering the company's expansion plans. The accounting department notifies the owner, executives, assembly-line foreman, and sales manager, all of whom deal with the items on the invoices, the invoices, or the vendors. The involved parties discuss the solution, implement it with all invoices in accounts payable, and solve the problem. They are also all on the same page when dealing with the surcharging vendors and strike better deals for products, improving the bottom line and their upside.

Such discussion also tends to improve understanding of the risk management process and its benefits to the company. This leads to greater implementation of the risk strategy throughout the company, better protection for executives and directors, and a strong inside-out communication pipeline between internal and external stakeholders.

Increased Employee Confidence

When risk is being managed at a company, and the rank-and-file know it, employees feel a greater sense of security. When workers know that the company leadership is looking out for pitfalls, their confidence in the company and their jobs within the company grows. Employees may also feel empowered to improve their skills for managing risk issues that come up in their own departments and to learn more about how management is dealing with issues. This increases their confidence even more, creating a stronger and more dedicated workforce.

A company that carries out well-crafted risk policies also tends to enjoy smoother processes, stronger workplace practices, and other features of a robust company. This is the "proof in the pudding" of risk management. People feel pride in being part of a better-managed operation, where the equipment isn't breaking down all the time and where the system works.

Manage Obligations

Bringing risk management into the business is like hiring an organizer to clean up the office. Before long, elements of the business are decluttered, providing a clearer picture of the operation. This creates a greater awareness of how obligations of all shapes and sizes can be managed in a more stable, secure way. The result? A stronger business.

Reduced Fines and Compliance Costs

Schedules, reviews, filing deadlines, and other key dates often get lost in the hustle and bustle of daily business. A risk management plan will turn these into priority items, resulting in fewer missed deadlines and overlooked requirements, thereby minimizing the risk of being fined, failing to apply for appropriate licenses, and so on.

Red Flags

Beware of compliance issues leaking into other risks or areas of the business. Once a regulator or other official identifies an issue in one area, he or she is likely to look into others. A single compliance ding can lead to numerous fines and potentially costly remediation projects—not to mention business interruptions due to increased scrutiny. This can result in negative media coverage and angry stakeholders, both of which will require more money and time to address.

Reduced Consequences

It is crucial to reduce the consequences of failed financial obligations. If a company misses just one critical financial obligation, the doors can literally close next month—or tomorrow. If you don't make payroll or delay payment, for example, employees may walk. If you don't make a credit payment, banks may call the loan. A bond call can shut down a company within a couple of weeks—that's what happened to Enron. A market call has the same impact, since all trading with the company will be suspended. When you can't pay a supplier, it won't be long before that supplier stops shipping critical material to you.

Reduced Litigation

A well-managed business that knows its current and potential short- and long-term risks and acts upon them is less likely to sit on either side of the litigation fence. Disputes between the company and suppliers, customers, regulators, and other authorities will be reduced. And when disputes do arise, you'll have clear, well-organized documentation to back up your company's claim. The expensive, reputation-threatening decision to litigate can be replaced by mitigating the situation.

Reduced Insurance Costs

With fewer and smaller incidents comes a perceived increase in company safety and reliability by the insurance industry. Consequently, managing risk well often leads directly to lower insurance costs.

Reduced Business Interruptions

Risky situations almost always slow down company processes. They can mean interrupting a sales manager for three critical selling hours or shutting down an assembly line because a financially strapped supplier sent watered-down materials to stretch their inventory.

The key to risk management is to build just enough measures and systems into place so that, ideally, nothing will shut down or be interrupted. Every time an incident occurs that takes an employee or employees away from their jobs, causes a delay in production, or makes it impossible to supply a new product, time and the opportunity to sell are lost to the business. The company loses money in two ways: from the lost wages of employees who had to deal with the situation and from lost potential sales.

The less these incidents occur, and the faster normal operations resume, the better the company's position.

The Least You Need to Know

- ◆ Good risk management can reduce earnings volatility and support successful growth opportunities.
- ◆ For most businesses, financial failure or difficulty amounts to the inability to manage cash flow.

◆ Business assets are the most vital organ of any company. They must be protected and the risk to them mitigated.

◆ Companies that carry out well-crafted risk policies tend to enjoy smoother operations and better workplace practices.

◆ Utilize risk measures and systems to improve competitiveness and risk-adjusted return.

Why Is Risk Management So Hard to Implement?

In This Chapter

- ◆ Overcoming resistance to change
- ◆ Seeing the benefits of transparency
- ◆ Balancing risk management
- ◆ Garnering upper-level support

Your business has been running well for 5, 10, or even 20 or more years. In fact, it has run very well. You've seen profits in all but one or two years. Your cash reserves have grown. You've made wise capital investments and good hires. You've built a customer base whose loyalty safely stretches far into the future—a secure feeling for any business owner.

Now, for some reason, other business owners, your best watchdog employee, and your most trusted advisors are telling you to implement a risk management plan. "You need to protect yourself better," they're saying. "You need to watch how money is spent, keep your vendors from charging you more money for inferior products, and watch what your former employees are doing with all the intellectual capital they built up under your roof … and, oh, by the way, the next economic downturn or hurricane could shut your doors for good."

Isn't your business the example of solid sales, solid operations, solid growth, and solid profits? Sure. Then, isn't the scenario described above alarmist, fraught with paranoia? Perhaps—but only to an extent. The fact that you haven't experienced a major *risk event* to this point means that you have likely used sound business practices. However, it also means you've been lucky. If you don't implement some sort of risk management plan, the next economic downturn or other unplanned incident could become that major risk event.

def•i•ni•tion

A **risk event** is a risk (or possible problem) that materializes into a real problem with tangible consequences, generally a loss of some sort.

Resistance to Change

It's hard to convince business owners and decision-makers, especially successful ones, to implement a plan to manage their risk. And it's rare for new companies to implement risk management plans, even though it's relatively easy to integrate risk management practices into a company whose organizational elements are still being formed.

The biggest obstacle to more companies adopting risk management is resistance. Resistance affects any change opportunity for a company, regardless of the operation or department involved. How many times have companies lost market share or been bypassed in technology development because of their decision-makers' resistance to change? Never has the old adage been truer than in today's business world: the only constant in life is change.

 Red Flags

Resistance is the mortal enemy of change. Consider any resistance to necessary decisions or new risk management practices as an enemy that must be vanquished to ensure success.

The seed of resistance comes from sustained success owing to consistent business practices. Why change if it's going so well? If a company has been working without any major mishaps for a while, managers will be proud of what they have been doing to prevent significant incidents or disasters. But ask yourself this question: How has the business been dealing with issues as they come up? Are they handled completely, or just well enough to get by?

Be sure you and your team feel that there is a need to make changes. Dive deeper into the organization to learn how it really works. Perhaps you will find a different picture of the processes and networks than you surmised. Perhaps not. Either way, it is certain that the business can benefit from better risk management capabilities, or techniques for managing risk. Start with a willingness to improve those capabilities.

Not Invented Here

Nothing tastes as good as home cooking—especially when it concerns a business system, operation, product, service, or risk management system that the owner, business team, or decision-makers cooked up within the company's four walls. Unfortunately, in the business world, continually feasting on home cooking can be a major problem. Businesses become blind to new risks and new techniques for managing risks. They tend to believe they are okay and have it under control. This often happens when companies make a new investment and then forget to manage the investment. The worst cases occur when firms forget to maintain their existing programs or models. Models may be implemented but not checked and improved, people may be trained once but not continually (so new people never get trained), or processes are put in place but are altered gradually or not even followed after a while.

Failure to maintain systems becomes even more troublesome if the organization has developed its own risk plan, no matter how basic. If a risk situation arises, decision-makers will assume they have the tools and measures in hand to deal with it.

It's okay to work in-house, but it is important to ensure that a company doesn't implement processes without following through on them. Companies always need to review, upgrade, test, check, and be prepared.

Risk Factors
Risk situations are like computer viruses—and human viruses, for that matter. They are often products of the present business environment or unsavory characters trying to defraud the business. Over time, they become "super strains" resistant to solutions that worked in the past. They can become as insidious as runaway computer viruses.

Make sure people within the organization understand the need to seek an outside solution. Bring people on board by including them in the process of identifying risk-sensitive areas and seeking outside solutions. Use them to help arrive at a solution that will integrate seamlessly into your business.

Transparency Is Scary

Many business owners and executives fear risk management because it involves transparency, a concept that scares the daylights out of many. But when it comes to risk management, transparency has nothing to do with divulging proprietary information. It is simply about identifying, quantifying, and reporting to senior management on how a company stands with respect to its risks and how well mitigated they are.

Best Bets

Create transparency in your risk management program. Identify, quantify, and report on how the company stands with respect to the risks it carries. Begin by setting up the risk measures or analyses. Understand the overall size of the company's exposure to risks, the likelihood that they will occur, and the impact that a risk event will have. Look for the upside to show how risk management might help the business. Use a risk versus return measure to flush out the big problems.

Very few businesses can produce a list consisting entirely of strengths and triumphs. Nearly everyone has a skeleton or two in the closet, a weakness that can affect relationships with stakeholders, suppliers, customers, and employees. At the corporate level, organizations resist more formal processes—like risk management practices—because they can uncover those weaknesses in operations and capabilities. They can reveal or break down power centers where one individual or group may currently enjoy a better market position due to relationships, capabilities, or information. Even more frightening, a transparent risk assessment can reveal limited knowledge among executives or business managers who have built their businesses on the perception of industry- or sector-leading knowledge. What happens when the expert proves to be not so knowledgeable?

This scenario implies winners and losers—with the losers being businesses and individuals who hide something or hold something back. However, transparency is not all doomsday and Armageddon. The transparent approach can also reveal divisions, practices, and products that weren't getting their due attention because they were managing in a lower-risk environment. When the risk management searchlight shines on them, they can rise to a better consumer or market position because their practices are shown to be transparent, safe, and well organized.

All business sectors, product lines, and services can benefit from transparency—unless, that is, they are really hiding a serious problem. But when exposing your risks, it is important to gain clear, strong support from the top—the owner or CEO, the board, executives, and other decision-makers. It is important to be inclusive and to clarify the benefits. Most of all, it is essential that your company take quick action to demonstrate the improvements made as a result of the transparent risk assessment.

Do We Have to Do It?

This question is the eternal bedfellow of resistance. It both solidifies and justifies one's resistance to change. Probably no other group of business professionals hears it more than risk management consultants! This is definitely the "out" question—as in, the way out of developing a better risk management program. It can prevent people from moving forward faster than a Nolan Ryan fastball.

You must consider opposition to implementing risk management strategies as toxic. Someone might try to undermine the importance of the new steps. When pressed, they might ramp it up a notch and compare the time and cost of a new risk plan to what he or she perceives as "more important" issues, such as pushing out a week's worth of orders or setting up for a factory-wide sale. However, when a regulator is knocking on your door, the manufacturing line hasn't made any product in three days because of inventory or cash shortages, or your customers haven't paid up despite numerous collection attempts, suddenly the time you could have spent on risk management doesn't seem like such a waste.

The answer to the question "Do we have to do it?" needs to be a resounding "Yes!" every single time. Everyone needs to participate on some level. Every business line and division needs to be considered. Why do we have to do it? Because it's a solution that protects the short- and long-term stability of the company.

 Red Flags

When evaluating and creating a business-wide risk plan, avoid the temptation to hive off a single sector, saying that they are special and don't have to participate. It creates disunity and strained communications. And at the end of the day, it exposes the company to greater risk.

Finding and Managing the Right Data

For many organizations, risk management's reliance on quantitative measures is a deal breaker. Who has the time to implement, much less act upon, a new set of measures, especially if they are hard to understand or don't jive with how you perceive the business? In this world of numbers and more numbers, who really wants to become proficient at reading another battery of … numbers?

Such resistance quickly changes to cooperation, and even to enthusiasm, when decision-makers realize that the numbers they have currently don't include the data they need most. In risk scenarios and actual incidents, the data that makes the difference often doesn't exist in any business accounting program or marketing metric. Owners and key staff quickly realize they are holding woefully inadequate data—or no data at all—that is relevant to the problem at hand.

Avoid becoming the unfortunate business manager who tries to solve risk problems with inadequate data. There are hundreds of ways to measure and assess risk. Some of the most common and easiest to implement are in this book. Learning the language of risk, becoming acquainted with the basics of each step in the process, and setting up a robust process is a journey in and of itself. It can add deep value to the business and to employees' knowledge of the possible risks in the operation, without requiring sophisticated measures.

Best Bets

To begin measuring your company's risk, you need some basic information. One is a simple breakdown of the profit-and-loss statement over a fairly short period of time. The variance in the P&L can reveal quite a bit. By reviewing it, a company may also be able to start collecting information on losses averted as well as exposures at risk (such as money pending on credit or days of inventory on raw materials, etc.).

Fortunately, implementing a risk management plan doesn't have to happen all at once. Your risk measures can be developed in steps over time, as can the data required to support them. The most important thing is to realize that risk management involves a different type of data analysis than normal business operations. It also involves different capabilities. As with everything else, a willingness to begin the process is the place to start. Then, in stages, you or a risk management professional can determine which data will best measure your risk appetite and risk portfolio.

How Do We Know It's Right?

As organizations begin to implement risk management practices, they sometimes become embroiled in bothersome questions, such as the following:

Are we taking the right steps?

Did we choose the most appropriate staff training for our company's specific issues?

Was it wise to task the best number crunchers in the company with yet another set of measures and metrics?

Are the measures implemented so far yielding accurate results?

Sometimes, the risk measurement calculations just don't feel right. Many a manager has said something along these lines: "I don't really know what's in the calculation, but I know this can't be right because if X piece of equipment breaks—just that one thing goes wrong—we would lose more money than that."

When concerns like this come up, all the key people involved need to agree on what's being measured. If the risk assessment suggests there are fewer risks than everyone thought, then it's okay to scale up the risk estimate until measures and organizational knowledge have advanced to the point where you feel more comfortable with the results. If the estimate feels "too big," then the problem becomes harder. It may be unwise to arbitrarily scale it down, but the company can break down the specific risk estimate into smaller pieces and focus on hot spots. Overall, people need to feel comfortable with the solution in order to buy in and move forward.

Other Tough Questions

Business leaders should ask the following questions, as well.

Can this plan be implemented? In other words, does the company have the capacity and skills to implement it? If the answer is "no," then further analysis of the "whys" needs to be conducted. Perhaps the plan needs to be ratcheted back.

Is the company getting the information needed to manage the risks? This can be tricky. Often the first steps of identifying and starting to measure and assess risks are a bit foreign and abstract. It is important for risk managers (or whomever is doing this assessment) to try to overcome the "so what?" questions for those with whom they are working.

Do we—including managers, board members, CEOs, and investors—fully understand the implications? Risk terms, concepts, and measures can often seem obscure and complex, particularly before an organizational understanding and common language is developed. It is important for risk managers to translate the implications of their work into clear terms and keep their messages short and precise. It is also important to ensure that communication and education at different levels accompany each risk implementation and that the communication is tailored to different departments and individuals within departments using a "need to know" approach.

Can I justify further investment in risk management measures, based on what I have? If the answer is "no," then there is probably something wrong. It is unlikely that the business doesn't have any important risks, so it is likely that the plan isn't well enough developed or that there is something seriously missing from the explanations or measures.

Stalling the Process

Let's face it: some groups or individuals will go so far as to use the perceived difficulty of implementing risk practices as an excuse to stall the process and cast doubt on the whole exercise. Besides costing the business time and money, this can be a dangerous action—especially when the business has been exposed and made transparent in order to effect risk management measures. Instead of looking at risk management implementation as an overwhelming obstacle, break it down into small, manageable chunks. Focus first on the most material risks affecting the company. These are the most important to rectify or mitigate, and they will be pretty clear.

Achieving a Balance

If a business owner were to ask a risk management consultant, "Show me everything you can do to address every potential risk you see in my company," the consultant's response would be lengthy. So lengthy, in fact, that the consultant might drink a couple pots of coffee while wheeling out everything from his or her bag of tricks, constructing measures and tools, and giving them back to the owner.

That owner would likely experience systemic shock. He or she might seize up even further when time and money costs are assigned to every possible risk scenario!

It's important to keep in mind that every business has risk potential. In all likelihood, every business has many potential areas of concern. They cannot all be addressed at once, nor should they be. To try to address every risk would put an undue strain on both management and the rank-and-file and bog down the company.

Upper-Level Support

Organizations often struggle to achieve the right balance in the degree of their measures and techniques. Overall, the best way to deal with most risk management implementation issues is to have upper-level support. If you are not the owner or part of the company's senior management team, make sure they have your support. Also make sure they and the board, key investors, and stakeholders are involved and are seen to be driving the effort.

Upper-level support is critical to the success of any risk management implementation effort. Everyone from the CEO to department heads need to believe in the program, support it, and do their part to implement it. A risk management program without widespread support from the top actually creates added risk, as different executives will offer different approaches that could prove disruptive or damaging.

Best Bets _____

Developing upper-level support involves establishing several points of focus: the right level of emphasis, the right level of seniority or senior attention, the right amount of reporting, the appropriate degree of specificity, and the appropriate degree of accuracy in measures and models.

The Least You Need to Know

♦ To prevent the next financial downturn or incident from becoming a risk event, you must implement a risk management plan.

♦ Resistance is a natural response to risk management practices. Understand that the process will benefit your company.

♦ Be sure to achieve a measurable balance when you implement risk management practices.

♦ You cannot address all areas of concern at once.

♦ It is crucial that any risk management program has the fullest support of upper-level management.

Chapter 4

Risk Management Guidelines

In This Chapter

- ◆ Learning the "rules of the road"
- ◆ How knowing your business reveals risks
- ◆ Defining hidden risks
- ◆ Finding the right measures to implement

Every business venture or practice has its rules of the road. Risk management is no exception. Not that this road is straight, mind you: if anything winds and bends like the road of life or holds as many surprises, it's risk management. After all, every business is different, and each specific set of potential or actual risks is unique to the operational environment of that business.

There are simple risk management guidelines, however, that will serve your company well. These guidelines are proven and practiced by risk managers worldwide. Whenever you hear about a catastrophic failure in a business—or a regional, national, or global crisis, such as the blackout in the northeast United States and Canada in August 2003—you can be sure that one or more of these guidelines were not followed. It is also fair to say that, in most risk events, two or more guidelines are disregarded simultaneously. When this happens, isolated incidents can turn into company-wide catastrophes.

The risk management rules of the road presented in this chapter are simple to remember. Heed them as you would traffic signs, whose meanings you grasp instantly and whose rules you follow without a second thought.

Know Your Risks

A cardinal rule that pertains to life, business, and any meaningful pursuit is this: know your risks. Understand the risks that exist in your company and be aware of how they may change over time. Many things can cause change, including rapid growth or decline, new product lines, new brands or divisions, mergers and acquisitions, new upper-level hires, upgrade in clients, and changes in materials or product suppliers, to name a few. Watch for strange or risky investments being made with capital. Reassess your business routinely and be on the lookout for new risks as they surface—or, better yet, when they appear as blips on the horizon.

Risk Factors

Metallgesellschaft AG, an old and famous German mining company, collapsed after losing $1.4 billion in commodities futures. How did this happen in a climate where precious metals and oil were booming? The firm's headquarters didn't know that the New York office was trading aggressively in futures. When oil prices dropped, the company was left paying prices that were far above market price, and it couldn't bear the load.

An all-too-common reason businesses get caught in risk events is because one division is doing something unbeknownst to management or the head office. Suddenly, there's a blow-up, a financial calamity of some kind. Capital is wiped out. To avoid such scenarios, you must be aware of *everything* that is going on throughout your business.

Also, be on the lookout for hidden risks. They exist wherever business is active—and they hide behind some truly alluring disguises. For instance, whenever something seems too good to be true, well … you know how the sentence ends! There is almost always a risk hidden in the fabric of the "can't miss" opportunity.

Take the 2000 merger of America Online and Time Warner. Analysts, investors, and pundits drooled in unison, and why not? The nation's two most popular (at the time) media behemoths were joining forces. Old-school media was merging with new media. Millions of subscribers were going to receive content that ranged from marketing e-mails to Warner Brothers movies. Corporate geniuses and visionaries Ted Turner, Steve Case, and Gerald Levin were going to work together. The vertical and horizontal integration of business practices, services, leaders, and smart staffers in both companies looked like the perfect combination of resources. Certainly, it felt more like a monster to competitors like Microsoft and Newsweek, whose executives wore very long faces—for a while.

Best Bets

Hidden risks can lurk behind your annual returns. Large returns might seem enticing, but they almost always signal risk. A rule of thumb: honor the 7 percent rule. Most companies, as well as stocks and other investments, would make no more than a 7 percent average long-term return if they were stable and operating at medium to low risk. As percentage points rise, risk increases. Strong companies return 12 percent to 15 percent when navigating a greater risk environment. Beyond this point, you've entered the high-risk zone.

Fast-forward 10 years. Why did Time Warner sell off AOL? Partial answer: two hidden risks reared their heads after the merger to create a most contentious decade. One was bringing together two entirely different corporate cultures (AOL's young, aggressive, casual team and Time Warner's older, conservative, more bureaucratic group). The dealmakers wagered that the overall impact of the merger would supersede the cultural clash. They were wrong. The other risk was the decade-long decline of *Time* magazine as an advertising center. Even in 1999, the signs were apparent, but Time Warner banked on its market position to carry it through.

Risk Factors

According to CFO.com, the online version of *Chief Financial Officer* magazine, 70 percent to 80 percent of mergers and acquisitions ultimately fail. The biggest reasons: acquisitions tend to destroy value for the acquiring company's shareholders; the two companies cannot reconcile their different industries, cultures, markets, or approaches to business; governance issues; and difficulty in streamlining operations. In 2004, McKinsey, a well-known management consulting firm, calculated that just 23 percent of acquisitions or mergers had a positive return on investment.

There were two other reasons for the failure of the merger, but they can't be labeled hidden risks, since they were complete unknowns in 1999. First, competitive online services popped up with more speed, easier accessibility, and more confidentiality, and they didn't charge any fees. Second, the AOL Time Warner union was only the first in a spate of mergers and acquisitions in the media world. It is safe to say that ESPN, ABC, Pixar, and 30-plus additional entities—and their top-to-bottom media and entertainment holdings—might not coexist under the Walt Disney Company umbrella had they not been shown the way by the AOL Time Warner merger.

As AOL and Time Warner learned, the risks that you take on will define your management approaches to risk. This holds true whether or not the risks are hidden at the time of the merger, acquisition, or working partnership.

Know Your Appetite for Risk

How much risk are you willing to take on? How much existing risk can you handle? By understanding the amount of risk that a company can absorb and handle, you are measuring the company's *risk appetite*.

def•i•ni•tion

Risk appetite is the amount of risk that a company owner, principal, or board is willing to absorb and sustain in order for the business to obtain its projected returns.

When figuring out a company's appetite for risk, review each type of actual or potential risk. Try to evaluate this in both quantitative and qualitative terms. How much money are you willing to lose? How much of a reputation hit are you willing to take? How much are you willing to let quality control be affected?

You need to ask these questions every time a risk is assessed and its mitigation or removal planned.

A simple way to think about this is the "front-page test," in which you imagine how the worst-case scenario would play out on the front page of a newspaper. The front-page test is a great way to bring everyone on board with the risk management process. It focuses thinking very quickly and creates greater awareness of the possible or actual risks and their potential impact on company, staff, and outside partners or vendors.

Use a Common Language

Nothing can derail the risk management process faster than inadequate communication resulting from lack of a common language. It even happens sometimes among risk managers! Some business practices require more exact communication than others, and risk management takes the cake for the need for everyone to be on the same page and use the same terms.

Develop a common risk language throughout the business. Start by developing a vocabulary of risk terms that everyone in the organization understands—particularly the people tasked with assessing and implementing risk management policies and tools. Set up a method for reporting or communicating where you stand at each step of the process.

With a common language, your company will experience the following benefits:

- ♦ Greater organizational acceptance of the risk policy or practice

- ♦ Heightened awareness of potential risks

- ♦ The ability to respond more rapidly to risk events

- ♦ The ability to prevent risks more efficiently

Develop Capabilities Right for You

Imagine assembling an oil pipeline. You walk into the materials yard, and pieces of all shapes and sizes sit in various piles. The object is to choose specific pipes and pieces with which to build the pipeline. The pipeline must not only connect the oil field to the refinery, but also account for present and future capacity.

Developing your risk management capabilities is like building that pipeline. The pieces need to fit together, and the finished product needs to be wide enough to handle present and future capability. When determining capability, focus on understanding the types of solutions and approaches for measuring, assessing, and managing risk that are appropriate for your business. These aspects are fully described later in the book. These should be considered as they pertain to the size and complexity of your company. Which solutions and approaches to addressing risk will best connect your business capabilities to your risk management program?

Consider the company's current stage of adopting risk management solutions. If you've never engaged in risk management before in any formal sense, it makes sense to start simply. As you gain competence (and confidence), you can further develop skills, capabilities, measures, and tools.

Best Bets

Take into consideration the specific types of risks that you face and the characteristics of those risks. Do they have the potential to grow quickly? Which areas of your business could be affected? Are the risks highly concentrated? Do they have a real potential for contagion?

Implement Simple Measures and Approaches

Many organizations see risk management as a science with lots of complex models to support analysis and projections of risk and loss. Their perception is correct—if they allow themselves to get lost in numerous complex approaches to managing risk. In that regard, risk management is no different than any other science. Chemistry, for example, can be as simple as combining air, a match, and a piece of wood to build a fire, or as complex as spending five years in the laboratory to perfect a new pharmaceutical drug.

Such research typically goes two ways: either the chemists make the process overly complicated and get lost in mountains of experiments or they break down the work to the simplest possible steps—and find solutions. Likewise with risk management.

Risk Factors

The devil lies in the details of risk management, a discipline that can develop details on top of data-saturated details. For that reason, many people have the urge to overdo it. They may build models or processes that are highly complex, believing that they will be more accurate. The reality, however, is that management and others will find these processes difficult or impossible to understand and implement as the company moves forward.

Develop risk measures, frameworks, and strategies that are simple and readily understandable. Start with the basics and develop more nuanced capabilities and measures if there is a good reason to do so. Create simple capabilities to match the natural growth of the company.

Fit Capabilities into Existing Processes

A risk management capability needs to fit as seamlessly as possible into the processes, systems, and organization that you already have in place. This is particularly true in the beginning, when the risk concepts may be new and untried in your environment. Management and staff alike are still learning and coming to accept the process. The best way to gain that all-important company-wide understanding and support is to keep measures and models, as well as the process, as basic as possible. This also creates a sound basis from which to build capabilities without overinvesting in an elaborate risk management program.

Once your basic models are in place, you may find that they don't provide enough specificity about the risks you're uncovering. This is especially true if they need to consider financial risks or financial mitigation. Nothing is more unique to each organization than the relationship between money and the present and future path of the business.

Best Bets

If the model you develop to measure risk is well constructed but not specific enough for your company's needs, consider the 80:20 rule: 80 percent accuracy can be obtained with 20 percent of the effort. In fact, most risk models—even those with very rudimentary frameworks—will work within 10 percent or even 5 percent error bands. A ratio of even better than 80:20 can typically be achieved. However, it's important to think carefully before investing in the next 5 or 10 percent of accuracy. The effort, cost, and complexity will rise exponentially and may not provide the expected cost benefit.

Don't Overdo It

Numerous companies have adopted extremely sophisticated measures, models, and overall processes only to discard them in favor of simpler frameworks or measures.

Many risk models evolve into such complex creatures that they become like black boxes. Nobody—not even the guys who run these risk models day-to-day—can understand what is going on inside them. They become perplexed about the issues or failings they have "baked" inside the model. These models sometimes create as many risks to the organization as they are supposed to be managing.

Provide Clear Direction

Another benefit of keeping it simple is in providing clear direction to the firm. No matter how advanced the organization becomes in the ways of speaking about, measuring, and managing risk, keeping it simple helps maintain transparency and clarity for management. Everyone can understand what is going on and how to interpret the information they are receiving. If the process gets too complicated, people won't be able to follow—or in some cases, believe—the results.

Risk management is like any other management technique in that it is important to set a direction, articulate that direction to the team, and send clear signals along the way. The more transparency you build into the process, the more clear the direction. Everyone needs to know what is happening, what the process is, what the decisions are, and how they will be implemented.

You can take four simple steps to achieve clear direction, or transparency, in your risk management assessments:

1. Use clear and complete descriptions of risk, issues, and decisions.

2. Develop a basic governance approach that allows for open discussion and reporting.

3. Understand where and how decisions are made.

4. Develop a simple reporting approach for material risks.

The goal is to create and use processes that are well described and documented, including all reports on risks and decisions developed as a result of those reports. In many cases, decisions about risk lead to one of two outcomes: major strategic decisions that are important for investors and other stakeholders to understand and major management decisions about operations.

Some of these management decisions may intertwine with regulatory or compliance requirements. If so, an authority could seek formal documentation. Some decisions may lead to outcomes regarding safety. In that case, an insurance company would want to see what is being done (and formal documentation with support can really help the case). As well, decisions could be made that affect quality and potentially impact agreements with, and the expectations of, customers.

 Red Flags

Some reporting procedures are more formal than others. Not every company needs a high degree of formality, but clarity of reporting should be considered and pursued wherever contracts, safety, and compliance/regulation are concerned.

Overall, the aim is to ensure clarity about decisions and elicit trust from the ownership or management team. If you are a larger company, that clarity and trust should extend to your employees and stakeholders.

Expect the Unexpected

Like a New Year's Day swim with the Polar Bear Club, risk management is for people with strong constitutions. When dealing with risk, you have to expect the unexpected. Risk management opens the doors to problems that companies don't yet know they have. It is not about managing recognized problems, but about anticipating issues and opportunities and understanding how to evaluate, manage, and capitalize on them. It is also about remaining vigilant to the possibility of new and hidden risks.

Adopt an attitude that enables you to see beyond the day's business. Tie your vigilance about risk directly to the overall vision and projections for your company. Consider what to do about risks that you know are out there but that you haven't addressed previously. Make them increasing priorities. Consider new ways that these can creep up or affect you. Maybe it's through an incentive package you receive or give. Perhaps the company's expansion in six months will require you to work with a different set of contractors, vendors, and suppliers. To fill new jobs for that expansion, you may need to hire people with skill sets new to the organization. All of these things can create risk.

Don't Be Afraid to Forecast

Don't be afraid to be a little paranoid. In fact, when it comes to risk management, projecting future risk events is essential!

Stay on top of how even the unlikeliest of events may impact you. If the impact is big enough, it may be worth considering some form of mitigation. Develop capabilities for considering future risks and considering unexpected scenarios. For instance, much of western Kentucky's infrastructure shut down for 10 to 20 days in the winter of 2009 because of a brutal ice storm for which few businesses or governmental agencies had planned—even though there had been an ice storm the previous winter. Though the 2008 ice storm was the first major ice event in 25 years, an owner or decision-maker wearing a risk manager's hat would have planned for the likelihood of another such storm. Instead, the prevailing sentiment seemed to be, "It won't happen for another 25 years." Don't fall into that trap. Consider unexpected scenarios. To paraphrase (and change one word of) the famous Kinks song from 1980, "Paranoia won't destroy ya."

Pay Attention

Every major crisis is somehow a story about how someone (or groups of someones) stopped paying attention to one sort of risk or another (or maybe groups of risks). However, companies that face serious risks with possible life-and-death consequences, such as airlines and high-rise construction companies, must be vigilant and careful about everything. They have to pay attention to all possible risks at all times.

Airlines have to consider check-in security, maintenance of the plane, pilots' rest time, weight of the plane, and the plane's flight track. They must factor this into an existing air space filled with crisscrossing planes that, during peak hours, looks like a five-year-old's Etch-a-Sketch rendering. There are countless other items to consider in a single flight—and there are thousands of flights daily—but you get the point. If an airline or a member of its staff fails to pay attention to one thing, it may cost people their lives.

Risk Factors
The negative domino effect that financial institutions experienced in 2008 and 2009 was a classic case of not paying attention. They failed to pay attention to the signals, either out of ignorance ("It's never happened before"), arrogance ("It can't/won't happen to us"), complacency ("We don't need to address that right now"), or a sense of invincibility ("We've had 30 strong, profitable quarters in a row; what can possibly hurt us?").

Imagine if your company focused on risk management with the same intensity as an airline. Can you imagine how much safer and more successful your business would be? This degree of focus may be a bit too extreme for most companies. However, the point is to understand and continually reassess the internal and external landscape and be prepared. Root out complacency, and replace it with attentiveness.

Continuously Make Improvements

When you think about it, human capabilities are just as important as material capabilities. Continuous improvement pertains to both of them, and incorporates measures, processes, and mitigation techniques. The bottom line is to avoid complacency and continually assess situations. Expect and plan for continuous improvement.

Risks evolve as organizations evolve. They change and morph daily. Personal and company skills and capabilities also change, hopefully in a way that increases an organization's competency over time. In addition, new measurement and management techniques become available as your industry and risk practices evolve.

Plan for and expect that your own capabilities and skills will change. Plan for and expect that there will be new risk management techniques. They are popping up everywhere, especially during the last few years, when businesses and industries began to face scenarios they—and the world—had never seen before. Plan for and expect that your equipment, services, assets, and intellectual capital may age or lose suitability.

Continuous improvement also means regularly tweaking the future plans you have laid out. The most successful organizations learn to build risk management into their ongoing processes and budgets. They assume that they will always be evolving their capabilities at every level. As you add this mentality to your approach, always keep in mind all of the points in this chapter. That way, when you implement new capabilities, processes, measures, and tools, they will still follow consistent principles. And in risk, consistency and redundancy are everything.

The Least You Need to Know

- There are simple guidelines to evaluate and handle risk.
- Know the risks in your organization and how much risk you can withstand. Be aware of how potential risks may change over time.
- Guide your organization with clear messages, using a common language.
- Develop capabilities that fit your organization and its risks.
- Plan to review and improve your risk management plan on an ongoing basis.

Chapter 5

Introducing the Risk Management Process

In This Chapter

♦ Recognizing and identifying risks

♦ Understanding four approaches to risk management

♦ Determining short- and long-term goals

♦ Making communication a priority

Imagine building a stronger, safer frame for an existing house but being able to leave the rooms intact in the process. Perhaps you've identified termite or structural problems and recognized that without reframing, the affected portion of the house might collapse or become unlivable or, even worse, the whole house might come down. But you now have the opportunity to check out every joint and groove and build additional safety into the structure.

The risk management process is similar. The business already exists; in many cases it has been around for years. Part of its structure will likely change to integrate risk management techniques that will add to the structural integrity of the whole company. By doing so, the process adds a new framework to think about risks and manage decision-making regarding risk. It guides the organization to practice continuous monitoring of all aspects of the operation. It helps support continuous operational improvement, and it helps explain to others what is involved with risk management.

What Are the Key Steps?

Like any other complex activity, the risk management process contains a number of key steps. The four main steps are as follows:

1. Identify risks

2. Measure and assess risks

3. Manage risks

4. Monitor risks

By taking the process step by step, you can begin identifying and reducing expected and unexpected losses in your business. This chapter serves as an introductory overview of these steps, with further discussion on implementing them to come.

The risk management process involves four actions: identify, measure/assess, manage, monitor.

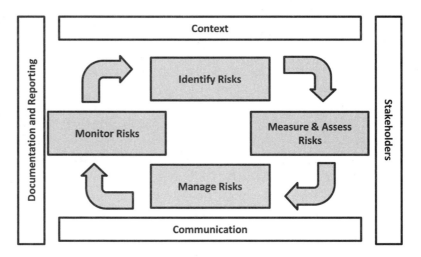

The risk management process also involves a number of other factors, including:

♦ **Context.** Setting the context is part of understanding the risk management process. It's important to consider the activities being focused on, whether the entire organization, one business line, or a specific strategy or project where the company is trying to assess and manage risks.

- ◆ **Stakeholders.** Stakeholders are a key consideration in terms of how to manage them through the process. What role do they play and what information do they need to know?

- ◆ **Communication.** Who needs to be informed? What sort of communication needs to be considered and to which people? Will it be necessary to communicate only with people inside the company, or with people outside the company as well, such as media or regulators?

- ◆ **Documentation and reporting.** It's important to consider what aspects of the risk management process will need to be recorded and what kind of reporting will be required. Reporting is key to ensure that the process is monitored and that key people are aware of the risks and how they are being addressed.

Step 1: Identify Risks

The world of risk seems fraught with shadows and ghosts. After all, how do you know something is a risk when its dark side hasn't even appeared yet? Without the sturdy guideposts of experience (previous problems in one area or another), how do you even know where the risks may lie?

Yet you can't manage what you can't identify. It is vital to understand the types of risks you face and to develop categorized lists of those risk types. This critical first step enables everyone in the company to discuss the situation internally. It also sets the context for everything to follow.

The first time you make a formal risk assessment, the approach will seem foreign. It might feel like you're traveling deep into a foreign country for the first time. The terms and signposts will be difficult to read. Once you become fluent in the language of risk, however, you'll find that this step is largely intuitive. You may never need a formal assessment again—or at least not for a very long time. In fact, after their first risk assessments, many organizations only take a new formal assessment when they are considering implementing a new strategy or building a more robust, formalized risk framework.

Best Bets

Buttoning down the risk assessment and identifying your risks enables your organization to set a baseline, understand the new language, and establish which risks will be prioritized for further assessment and mitigation.

Step 2: Measure and Assess Risks

With assessments come measurements, as well as tools for doing the measuring. By measuring each risk, you can determine how important it is to the company's present and future course. You can also assign a priority to mitigating or solving it.

There are eight basic steps for determining risk likelihood and impact:

1. When risks materialize, determine why losses have occurred and whether they may occur in the future.

2. Understand what contributed to the losses and whether those causes are appropriately mitigated.

3. Collect information on recurring risks (and losses) and use it to test previous assumptions and to update the assumptions you use in your models and measure.

4. Consider how important risks may be in the future.

5. Test risk assumptions under many conditions to understand if the risk is still relevant—or even more important than before.

6. Monitor risks to determine if the threat has changed.

7. Consider the balance between the degree of risk and the benefits associated with addressing the risk.

8. Determine how risks compare to returns.

For organizations that take a more structured view, risk measurement becomes an area in which they may make major investment —at least eventually. This is especially true of companies that are regulated, because reporting and documentation is essential. In those cases, formal approaches are required. Don't get too carried away, though. Keep your eyes on the goal of any risk management process: to determine how risks may affect your organization or project.

Step 3: Manage Risks

Like a well-run business, the management of risk follows its assessment. It cannot be stressed enough how vital it is to move into a management mode immediately after determining your *risk assumptions* and making an assessment. Any wasted time can enable a potential risk to become very real—and very costly.

def•i•ni•tion

Risk assumptions are evaluations of existing risk that are developed as part of a risk assessment. To create them, you or a risk professional determines how relevant and potentially costly a risk is and what, if anything, should be done to mitigate it.

Once risks are assessed, the company can determine the best approach for managing them. This is usually achieved by one of the four broad categories of risk management discussed in Part 4.

Best Bets

When you consider ways to reduce risk, ask yourself which risks can be transferred. Determine whether or not the transfer is worth its cost when weighed against the gain made by moving the risk. If the company takes fewer losses and your employees and management can refocus on necessary tasks instead of managing risk, then the transfer of risk was valuable. If the transfer doesn't reduce your risk at a reasonable enough cost, consider other alternatives.

Step 4: Monitor Risks

The final step in the risk management process involves continual monitoring of those risks the company has chosen to focus on. Perhaps many risks have been identified. Perhaps only a few. Those risks have been prioritized, with some rising to the top of the list. Some have fallen off the list because they were not considered significant or potentially damaging enough to warrant close monitoring.

With the remaining risks, monitoring is the name of the game. This includes monitoring each risk or group of risks and the operation or system they might affect and a regular review of the risk to the company overall. You can monitor most efficiently by repeating the measurement and analysis activities used to identify them. This also is the trigger to create an *iterative process* for monitoring the risks as they grow, shrink, or dissipate.

Because of the shifts in risk revealed by this iterative process, you will need to reconsider the level of management and mitigation each time through the process. Even if the risks have stayed the same, you will need to factor in future activities or the future environment, which may require changes in management and mitigation.

def•i•ni•tion

An **iterative process** is a repetitive process. As it pertains to risk management, it involves repeatedly monitoring risks as they grow, shrink, dissipate, or appear anew. Every time the process is repeated, new risks or new manifestations of the old risks are identified. The risks may have reordered themselves in terms of materiality or criticality. In other words, they might be bigger or smaller and more or less significant.

Establishing the Context

When entering any venture, it helps immensely to know the overall goals of the work. What are the objectives in terms of business growth, the market, and your financial strength? What is expected? Who are the key players? What are the short- and long-term goals?

All of these questions can easily be transferred to risk management. When assessing risk, establish its context and scope. Understand the objectives of the organization with regards to risk management, the scope of the activity, and the environment in which it is being conducted. Many companies only conduct the risk management process to evaluate key projects. Others might build an entire implement the risk management process throughout the entire company.

Companies often start with a segment of risks, or a pilot with a specific business or product line, and branch out from there. Every company will approach this somewhat differently, in relation to its specific concerns.

 Red Flags

It is very easy to lose yourself in the countless directions that risk assessment can take you and your business. Be sure to ascertain if you are dealing with an isolated project, business segment, or set of risks. If you fail to grasp the scope of the project, you run the risk of overspending and overtaxing your business and employees. Work within the parameters and context of the project or company goals for risk management.

Regardless of your initial approach, stay focused! It is quite easy to start branching out, particularly if the company has not done much in the way of risk management in the past. As in any other activity in business, it is unlikely that you will have unlimited resources, so it is important to be clear about the scope and the available budget and resources. Know the considerations for key types of risk management, make sure they are clear and appropriate for the risk at hand, and address them.

Dealing with Stakeholders

Any risk management operation will involve stakeholders. Whether you're considering the risk involved with a single project or an entire business, the people and outside companies that create and drive the work will be affected. It is important to determine the stakeholders associated with any risk management activity.

If you're building a company-wide risk management capability, stakeholders will be widespread and will include both external and internal parties. For instance, if a regulatory requirement drives the risk management process, external parties will include regulators, who will demand a greater degree of governance and documentation. Know those requirements and expectations at the outset.

Understand each party in the process and their interests. Look for hidden agendas or areas where the outside interest may have particular issues. If you are dealing with a regulator, make sure you fully understand what the regulator needs from you. Make it part of the management plan to engage in regular discussions with regulators and be prepared to guide them through the process.

> **Risk Factors**
>
> Stakeholders can include executives, managers, employees, suppliers, distributors, regulatory agencies, service providers, shareholders, media, and more.

Communicating with Stakeholders

Does it seem like communication keeps popping up in our discussion of risk management? The C-word is everywhere. Different forms of communication are needed for different stages in the risk process and for different participants. In no area is it more important than in rolling out a risk management process, especially where stakeholders are concerned.

Stakeholders may be widespread and yet critical to the success of the risk management process. Because of that, it is vital to know what types of communication are required for each type of stakeholder. This will largely be driven by the context in which the company is conducting the risk management process. If it's being contained within a project, the number of stakeholders who need to be in the communications loop is likely to be far fewer than if the process stretches across the enterprise.

The Process

Communication itself is a process. It enables a company to identify stakeholders and understand their roles and requirements. From there, the company can and should develop a consultation or communication plan. This might include an educational process, an information bulletin, regular program updates, or executive review and briefing sessions. Regardless, communication in risk management works best if it is clear, thorough, and ongoing.

The Form

It is important to understand what type of communication works best for your project. The key forms of communication for the risk management process include the following:

- **Notices.** One-way information bulletins.

- **Education.** This can vary from instructive one-way updates to detailed multisession classroom education. Often there is a wide variance, tailored to every level of the organization and each major type of user. It is very useful to make sure that the CEO, management, and even board members are reasonably well educated. After all, they need to make key decisions and drive support from the top.

- **Updates or program reviews.** These are usually progress updates on the implementation of risk management capabilities, measures, mitigation, etc.

- **Routine risk reporting.** These are reports provided at specific, regular time intervals describing the state of risks, their potential size, what is being done to mitigate them, how they have changed since the previous report, and whether any are becoming serious or mission-critical situations for management. Risk reports also can take on a variety of targets and levels. Once measures are in place, the organization should routinely monitor risks.

  These reports can be developed for specific business personnel who have responsibility for day-to-day management. They normally range in size from 2 to 5 pages. The idea is to keep them concise. They can also be developed and delivered as high-level overviews for senior executives, the CEO, or board members, who are more interested in overall progress than specific details.

Best Bets

What type of risk report should you prepare? Focus the report on delivering key messages succinctly. It should provide an overview of the relative (or ideally, absolute) size of each of the risks being reported and their growth over time. Ideally, the cause for their movement toward the danger zone should be identified and described. It is most effective if the reports are less than five pages (some organizations even shoot for two-page summaries). Another effective technique comes from the streets—literally! Use "traffic lights" to identify high (red), medium (yellow), and low (green) risks. Then use arrows to represent rising and falling risks. This method is particularly valuable when risks are hard to quantify.

How specific and particular should the communication be? Who is entitled to receive this information? How often? Will this communication be ongoing?

Let's say you are establishing a firm-wide risk management capability. Communication will most likely include various types of discussions with different groups of stakeholders. Some talks will concern the progress of implementing the overall capability. Other dialogue will focus on specific reporting on outcomes. What risks are manifesting at what levels, for example, and how are they being addressed? Discussion might also refer to routine reports that persist over time.

Valuing succinct, regular, progressive communication is critical to ensuring success for any risk management process. It is vital that everyone understand his or her roles and responsibilities and no one attempt to block the process. If you communicate every step and establish clarity and trust, real risk issues can surface and be constructively addressed.

Communication needs to be considered a treasured part of each step of the risk process.

Things to Remember

Risk management might seem like an exclusive process, a self-sustaining piece to add to an existing business, akin to a new division or product brand. It is not. Risk management does not occur in a vacuum; it is integrated into your organization, business, or project. For that reason, it is important to understand how it relates to every segment of the business, the objectives it is trying to serve, and the scope of the activity.

This process must always show positive value to the business—in terms of operational flow, productivity, and financial return. Even in a compliance context, where risk management is mandated, it should still seek to add business value. Risk must add value to the activity and value to the business and become an invisible (but mighty!) supportive arm. It should never become a burden.

Red Flags _____

> While you must know, manage, and mitigate your risks, you must also be aware of both their relative and actual sizes. Beware of spending thousands of dollars (or more) thwarting a risk that has little chance of harming your company. The consequences can be rough, in terms of both cash flow and the impact on sales, services, and production caused by tying up employees and resources.

The challenge in risk management is achieving a balance—striking the right level of integration with the business. You will know when you achieve that balance, because the process will become indispensable to each part of the business to which it is connected. Ultimately, a well-run risk management process can become a critical function for running the business on a day-to-day basis.

The Least You Need to Know

- The risk management process integrates with the targeted areas of your business. It is not a separate activity.

- The risk management process establishes an iterative approach that leads to routine review and continuous improvement.

- Understanding the context of the risk management plan you are building helps focus your efforts and increases the probability of a successful implementation.

- When dealing with risk, you must communicate with every key stakeholder in your company.

- When developing your risk management plan, be sure to tailor your reporting to your audiences.

Part 2

What Causes Risk?

By now you have a general sense of what the risk management process is all about and why it's necessary to assemble a plan to make sure that your business captures risks before they turn into major disruptive events.

Now it's time to dive into the details of risk as they pertain to your company. The following two chapters identify specific categories of risk that can afflict your company and your industry. You'll discover what causes these risks to materialize, either as separate events or in groups. Finally, you'll get a firm grasp on why businesses need to pinpoint their most potentially damaging risks and understand the relationship of those risks to the company.

Chapter 6

Categorizing Risk

In This Chapter

◆ Identifying risk categories

◆ Distinguishing among subcategories

◆ Determining strategic, financial, and operational risk

◆ Working with risk categories

It is human nature to name, label, and categorize. Every home, school, wood shop, museum, or business contains labels and categories for organizing specific items. Remember those baseball cards? That butterfly collection? Or the way you used to label your notebooks at school? Labels and categories help to develop a connection and sense of familiarity with new things, ideas, or concepts. They also help to organize thoughts around a common, familiar theme.

So it goes with risk. It is very helpful to categorize risks in business, to organize them so that solutions can work more effectively. While many business owners have created their own names for specific risks, the risk management profession has developed a set of formal categories, which will be introduced in this chapter.

Why Categorize Risk?

When learning a new language, one of the first steps is to categorize specific word patterns that remain consistent in their meaning. By categorizing those patterns you can quickly build vocabulary and understand better how the language is spoken.

Likewise, categorizing risk provides a specific way to reference information so that everyone can understand. It is the key starting point for learning the language of risk. It also provides a structured approach for identifying risk. As with languages, categories of risk can be quite different from one another. Different categories usually employ somewhat different techniques for measurement and management.

Rules of Thumb

When categorizing risk, it's useful to follow a few simple rules of thumb.

Mutually Exclusive, Collectively Exhaustive

The first rule of thumb is to use an approach risk management professions call *mutually exclusive, collectively exhaustive (MECE)*. The MECE approach categorizes risk in such a way that all risks can be covered without developing overlap.

def•i•ni•tion

The **mutually exclusive, collectively exhaustive (MECE)** approach to categorizing risk addresses every risk in your company or department (collectively exhaustive) while respecting the unique threats or issues posed by each (mutually exclusive). It helps to prevent overlap in measures, resources, or actions.

When it comes time to measure and manage risk, companies serve themselves best when the risks are measured in independent groups. This puts the risks in their proper categories, but also enables the assessor or assessment team to add up the groups to arrive at a "total" risk.

Industry-Specific Risks

When categorizing your company's risks, also keep in mind that specific risks tend to follow certain types of businesses. This is usually driven by the industry, but the company's size, growth, changing business climate, and other factors also come into play.

Most businesses also face risks in each of the different main risk categories. The question for any company implementing a risk management plan is "What specific risks do you have, and which are truly material?"

Risk Categories and Subcategories

The world of risk funnels down into three major categories:

- ◆ Strategic/business risks
- ◆ Financial risks
- ◆ Operational risks

Each of these risk categories contains unique characteristics that require different measurement, analysis, and management techniques. Each category fans into a group of subcategories that help more specifically nail down what is happening within the business and where the true risks lie.

Major Classes and Subclasses of Risk

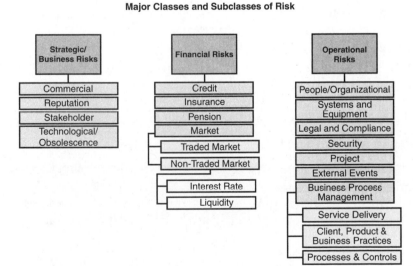

The Major Classes and Subclasses of Risk chart shows the three major classes of risk and the types of risk that derive from them.

Best Bets

When identifying risks, be sure to determine what category of risk each fits in. You can adopt the categories and subcategories presented in this book or you can use a variant—but be sure that all the categories are MECE.

Most likely, your business faces risk in the main categories but not necessarily (or likely) in all of the subcategories. If nothing else, subcategories form worthy checklists, serving as a mechanism for determining whether you face risk in this area. Although the subcategories listed in this chapter are not all-inclusive, they do provide a good starting point for understanding what risks may lurk in your business practices.

Strategic/Business Risks

Strategic risk, also called business risk, is both the broadest and murkiest category of risk. It encompasses every type of risk that can appear as a result of changes in the business environment, how the business addresses those changes, or how the business makes and implements strategic decisions. Since every company has a different strategy, the specific risks vary from organization to organization. The concept is fairly straightforward, but as we'll see later, strategic risk is one of the toughest types of risk to measure, assess, and manage.

def•i•ni•tion

Strategic risk is the current or prospective risk to earnings and capital arising from changes in the business environment and from adverse business decisions, improper implementation of decisions, or lack of responsiveness to changes in the business environment.

The major subcategories of strategic risk include the following:

Commercial risk. This category includes the risks associated with market placement, business growth, diversification, and commercial success. These risks relate to the commercial viability of a product or service and extend to the ability to retain and grow a customer base. Commercial risk can also include the presence of competitors, competitive responses, regulatory responses, and other factors.

Reputation risk. Reputation risk entails a threat to the private and public reputation of the business due to the conduct of the company, the quality of its products or services, or the conduct of employees or other individuals associated with the business. This risk often accompanies other risk events.

Stakeholder management risk. This category relates to the management of relationships with internal and external stakeholders, including shareholders and investors, unions, partners, employees, regulators, community interest groups, the media, and so on. As with reputation risk, this type of risk frequently accompanies other risk events.

Technological/obsolescence risk. This risk category involves the viability of products, production methods, or business management methods. It extends to recognizing the need for and the cost benefit associated with technology as part of a business development strategy.

Strategic Risk at Work

A local chain of hardware stores is evaluating expansion into other products and services in order to compete with bigger warehouse-style national chains. The decision-makers want to construct a strategy. In doing so, they decide to evaluate their strategic risks, of which they have several:

Commercial risk. Their commercial risk is large, as they could make an investment and discover that their market does not respond accordingly.

Reputation risk. They don't want to lose their glowing reputation as a trusted supplier that provides individual attention and good advice.

Stakeholder risk. The company has investors on its board as well as community support. They also will be dealing with contractors, some of whom are unionized. They will need to consider their current stakeholders as well as any potential new stakeholders that come aboard.

There will ultimately be other risks if the company chooses to move forward. These include numerous operational and financial risks as the store chain seeks to manage its capital position through the implementation. The company is aware of these risks, but wants to review the strategic risks as a first step.

In conducting the review, the decision-makers became aware of some issues that they hadn't previously considered, particularly the reputation and stakeholder risks. Realizing these risks are considerable, the chain plans to manage them carefully as it moves forward with expansion plans. The chain will also factor all of these risks into its budget and project plans. With this knowledge in hand, the decision-makers have a more accurate sense of the full costs involved in expanding. They can build a more robust plan and budget to address all of the risks.

Best Bets

When you conduct strategic risk reviews, be prepared to uncover additional risks, either strategic risks or risks in other categories. If these risks surface during a high-level assessment, which only addresses major risks and issues, then they likely are significant and need to be addressed.

After completing the review, the chain determined that the expansion project still looked viable on a cost-benefit basis and decided to move forward. As a result of using risk management techniques, their implementation benefited by increasing communication to stakeholders. Thanks to their efforts, the chain actually garnered higher sales in their new service offerings than they anticipated. The extra effort of running a risk management plan paid off.

For more information on measuring on managing strategic risks, see Chapter 14.

Financial Risks

Most business owners know what their *financial risks* are. Catching them on time and remediating them is the challenge.

def•i•ni•tion

Financial risk is any threat to a company's monetary strength, profit margin, or capital investment. Such risks include cash flow, budgetary requirements, tax obligations, regulatory capital and reserve requirements, creditor and debtor management, direct capital markets effects, remuneration, and other general account management concerns.

This category of risk garners the most attention by regulators and business investors. It also has the best developed capabilities in terms of measurement sciences, management, and mitigation techniques.

One of the fascinating qualities of financial risk is that each and every subclass of it can be analyzed, measured, and modeled separately. This is why businesses can wind up investing a lot of money and time in this area if they so choose. The two financial giants Citibank and Barclays, for example, each dedicate hundreds of people to the measurement, management, and monitoring of financial risks and subrisks.

The following specific subcategories of financial risk are familiar to most business owners or accountants:

Credit risk. Credit risk is the potential for economic loss due to the failure of a borrower or counterparty to fulfill its contractual obligations in a timely manner. This usually happens because of an inability or unwillingness to pay. Examples of credit risk areas include business banking, middle market lending, small business lending, retail lending, settlement risks, project finance risks, credit cards, and residential mortgages.

Market risk. Exposure to potential loss often results from changes in market prices or rates. The two main subcategories of market risk are traded and nontraded market risk.

Traded market risk concerns financial instruments that the company holds and how interest rate changes and other economic and market factors may affect their value. This is important to any business that carries traded instruments, whether for investment or hedging purposes. These risks are also associated with commodities, equities, foreign exchange, and fixed income.

> ### Risk Factors
>
> Breaking down financial risk categories and subcategories can feel like calculating the square root of pi. There are more than 200 subcategories of financial risk that institutional giants monitor, each of which has separate models.

Nontraded market risks are any financial risks associated with the business structure. Nontraded market risks can be further divided into two smaller categories: liquidity risk and interest rate risk.

Liquidity risk focuses on whether the business has enough liquidity to cover its obligations. Many market and financial management factors can create cash flow problems. This is a very important risk category for many businesses, particularly small businesses. Technically, this risk is associated with the inability to rapidly liquidate assets, products, positions, or portfolios. Every business tries to get beyond the worst-case scenario, which is having obligations to cover but not being able to sell products or other assets rapidly enough to cover them.

Interest rate risk concerns the strain on a business's coffers brought about by rising (or falling) interest rates. For most businesses, interest rate risk is relatively small, but there are a few notable cases where it can become large and very meaningful. This is particularly true if incoming cash flow is dictated and determined in a relatively fixed manner. When cash requirements, such as loans, are denominated in floating rates (rates that rise and fall with external market rates, such as the prime rate), a rise in interest rates can cause real problems.

If interest rates move, how would they affect the business's financial strength? If the business is servicing a floating rate loan, it may have difficulty meeting interest payments on the loan. If the company provides financing to customers—say, a furniture company or auto dealership—terms may change if interest rates increase. Or customers may have trouble paying the increased monthly installment.

Other financial risks. Other financial risks include insurance risks (there are a whole set of these) and pension risk. Insurance risk really only applies if you self-insure or are operating an insurance firm. Pension risk applies if you assume long-term pension responsibilities for your employees.

Financial Risk at Work

A consumer products company that sells small electronics and appliances has been expanding its offerings to sell larger products, such as bigger TVs and white goods (large appliances such as refrigerators, dishwashers, etc.). As a result, the company has started offering credit. It has been expanding its initially successful credit program to offer some lines of credit and other loans. The company realizes that its credit offerings are expanding rapidly and that it is starting to see a large credit exposure. The company hasn't suffered any negative consequences so far, but company leadership knows that they have been fortunate.

Risk Factors

Primary risk concerns vary from industry to industry. If you are in financial services or high-tech, you are more likely to experience a higher degree of strategic risk. Businesses in financial services, shipping and transportation, and telecommunications all have a high degree of financial risk. Health care, manufacturing, shipping and transportation, and construction businesses often experience a higher degree of operational risk.

Company leadership decides to assess their financial risks. In doing so, they discover that they not only carry the retail credit risks of which they were previously aware, but that they also have exposed themselves to interest rate risk and liquidity risk. They realize that they will need to put in place a more robust team to manage the treasury or change their credit terms. They decide that the investment in treasury is more than they are ready to handle for the time being. However, they strike up a relationship with a local bank that enables them to continue to offer the favorable credit terms. In exchange, the bank convinces the company to outsource the management of the credit, and with it the liquidity and interest rate risks that it created, to an outside firm. Doing so allows the company to offer the same great services and product support that were helping it grow, while eliminating many of the increasing financial risks. After all, the company's core business is selling consumer products, not banking!

See Chapter 15 for more information on measuring and managing financial risks.

Operational Risks

By far the most ubiquitous risk category is *operational risk*. Businesses face operational risks in myriad shapes and forms every day.

Operational risks cover every aspect of internal operations, as well as certain non-strategic external events (such as natural disasters and security breaches). All front office, back office, and factory/assembly line activities and all activities associated with the outer extensions of the company's four walls (suppliers, distributors, etc.) carry operational risk.

The risk management profession breaks operational risk into a number of subclasses, as follows:

def•i•ni•tion

Operational risk is the risk of loss resulting from inadequate or failed internal processes, people, and systems or from external events. This includes fraud, security issues, and outside occurrences, including natural disasters, political upheaval, and widespread power outages.

People/organizational risk. Every business has personnel requirements ranging from job descriptions to company-wide policies. These internal requirements extend to cultural, structural, and people issues associated with the effective operation of the business. Since every worker is human, and thus prone to occasional mistakes, risk is inherent. This subcategory also includes risks that may arise due to employment practices, staffing inadequacy, and loss of key personnel (including *key man risk*), employee errors, wrongful acts, and workplace safety.

def•i•ni•tion

Key man risk is the operational and strategic risk that results when a well-placed, indispensable employee (the "key man") leaves the company, and either retires, goes to another company, or starts a business. The key man likely holds proprietary information and strategies that he/she helped to develop. Besides being difficult to replace, the key man can literally take away trade secrets and affect operations if the operational steps he/she has mastered have not been written down. Either way, it poses substantial risk to the company.

Business process management risk. A business's ability to consistently manage its day-to-day operations and deliver services and products is crucial. Disruptions of these core processes can be costly not only to the bottom line but also to the company's reputation. Business process management breaks down further into risk potential resulting from service delivery (customer service, product and service delivery, poor response to customer complaints, etc.); client, product, and business practices (documentation, disclosure advisory, product flaws or inadequate specifications, improper business or market practices); and processes and controls (failed transaction processing, vendor and supplier miscommunication, process control failures, inadequate or failed internal documentation).

Systems and equipment risk. This subcategory concerns business disruption and cost due to system failures or lengthy maintenance or replacement of equipment. When businesses are running well, they often fall into a comfort zone, focusing on servicing customers but failing to upgrade or adequately maintain their systems and equipment.

Legal and compliance risk. This category includes compliance with legal requirements such as legislation, regulations, standards, codes of practice, and contractual terms. This category also extends to compliance with additional rules that may be established through contracts, customer requirements, the social environment, or internal management. These rules come in the form of policies, procedures, or expectations.

Security risk. The greatest security risks to businesses concern premises, assets, and people. They extend to security of information, intellectual property, and technology—a huge subcategory for companies working in the IT field or dealing with foreign governments or markets. The information/intellectual property/technology triad has become a major issue in the era of the laptop, Internet, and instant information transfer. For instance, the second you enter some foreign airspaces while traveling for a meeting with your product manufacturer, everything on your computer and the Internet can be monitored and intercepted by that country's government.

Project risk. Project risk concerns threats to the management of equipment, finances, resources, technology, time frames, and people associated with those projects. It extends to internal operational projects, activities relating to business development, and external efforts such as those undertaken for clients. Whenever a project involves another business, the risk stretches into your relationship with that other company.

Risk Factors

Unlike financial risk, which employs different sets of numbers and instruments for literally every subcategory, operational risks are not generally modeled separately.

External events risk. External events are what are known as "acts of God" or other natural and non-natural disasters and events. They are risks by virtue of their destructive potential and their unpredictability. Earthquakes, hurricanes, ice storms, fires, floods, airplane crashes, and other disasters fit into this category.

Operational Risks at Work

A small manufacturer of special fabrics decided to conduct an operational risk assessment. The managers knew that, as a manufacturer, they faced numerous operational risks, but they had always managed them as they materialized. In essence, they were firefighting each day's problems. They conducted an assessment and confirmed the myriad risks associated with their equipment and management of their suppliers. They also discovered a few notable risks they hadn't previously considered.

One risk that hadn't been considered previously was key man risk. A single employee, who had been instrumental in the development of the core product line, single-handedly tweaked the machinery several times a day to ensure that the product was being generated at its highest quality. He was viewed as a magician. He never wrote down what he did or the logic behind his adjustments. As an additional risk, the manufacturer was operating in very old wood buildings. With all of the fabric dust, they faced a serious risk of fire.

 Red Flags

Operational risks are notorious for starting small, multiplying, and turning into large risks—risks that can become contagious to the entire company. They tend to pop up and cause immediate trouble.

The company's managers decided to establish two parallel efforts. The first was to document and create procedures around the old trusted employee. They developed process control procedures and assigned two employees to be the old hand's apprentices to learn his approach to quality control. On the second front, the company took several actions: increasing insurance, establishing a backup manufacturing site in a more modern building, developing a plan to move some of the manufacturing to lower floors, and improving safety procedures in case of fire. The company also beefed up its sprinkler systems and smoke detectors. In turn, this move supported capacity needs and allowed for more efficient deliveries. Most of all, the new environment simply didn't contain as many operational risks.

See Chapter 16 for details on measuring and managing operational risks.

Who Holds These Risks?

The preceding pages outlined numerous serious risks. List all of them on one sheet of paper, and any sensible person might ask, "Why go into business at all?"

The Heat Map of Industry risks enables companies to consider risks stretched across their industry when identifying and mapping their own risks and evaluating action steps.

Heat Map of Industry Risks

Industry	Strategic & Business Risk	Operational Risk	Financial Risk
Agriculture/Agribusiness	Medium	High	Medium
Financial Services	High	Medium	High
Business and Professional Services	Medium-High	Low	Low
Hotel and Hospitality	Medium	Low-Medium	Low-Medium
Industrial/Manufacturing	Medium	High	High
Personal Services	Low-Medium	Low	Low-Medium
Construction	Medium	High	Medium-High
Retail Merchandise	Medium-High	Low-Medium	Medium
Wholesale Merchandise	Medium	Low	Medium-High
High Tech	High	Medium-High	Medium
Non-Manufacturing High Tech	Medium-High	Low	Low
Entertainment	Medium-High	Low	Medium-High
Health Care	Medium	High	Medium
Printing and Publishing	Medium-High	Low-Medium	Low-Medium
Real Estate	Medium-High	Low	Medium-High
Shipping and Transportation	Medium-High	High	High
Telecommunications	Medium-High	Medium	High
Utilities	Low-Medium	Medium-High	Medium

It's not as scary as it seems. Unless the company serves all industries, has bottomless financial reserves, and employs a team of risk-taking daredevils managed by equally adventurous executives, it will never see all of these risk categories materialize at once. Virtually no company will. However, every company holds some combination of these risks today, with other sets of risks certain to pop up as the business grows and expands—or as the industry, market, or social environment changes.

Knowledge of the industry and its risk profile over time can help a company identify, categorize, and prepare for specific risks. Those risks may or may not be material at the moment, but it's important to know whether or not they are. In the world of risk, ignorance is most certainly not bliss.

Beyond that, a company's particular position in the marketplace and its overall life cycle will determine most of its risks.

The Least You Need to Know

- Risk categories enable companies to label potential risks and group them for assessment and action.

- Strategic risk appears as the business environment changes. It affects how businesses make and implement strategic decisions.

- Financial risk affects cash flow, credit, invoicing, and the money supply of the business.

- Operational risk affects the way companies operate day to day in every activity. It must be identified and monitored closely, since it can quickly paralyze production and infect the entire company.

- Knowing the history and business dealings of the industry helps companies identify and categorize potential risks.

Which Risks Are Lurking in Your Shop?

In This Chapter

- Identifying potential risks inside your business
- Differentiating risks for new and established companies
- Uncovering competitor risks
- Rooting out risks in your supply chain
- Making assessments that work for you

Now that we've explained what risk management is all about (Chapters 1 through 5) and identified the three major risk categories (Chapter 6), we arrive at one of the biggest questions you can ask when it comes to your business: How do you identify your potential risks?

What you do to address today's potential risk determines what your business will look like next year. If you do not identify a risk when its early symptoms present themselves, then you may not be around to swing your doors open next year, let alone five years from now. On the other hand, if you identified and planned for potential risks you will be in a far better position to have expanded and increased your business markedly.

To be prepared, it is important to take a systematic review of your business and focus on identifying the most significant risks you are likely to face. Don't be afraid! This is a normal part of doing business. Keep in mind that risks can be both positive and negative. And remember that if you don't take on some risk, you won't grow and make money. The objective here is to identify your business's core categories of risks so that you can take an informed view on how to manage them.

Know Your Business

Wise business owners, managers, and executives always keep an eye on their business structures as they pertain to the larger industry and marketplace. Knowing your business landscape makes it easier to understand the framework of risks you are likely to encounter, which include your overall risk profile, specific types of risks, and interactions that might take place between risks or risk categories. These interactions can be as harmful to your business as a mixture of prescription drugs can be to your body.

In order to see your business in the context of risk management, try looking at tools such as Porter's Five Forces, which was developed to show the relationship between your business and the various threats to its stability. Always maintain a keen awareness of the risks inherent in dealing with your industry, competitors, suppliers, and buyers. By knowing and understanding the business structure in good times and bad, companies can better prioritize which risks must be addressed first. That enables you, or your team, to define the types of measures, analyses, treatments, or mitigation strategies to apply. Consequently, you know what types of risks to monitor.

Porter's Five Forces is a great tool for understanding and identifying the strengths and weaknesses (read: risk) of your present competitive position.

(From Competitive Strategy: Techniques for Analyzing Industries and Competitors *by Michael Porter [1980: Free Press].)*

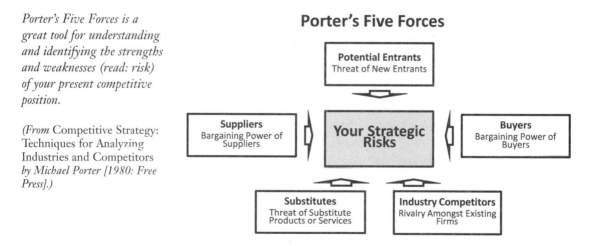

Porter's Five Forces

Industry Risks

Whether you are CEO of a large multinational media conglomerate or the owner of a local clothing boutique, it is vital to know the risks particular to your industry. Be sure you are acquainted with your industry, its history, and its responses to various economic and social situations. When you know your industry and the risks associated with it, you have taken a critical first step.

If you sell products into different markets, identifying your industry might not be as simple as it seems. For example, if a company makes dinner plates and sells them through retail distributors, is it a ceramics company or a consumer products company? The answer will shape that company's view of its competition, products, customers, and distribution channels—each of which has its specific set of potential risks and strategies for managing or mitigating those risks.

An example is the famous De Beers diamond company, which has long prided itself on its position as one of the world's primary sources of diamonds. But is De Beers a diamond supplier or a retailer of fine jewelry? When De Beers ran into strategic challenges, the company reassessed its risks and realized that it needed to rethink what business it was in. De Beers repositioned itself as a customer-oriented diamond jewelry retailer. This changed not only its strategy but also its risk profile. With this view in mind, De Beers reduced its massive inventory and supply channels. The action enabled the company to reduce specific risks and focus on the core risks of retail, which lessened its overall risk profile.

Most risks can be identified and understood by reviewing the dynamics of the industry—how products have traditionally been developed, how competitors have thrived (and failed), how the industry is moving against the overall market landscape, fluctuation of price points (and why), industry or government regulations, best practices, and how the seasons and economic upturns and downturns work for and against you. These dynamics will inevitably shape the risks you face.

The key is to identify your industry, develop a clear picture of it, and understand the relationship of your business to the dynamics of that industry.

Size and Growth Projection

Risk is like a vessel that sails to sea. If the boat is small (a small company) and heads into open water (large, expansive growth), chances are that the boat will face high-risk situations almost daily. On the other hand, if the vessel is a huge cruise liner (a large company), the chances of single open-ocean incidents turning into full-scale disasters are proportionately smaller.

Every company wants to grow; growth is often synonymous with success in business. However, even for big companies, aggressive growth relative to the rest of your industry can present problems.

A great way to identify potential risk is to measure the current size of your company compared to other companies in the same industry. Included in this measurement would be growth projections and typical short- and long-term industry growth.

Smaller companies often experience rapid growth until they reach a standard scale for the industry. During this period of rapid growth, their operational risk increases as the need to manage people, processes, equipment, and technology grows to support demand. Along with that comes financial risks pertaining to need for stronger cash flow and more investment capital.

Smaller companies also face a host of new challenges larger companies can typically avoid. For instance, small companies can experience less leverage in negotiating with suppliers, greater difficulty in developing a supplier base, less power in negotiating with customers, greater dependence on single customers, greater difficulty developing new products or entering new markets due to the costs and resources involved, and greater difficulty weathering financial storms. All of these are necessary hurdles to overcome in a small business.

> **Risk Factors**
>
> Growth of more than 20 percent annually is considered high growth and is often difficult to sustain. Companies growing this fast need to be particularly alert to operational risks creeping up.

If you own or operate a bigger company, you can probably handle more risks and greater swings in those risks, including shifts in your overall financial condition, because you have more resources at hand. This doesn't mean that you don't need to be wary. You may handle competitive demands, including growth, better than a smaller company, but excessive growth can still generate real risks.

How Established Are You?

Time in business, level of marketplace establishment, and life cycles are the long-term measuring blocks of any company. They require different planning, operational, and management strategies—all of which bring into play different types of risk.

For example, if you're a new company, you are (hopefully) spending a considerable amount of time and resources developing your staff and structure, and also creating markets and securing new business for the company. This creates a broad variety of clear operational and financial risks associated with spreading precious resources and manpower too thin.

If the business is more established and well-rooted in the community, industry, and greater marketplace, then you may face fewer risks overall and have greater experience in managing them. However, the risks will be different and no less serious. They typically include strategic risks associated with maintaining viability, generating sources of diversification, and creating new growth.

Competitive Landscape

Whether conducting business or playing sports, we tend to focus on our competition. Thus, we tend to more readily recognize business risk from competitors than from inside our own office, store, or plant. Knowing the competitive landscape is not only vital for promotional and marketing purposes, but also for assessing the risks to the bottom line.

Ask yourself the following questions regarding your company's competitive landscape to accurately gauge the risk to your short- and long-term success:

Are there many competitors?

Are they large or small?

How aggressive are they?

Do they have a pattern of taking over companies, price discounting, or flooding the market with product to turn back competition?

What expectations in service, location, and reliability have competitors within the industry set for customers?

Be wary of certain behaviors in competitors. In marketplaces with many competitors, there's a higher likelihood of aggressive practices that can lead to mergers, takeovers, and other forms of industry consolidation. In some industries, larger companies might acquire smaller companies to take them out of competition and absorb their unique products; a perfect example is how Microsoft has bought out and then absorbed the innovative products of numerous small outstanding software companies over the years. Or, to flip the coin, beware of companies that must merge with another company or else go out of business. Other aggressive practices that can put your business at risk include slash-and-burn discount pricing, poaching of your top employees, and offerings from competitors that compromise your most recent product line.

80   Part 2: What Causes Risk?

Suppliers

Suppliers provide the lifeblood of the business world, whether it flows as raw materials for a manufacturer, parts for an assembly line, or products for a retailer. Because of their importance to your business, suppliers can pose considerable risk. Their ability to deliver to you in a timely manner is crucial, but you don't have any control over their operations! Imagine if you ran a Dairy Queen and your supply truck failed to show up for its scheduled afternoon delivery, leaving you without any ice cream to serve your customers on a hot summer day. In this case, no control means lost sales and irritated customers.

Every well-managed business uses a core group of suppliers but also knows its product supply market well enough to call on backups when necessary. To determine how susceptible you are to supply risk, ask yourself the following questions:

> Do you know the major suppliers in your industry besides those that serve you?

> Do you know your suppliers' track records with other companies?

> How about their ability to keep the supply pipeline open—even during challenging times?

> Can you guarantee the quality of your suppliers' products to your customers?

> Do your suppliers offer you flexible terms, service, and ordering options?

Like so many other aspects of risk management, knowledge of suppliers, the quality of their products, and their highest and lowest inventory seasons—and cost variations—becomes a powerful way to reduce potential operational, reputation, and other strategic risks.

By understanding the risks associated with suppliers, a company can identify actual and potential risks and plan accordingly. The business can also alleviate the crippling pain of losing customers due to unforeseen kinks in the supply chain.

Customers

Customers come in all shapes and sizes, from individuals to large companies, and so it makes sense that the ways to identify and mitigate risks posed by those customers are equally varied.

Red Flags _____

In retail industries, customers usually show payment problems between two and four months after Christmas. Why? First payments aren't due until one month after Christmas, and most companies don't or can't track payments for another month after that. After four months, banks will intensify their collection effort and make sure they are the first creditor to be paid—making it harder for you to get paid.

The most effective way to identify risks that your customers generate is to know a lot about your customers. Answer the following questions:

How often do they need credit?

How much credit do they need?

What do their payment histories look like?

Who pays invoices early to take advantage of discounts offered?

What other costs do your customers generate?

Are some customers more likely to require customer service than others?

What are their average purchases? What times of year do they do most of their purchasing?

Best Bets _____

Look out for customers that might be too large! What seems like good news for your revenue can also pose serious risk to your business if variances in payments or orders affect cash flow and product volume thresholds. A large aggressive customer can also pressure prices downward.

Know Your Organization

We've spent the bulk of this chapter focusing on outside forces, conditions, or activities that require businesses to be flexible and razor-sharp in identifying associated risks. Sometimes, however, the greatest risks to continued growth and success lie within a company's walls. Evaluate the condition of your people, processes, systems, and products for further insight into where your risks lie.

Company Mission and Product

Ever since Leonardo da Vinci sketched out a helicopter and countless other visionary devices during the Italian Renaissance, the business world has been rife with stories of brilliant, innovative minds that developed great products—but never figured out how they fit into available markets. Even Thomas Edison had his problems, trying 2,000 failed iterations of the light bulb before stumbling on the one that changed the world.

Understanding how a company's products fit into the market and the company's overall mission is both necessary strategy and good risk management. It enables a company to differentiate itself and remain relevant.

A fine example of this comes from Volant, a manufacturer of high-end steel skis that would be considered a small business in terms of volume. Volant's skis run from $2,000 to $3,000 per pair, which is fairly expensive. In the hyper-competitive ski market, Volant would seem to be at risk of never selling a single pair of skis. However, Volant executives know that the industry includes a customer segment that appreciates the finest quality and function in the products they buy. Volant identified its greatest risk: losing sales to lower-priced fiberglass skis. The company devised a market strategy, complete with a brand book given to all buyers, that celebrated the story of 150 years of luxurious, classy products made with fine steel. Volant established a niche for itself within the broader ski marketplace and worked hard to become the premier manufacturer in that niche which, in itself, reduces risk. Consequently, the company bypassed the price-point objection, branded itself, and ameliorated what should have been its greatest risk.

You might ask the following questions about your product or product line:

Is the product too new, its effectiveness not yet known by the market?

Is it technologically stable enough for the marketplace?

Is it too old or obsolete?

What expense is involved in developing or launching the product or product line?

The answers to these questions mainly reveal potential strategic risks, specifically commercial risks, reputation risk, and risks associated with technological obsolescence. If you are launching new products, you will also experience financial and operational risks in project management, building new business processes, and funding. Be mindful of these when setting the world afire with your new product!

The Workforce

The most important aspect of any organization is its workforce. Your ability to find the right people for particular positions is directly proportional to the overall efficiency—and stability—of your operations. This is true whether you own or operate a large corporation with 10,000 employees or a diner with 10 employees. It also explains why larger companies create entire departments to deal with the recruiting, interviewing, qualifying, and hiring of employees.

Workforce management is, in essence, a part of risk management. After all, a troubled or underperforming employee is a potential risk, as is an overly ambitious employee wishing to rise to the top, no matter what (or who) might stand in his or her way. By the same token, overdependence on an exemplary employee—key man risk—can weaken the organization as well. Thus, it is vital to occasionally ask questions to identify potential operational risks stemming from the relationship between the organization and its people.

When evaluating your workforce, don't be afraid to ask the following tough questions:

> How stable is the workforce?
>
> How likely are workforce members to leave?
>
> How specialized is the workforce?
>
> Are there individuals who would cause major problems or critical holes in the company if they left (key man risk)?
>
> Are there existing challenges with human resources practices or relations (e.g., union rules and relations)?
>
> What type of people work for the company?
>
> How much care do they take with the business?
>
> Are they likely to cause issues with customers, suppliers, or stakeholders?

The answers to these questions can expose such issues as staffing inadequacies, potential loss of key personnel, employment practices, employee errors, wrongful acts, and workplace safety. Turn these questions into priorities. It is critical to the company's reputation, operations, and bottom line that all risks associated with employees be identified and acted upon in short order.

Governance and Decision-Making

Top-down businesses controlled by a hierarchal CEO, president, or management team and businesses in which the employees are highly empowered and share decision-making capability face equal amounts of risk. The specific types of risk often include compliance, stakeholder, and sometimes even operational risks to business processes. The best ways to identify these risks are to review how communication flows between management and staff and how rules and regulations are governed; that is, monitored, managed, and enforced. This happens whether they are company policies or best-practice standards set by the industry.

Risk Factors
Many people think that risk is greatest at the highest and lowest rungs of a business: with decision-makers, who determine the future types and course of business, and entry-level employees, who are susceptible to making mistakes. However, risk runs through the entire workforce, requiring attention to governance and decision-making at every level.

Examine the way the organization makes decisions. Its flexibility or responsiveness to change may be a risk if the process is too hierarchal or formal. On the other hand, having too many decision-makers can lead to mixed agendas, impasses, and paralysis of the business. Organizations develop over time, and their policy-makers need to adjust accordingly, or their decisions may impact negatively on the future and create risk.

Processes and Controls

Although most managers are intuitively aware of every process and control in their businesses, it is easy to forget the finer points of individual processes, which makes it harder to assert quality control and other risk-alleviating steps. When reviewing core processes for potential risks, it is very important to evaluate the stability of each process. In addition, be sure each process includes adequate controls and documentation. Accountability can minimize risk.

Systems and Technology

Nothing ruins a good day faster than a computer crash, especially when the data hasn't been adequately backed up. Crashes cause instant pain—and with it, potentially high costs and loss of crucial data! In this age of connectivity, identifying the risks associated with core systems and technology is just as important as making sure products and services are delivered on time. Yet, it's the old "you know how it goes" syndrome: Things get busy, employees type away, files aren't saved to redundant servers, daily or weekly virus checks are overlooked, or scheduled tune-ups on critical machines are skipped to save a few bucks. The next day, the systems are toast.

Learn and review the risks associated with all of the company's systems and technology. Hand the latest software or firmware manual to the company IT expert, and make sure he or she knows the technology well enough to troubleshoot it. With that same IT expert (it could be you) present, ask these simple questions to help identify other potential risks:

- Are the technology and systems adequate for current and future operations?

- What sorts of failures can occur with these systems and equipment?

- Do any of the potential failures present safety risks?

- What systems are out of date or beyond capacity?

- What equipment needs to be serviced—and when?

Rolling Up Your Sleeves

Now that the types of potential risk associated with competitors, the industry, suppliers, customers, and operations have been recognized, what is the best way to get to the bottom of the pertinent questions for each of these risks? There are a number of strong approaches, a few of which are key to conducting the right assessment. Most companies find that the quickest and easiest approaches are qualitative assessments that leverage your own knowledge and your own people.

Strengths, Weaknesses, Opportunities, and Threats

A great way to identify strategic risks and many other core operational and financial risks is through an analysis of strengths, weaknesses, opportunities, and threats, what risk managers call a "SWOT analysis" for short. When performed by the key management team and/or operational team, a SWOT analysis can quickly highlight key risks across the business.

A SWOT analysis is conducted by asking questions related to each category, such as the following:

- ◆ **Strengths.** What are my businesses strengths? What makes the business most successful? Is it reputation, good products, good prices, good service, good location? Something else?

- ◆ **Weaknesses.** What does your company worry about the most? What causes your greatest problems? What is noticeably weak about your company versus other competitors?

- ◆ **Opportunities.** Where is your company's next opportunity coming from? Are there changes in your industry or market likely to open up new opportunities?

- ◆ **Threats.** Are there any notable changes that are looming and could seriously hurt your business or your industry more generally?

Use Your Organization

Go inside your company walls and start assessing! Brainstorming sessions, focus groups, and structured interviews with the top executive or operations team work well. These can be conducted with a SWOT framework or using the questions laid out earlier in this chapter.

What Keeps You Up at Night?

Undertake a *scenario analysis* to focus on key risks as well as how they might manifest themselves. This process provides powerful insight into measuring, assessing, and managing risks down the road. This is often best conducted with your key business teams, your advisors, and your board.

def•i•ni•tion

Scenario analysis is the process of identifying and evaluating potential risks to your business and thinking about how they might play out before they actually occur.

Here's an example: Suppose your company loses a key supplier or encounters a major quality control problem with that supplier. What are the possible repercussions? Identify them, then ask, "What alternatives do we have, and what are the issues with those alternatives?" Maybe you can find a supplier that delivers product faster. Perhaps another supplier provides greater quality.

Explore these possibilities, and make lists of suppliers you can actually use if this situation arises. Then ask, "What risks could be generated by making this move?" Think of what might happen if the new product or material is inferior to the current supply. Would it shut down your process? Hurt your business's reputation?

War-Gaming

War-gaming is similar to scenario analysis, but it is done from the perspective of both the competitor and the company. Set up competitive teams (a "competitor" and the "home team"), and work through competitive scenarios and responses. This helps bring to light key strategic risks.

Call the Experts

Some companies seek risk assessment through outside experts and sources such as auditors, specialists, insurance claims reports, post-event reports, and other methods. Even without a formal risk assessment, standard reports provided by outside experts can provide great insight into where your business's deepest challenges lurk.

Best Bets

An expert or consultant can come into your business and provide a fresh, yet experienced, set of eyes. The information you need to identify risks to your business might be lying out in the open. An audit report, insurance report, or similar evaluation may already be in your hands—and may be ready to provide powerful insight into your key risks.

Why call an expert? Companies will make the call if they experience more severe issues or feel they need help the first time they encounter a risk situation—especially if theirs is a specialty business. If a company is regulated in any way by industry or government, it may want an outside opinion to provide a third-party view that satisfies an inspector.

The Least You Need to Know

- ◆ Risk identification requires a comprehensive view of internal and external factors affecting your business.

- ◆ Many of your key risks will be defined by the risks inherent to your industry.

- ◆ Use your workforce to obtain the best view of the key risks you face.

- ◆ Determine your key risks and how they might manifest in your business by using exercises such as scenario analysis and war-gaming.

Part 3

Assessing Risk

You've identified your specific risks and organized them into their appropriate risk categories. You know some of those risks are on the horizon, and you've identified others that are of only minor concern. Some risks, however, are imminent and need to be addressed ASAP.

Now it's time to determine the appropriate level of mitigation or action for each of the risks you face. At first glance, risk assessment might seem like a college-level calculus course, but it doesn't have to be that complicated. The following chapters show you ways to build simple measures and assessments that will provide the data you need. Of course, if you want to be a complete risk management maniac and go for complex, intricate measures, you'll be introduced to those tools as well.

How Do You Measure Up?

In This Chapter

- ◆ The reasons for measuring risk
- ◆ The rules for building models
- ◆ The core building blocks of risk measurement
- ◆ Deciding what to focus on

If risk management was simply a matter of identifying and fixing problems, then countless businesses might be more secure. There wouldn't be any need to write books on the topic. The most critical step of risk management, however, is measuring and assessing risk. This process is part art and part science, particularly for certain risk categories. Consequently, measurement and assessment is the most difficult aspect of risk for most people to grasp, and it is also the aspect that feels the most unnatural to a normal business flow.

Risk measurement and assessment grabs all the headlines and cameras when the media asks about troubled companies. We've all heard reporters ask these questions: "Did their risk models fail?" "What risk measures were taken?" "Did they pass the stress test?" This is the aspect of risk we hear most about when a financial crisis grips the globe or a company is in serious trouble.

Why Measure Risk?

There are many reasons to measure risk. Measurements allow companies to grasp the importance of the risks they face. By measuring risk, companies can more easily compare risks on many different levels and note declines or improvements in either their overall situations or specific problem spots. After all, the goal of measurement is to understand the nature of risk and pinpoint problems.

Best Bets

In your risk planning, always try to remember the key reasons for measuring risk. They include understanding how large or small specific risks might be, the possibility of contagion or concentrations of risk, monitoring, supporting mitigation methods, pinpointing causes, and evaluating future investment in efforts to reduce risk.

Measuring risk even allows companies to gain perspective on how much they want to invest in future risk management technologies, people, and processes. Since risk management can call for either a simple solution (always the goal!) or something complicated enough to twist a math professor into a pretzel, it's best to measure and size up the issues first. Measurement also allows you to determine materiality, a key concept that helps to focus on risks and groups of risks that are most important and significant.

How Much Mitigation Do You Need?

The other key reason for measuring risk is to decide how much mitigation and management is required. This is the big money question, quite literally. Measurements will be a waste of time and money if mitigation plans and proper management are not assigned to their results. Likewise, overly mitigating a not-so-serious risk can shrink profits and productivity. The balancing act between measuring and mitigating is perhaps the most vital task for a company's risk manager, whether it be the company owner or an executive, director, department, or outside consultant.

def•i•ni•tion

Immaterial risks are smaller risks that are not likely to present any problems now or in the near future.

In this review, look at both *immaterial* and material risks. With immaterial risks, mitigation and management may not be needed; after all, they're barely a blip on the radar. Material risks, however, may suggest that serious management and mitigation is in order. It is important to spot risk concentrations and evaluate how material or immaterial they may be.

Within those risk concentrations are the so-called small risks, those radar blips that can become screen-consuming blobs as they reach problem levels.

With material risk, the focus becomes different: How does the company mitigate it? At what cost? Most of the pitfalls described here and in earlier chapters can be avoided with good measurement and assessment techniques.

Using Risk Measures

While using risk measures can be a good idea, realistically, it's not for everyone. For smaller businesses or those with very little financial risk, just prioritizing risks and keeping an eye on them may be enough. Alternatively, you can seek a one-time assessment of risks when you're preparing to evaluate strategic decisions or projects. For many other businesses, though, setting up a program of routine measurement and analysis is very helpful, particularly when a considerable amount of financial risk is involved.

Risk measurement can be daunting at first. It involves some fairly complicated math. If you and those in your business are not able to look at risk in a quantitative manner and to communicate with each other about it, then even the simplest measures and analysis approaches may seem overwhelming.

Unfortunately, risk management professionals often make matters even worse. They have a bad habit of taking simple concepts most of us learned in grade school and complicating them. Simplicity sometimes escapes them, which can present a big problem for people who just want their risks measured, assessed, and mitigated already! The risk term "expected loss," for example, is another way of saying "mean" or "average."

Red Flags

Financial risk is the bellwether: if it cripples your business, nothing else is going to matter. Use risk measures to evaluate your financial risk often. Your business will be more stable because of your effort.

In addition, some business owners or those assigned to risk management must learn how to acquire the hard data that makes analyses more meaningful. They must also try to develop basic models or calculators that can be used repeatedly and set up systems such as scenario analysis.

Yet, as with any new skill or discipline, there are some ways to make the risk measurement process simpler and more effective for your company.

Some Basic Rules

Here are some basic rules for measuring risk.

Start with a clear goal. What are you trying to measure or assess? How much of your business do you want to involve? Which risks are you focusing on for each measurement?

Define your objective as narrowly as possible. Confine the objective to a single risk, or even a single sub-risk.

Understand your risk assumptions and document them. Record the assumptions you have made about the risks you are measuring, the data you are using, and the measurements you are making. Make sure others review and understand these assumptions.

Use as much data and data history as you can. A minimum of three years is ideal. However, if you don't have three years of data, don't let that stop you. Having some data—even a well-constructed guess—is better than nothing.

Build simple measures. Start with basic equations that are simple to understand.

Use consistent measures and assumptions. Make sure that your framework is the same for all risks. It becomes impossible to measure if each risk is assigned different definitions, measurement approaches, and horizon times. Using consistent measures and assumptions streamlines the process so you can readily add up your risks.

Update and maintain assumptions and data regularly. This helps improve the accuracy of your models and measures over time.

Validate the model. Get someone else to check the calculations, the inputs, and the logic. If your model is a predictive model (a model that tries to predict future behavior using past behavior), backtest it. (Backtesting is checking the effectiveness of a model's predictions by verifying how its predictions compare to actual results.)

Stress test the models. Apply extreme data points and assumptions to test the model or measures. Doing so will help to demonstrate how you will be impacted by situations beyond your current assumptions and may also highlight weaknesses in the model.

Avoid black boxes; make your process transparent. Try to break down calculations into clear, easily understood steps. Document each step so that others can make sense of them as well.

Document, document, document! Each step and each output should be documented so you can review the findings at a later date.

Best Bets

Do you recall hearing the term "stress test" to describe the evaluation the federal government put the nation's top banks through during the 2009 financial crisis? Now it's your turn. Stress test your risk measurement models. Put your models and assumptions in extreme situations to see what they tell you. This has two benefits: 1) It helps you see if your models have flaws and 2) It provides some idea of how risk materializes in extreme situations.

Keeping It Simple

Once again, it's time to repeat the mantra of the risk management process: *Keep it simple*. Not easy to do when everything feels daunting and complicated, is it? Risk can be very complicated under certain conditions. However, whether you're a risk management expert or a small business owner trying to understand your risks and how to manage them, it is critical to remind yourself that simplicity is the smoothest and most efficient course. Experts would do well to remind themselves of this also.

Simplicity starts with the information that will be input—the types of measures and data to be collected. It should be clearly defined. The measures should be clear, easy to describe, and transparent. A single piece of data kept out of the measurement, for whatever reason, can ruin the entire exercise. Use simple formulas unless the type of risk, or measurement, requires a complicated approach; even then, make sure you understand why the approach has to be more complicated and that the approach used is documented and clear.

Likewise, know how much risk or error you can absorb. Define and work within those boundaries. Unless you are trying to manage pricing decisions or large financial moves where *basis points* or tenths of percentage points matter, simple measurement models will likely suffice for you. Keep it simple.

def•i•ni•tion

Basis points are units of measure used to describe the percentage change in the rate of a financial instrument. One basis point is equivalent to 0.01%. Most people have heard the term in connection with the prime interest rate, which is set by the Federal Reserve, and the overnight London Interbank Offered Rate (LIBOR).

Key Measurement Concepts

When deciding what types of simple measures can best quantify your risks, be sure to grasp the overall picture of those risks as they occupy, affect, inhibit, or grow your business. Ask yourself, "What is my exposure to risk?" There is also a direct and personal way to ask this question: "How much money can I lose as the result of one risk event or a group of risk events?"

To answer this question is to stare into the dark side—the total potential downside loss associated with a specific risk or group of risks. Since risk translates into cash in a business setting, figure out the total financial impact you can withstand. This will set the priority level for your measurement and assessment.

Another key question to ask is this: "How likely are these risks?" Throughout this book, you have learned about risk management as it pertains to the likelihood of a risk event or events in your business. Now it's time to heat up the conversation and study the hard facts: how probable is the risk scenario?

Likelihood and Probability

"Likelihood" and "probability" mean virtually the same thing. Risk professionals often use the term probability to refer to the probability of a risk event occurring, often described as the probability of loss or the estimated percentage of financial and material loss occurrences due to a risk event. It is usually measured as it relates to the number of loss events per total number of potential incidents or the likelihood of an event occurring across time. This is a critical component in risk, because it is a key component of virtually every calculation or other form of analysis. After all, how can you take steps and authorize the money to mitigate a risk if you're not even sure how likely (or unlikely) that risk is to occur?

How Will They Impact Me?

Calculate the potential impact, or *severity*, of a risk event. Determine how much money you will lose from expenses associated with cleanup from the event and costs of mitigation. There are other impact questions to answer for this measurement, all of which are related: What if the risk caused you to be fined by a regulator? What if you lost one or more customers? What if your line of credit was reduced?

Imagine a critical piece of equipment failed and crippled your production process. That single event triggers a wave of impact measurement questions. How much does it cost to repair or replace the equipment? How much material that was being produced beforehand cannot be utilized? What is the cost of that loss? How much overtime will be required to get back on line quickly? How many orders were missed? Delayed? Are you looking at a sudden inspection and likely fine? If so, how much?

def•i•ni•tion

Severity is a risk management term that describes a potential loss when added up, plus the costs associated with cleanup, contagion, and mitigation. From that sum, subtract the amount of money you received, or saved, from the effect of mitigation.

Let's explore this scenario further. You might lose all of the material that was being produced at the time (and beforehand), plus the cost of fixing the equipment. That would probably require overtime hours associated with getting back on line quickly. It might include other costs, such as those associated with a damaged reputation or missed orders. A visiting inspector also might levy a fine. However, if you had controls in place that allowed the defects to be caught quickly, a circuit breaker in place to prevent problems in other locations of the plant, or insurance that covered part of the repair, then you would subtract the recovered or mitigated amount from the impact costs to create a net risk cost.

What happens when it all comes together? Every time you receive the inferior grade raw material from your supplier, it causes you to shut down the production line, clean out your equipment, and lose precious time and labor. You can't fill orders, which means you can't invoice, hurting your revenue. Add it all up: there is your degree of impact or severity, less the cost and effect of mitigation. If the supplier then compensates you for the cost of the raw materials that did the damage, then you would be able to subtract that from the total cost of the cleanup.

Estimating Severity

Here is an equation for estimating severity:

Total Loss Exposure (immediate plus related additional effects) + Costs of Recovery, Cleanup, and Mitigation = Gross Loss. Next, subtract What Is Recovered (through returning what was lost, insurance settlements, or other restitution). The sum is your estimate of severity.

Here's how it looks as an equation:

$$S = E + C - R$$

E = TOTAL LOSS EXPOSURE

R = WHAT IS RECOVERED

S = SEVERITY

C = COSTS OF RECOVERY, CLEANUP, AND MITIGATION

You can also estimate severity by multiplying the Total Loss Exposure (E) by the percentage of Total Net Loss (L):

$$S = E \times \%L$$

Or you can multiply Total Loss Exposure (E) by 1 minus the percentage of Total Recovery (R):

$$S = E \times (1 - \%R)$$

Sometimes severity is expressed as a percentage. In this case, severity is simply the percentage that was lost after all recovery activities have taken place. It is expressed as follows:

$$\%S = 1 - \%R$$

How Do They Relate to Each Other?

When risk events occur in groups through contagion or concentration, the likelihood of a very bad day or string of days soars. Unfortunately, more often than not, multiple events occur simultaneously or nearly so. For instance, take a customer with credit problems. If a recession hits, he will see a rise in credit card interest rates. Perhaps his job will be in jeopardy, or his hours cut. Suddenly, yesterday's ability to pay the bills has become today's hand-wringing exercise in juggling financial balls. Likewise, a supplier may be mining the same location for all of the raw materials she supplies. If she has problems with material quality, all of the products and companies that rely on her supply will suffer the same types of problems. This is called a *correlation*.

def•i•ni•tion

Correlation is the degree of relationship between two variables. Positively correlated events move simultaneously in the same direction. Counter-correlated events move simultaneously in opposite directions.

The degree of correlation between risk events is not described by words, but by a number, called the correlation coefficient. This number is between negative 1 and positive 1. Negative 1 describes perfectly counter-correlated variables. Zero indicates no correlation between variables. Positive 1 describes perfectly correlated variables.

Correlation often occurs across risk events as well. If your business customers and retail customers both have trouble paying their invoices, then there is a strong correlation between the payment behaviors of both business customers and retail customers. This happens frequently when the economy is in the doldrums and everyone is affected, particularly when a single industry dominates a town.

How Will They Look over Time?

When measuring and assessing risks, risk managers consider two business baselines. One is financial. The other is time: for how long do risk events need to be considered? When will their probability diminish? Will it take 1 year, 20 years, a lifetime? How long is the life of a piece of equipment?

In the life of a business, time is measured in many different ways. For risk management, assessment usually begins with a one-year horizon. That provides a simple way to anchor the measures, to use the same baseline for reviewing the data.

More advanced approaches address the time value of money. Some folks even model specific frequencies of events that occur over set periods of time. Even these are often initially based on the one-year time horizon and then later updated with more sophisticated models.

It is important to create a horizon time for measuring risks and to stick to it. The key number here is a one-year time horizon, no matter whether you're measuring a single risk scenario or evaluating the entire enterprise. It's particularly vital when measuring multiple risks to keep the same time horizon, so the risks can be added and compared readily.

What to Measure

Countless things can be measured as part of a risk assessment. In the end, the law of simplicity is the best for this potential jungle: a few basic types of measures apply to most of the enterprise.

When considering a risk event, it is important to understand when it is likely to happen, how big it will be, and its probability, or likelihood, of occurring. You will also want to make these estimates as accurate as possible. (Remember that it is the variance around predictions that causes the most concern in risk.) Try to focus on measuring one risk or group of risks at a time—and understand the distributions of those events.

How Risks Are Distributed

Distribution is one of the most common mechanisms for measuring uncertainty. It is the range of events that may occur—their frequency of occurrence and their range of impact. It is generally shown as a chart with frequency (or likelihood) on the vertical axis and impact on the horizontal axis. This produces a distribution.

Two common loss distribution curves, normal distribution and beta distribution, which illustrate the behavior of risks.

Two Common Loss Distributions

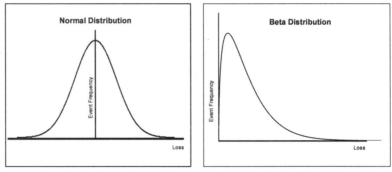

Distributions foster a clearer understanding of the behavior of risks, and risk managers make frequent use of them to aid in measurements. Some distributions are symmetrical (called normal distributions); there's a roughly equal chance of uncertainty above and below the most common result. Some distributions are skewed, with long tails (for example, one called a beta distribution is common); this generally means that, although overall risk may be lower, there is a small chance that something very, very bad might happen. There are many other types of distributions, but these are the most commonly used in risk management.

It is helpful to become familiar with the basic concept of distribution and its key qualities. Distributions are used to describe the way risks behave and how they may change over time. Distributions are also used to demonstrate the relationships between the core measures of risk that will be discussed later in this book.

Risk vs. Return

Every business owner knows that higher risks yield higher returns or greater losses. That's the risk of going for it. Ask yourself the following questions:

How much higher is the risk associated with the return?

Is it worth taking the risk for the increase in return?

The answers come as a "risk-adjusted return," another critical measure (also referred to as risk versus return). This allows owners to understand and compare products, customers, and even projects and strategies as they relate to risk and return. What type of return will they bring to the company? How much risk comes with them? Is the risk worth it?

Many people ask, "Why not take lots of risk as long as we are adequately compensated for it?" Often true, but with a caution: in the high-octane world of higher risk, one risk will start to intertwine with other risks and present more opportunity for contagion effects. Most likely, none of those costly extra zeros were factored into your initial risk-adjusted pricing. It is easy to get the overall evaluation wrong and wind up being undercompensated for risks you take, even though you thought you covered them.

With risk versus return, the focus on money causes many owners to forget about other possible fallouts, including reputation and stakeholder risks down the entire spider web of company contacts. When things go wrong, they can draw a lot of unwanted attention—creating unforeseen issues that can bring the company down. A perfect example is Enron, just a decade ago one of the most successful companies in the world. When media and regulators began to believe that something was awry, the company lost market confidence. Its bonds were called, nervous investors stepped forward, and Enron was unable to support its obligations.

Red Flags

The more risk an enterprise takes on, the more extreme the possible outcomes and the harder it is to measure and manage them.

The Least You Need to Know

◆ There are many reasons to measure risk, all of which pertain to the short- and long-term health of your company.

◆ Measure your current and future risks in order to determine how much mitigation will be needed.

◆ Learn the correlation between risk events: how your risks behave in relationship to one another.

◆ Clearly understand the relationship between degrees of risk and the potential returns they can bring your company.

◆ Distributions show the behavior pattern of risks over time, and are a vital part of the risk measurement process.

Chapter 9

Forecasting Risks

In This Chapter

- Comparing your risks
- Choosing the right forecasting tools
- Creating a total risk profile
- Calculating the likelihood of risk

A big storm looms on the horizon, threatening punishing winds and flooding rains. Tornadoes are possible. Residents prepare quickly, sealing their windows and moving their belongings to higher ground. The storm spins furiously off in the distance, yet no one can feel it in the preparation area. At least a day remains before it arrives.

How does everyone know that the big storm is approaching? Simple: they watched TV, listened to the radio, or checked a weather site on the Internet. They received an accurate forecast, and they acted upon it.

Just as you use forecasting to plan for future weather events, smart business owners and managers rely heavily on forecasting to predict risk and minimize its impact in their companies.

Comparing Risks

Forecasting is the key to any businessperson's ability to weather "risk" storms. Yet even seasoned risk professionals sometimes lose sight of the importance of looking to the future. All too often risk managers fall into the trap of relying only on analyses of *past* behavior to make assumptions about future behavior. Sometimes, however, the only way to predict the future is to stare straight into it, rather than turning our heads to the past.

When forecasting risks, you need to understand and try to gauge the following four essential characteristics:

- ◆ How risks behave
- ◆ When they are likely to materialize
- ◆ Their potential size
- ◆ What can be done about them

In this chapter and Chapter 10, you will be introduced to some specific measures and analytic approaches for forecasting risks. By the end of these chapters you will have learned about the basic forecasting tools and how to combine these measures with a broader set of risk management information to create your company's total risk profile.

The Risk Matrix

The most basic forecasting tool is the risk matrix. Regardless of your current level of sophistication when it comes to risk management, you can use the risk matrix to create a visual representation of relative risks.

To create a risk matrix, rate each of your risks with respect to its likelihood. Then rate each again with respect to its relative consequences or severity. Once you have done that, you can plot them on a matrix of likelihood versus consequence, as shown in the following illustration.

Risks with both high likelihood and high consequence (or severity) are high risk. Conversely, risks with low likelihood and low consequence are considered relatively low risk. The risk matrix provides a means of seeing the risks relative to one another for the sake of comparison.

The Risk Matrix

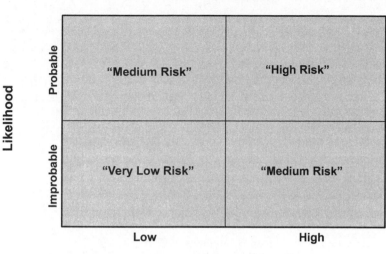

A risk matrix gives you a quick visual snapshot of your risks, the likelihood of each, and the level of severity of each.

Cell Values – Ranked Risks

The risk matrix can take on any level of sophistication, from very simple qualitative assessments to highly quantitative rankings on each axis. Start simply by using the risk matrix to sum up the varying risks you face.

Risk Factors
Remember that in risk, *likelihood* and *probability* are synonymous terms, as are *severity* and *consequence*.

Best Bets

Risk matrixes are particularly useful if you are presenting information on your company's risks to senior management, the board of directors, or another oversight body. Busy executives tend to relate much more quickly to a visual image with relevant data.

Consequence and Likelihood Tables

Risk tables are another type of forecasting tool in the risk manager's toolbox. There are actually two types of risk tables, the risk likelihood table and the consequence table. Both types of tables offer a nice way to better understand and predict the risks. The consequence table also helps to forecast or describe the ultimate outcome (or severity) of a risk event.

The risk likelihood table, or matrix, helps to forecast or describe the potential likelihood (or probability) of a risk event occurring.

Likelihood Matrix

Likelihood Score	Probability	Description	Example
1	<2%	Very Rare	Little evidence to believe that the event will occur but theoretically possible
2	2-5%	Rare	The event has been known to occur elsewhere
3	6%-10%	Unlikely	The event has been known to occur before: once in five years
4	11%-20%	Possible	The event occurs occasionally: once every few years
5	21%-40%	Likely	The event occurs periodically: once or twice a year
6	41%-80%	Almost Certain	The event occurs frequently: once every few months
7	>80%	Imminent	The event occurs on a regular basis: weekly or monthly

The risk consequences table, or matrix, shows the types and scales of consequences and how severe they can be to your company.

Consequence Matrix

Severity Level	Loss Potential	Health & Safety	Legal	Environmental	Reputation	Government/ Compliance
A	<$1000	No medical treatment required	Little or no legal issues	Little or no effects on physical environment	Minor complaints; little or no public or media attention	Minor breaches of noncompliance
B	$1000 - $10,000	Minor Medical treatment—no hospitalization	Minor legal issues—readily settled	Minor, short-term effect; readily reversible	Concern expressed by local community and/or NGOs	Minor breach of regulation
C	$10,000 - $100,000	Minor Reversible—but hospitalization required	Moderate legal issues— potential court action	Short- to medium-term effects; potentially reversible or treatable with moderate reparation	Attention from local newspapers	Moderate breach or regulation; difficulty with authority and/or remediation required
D	$100,000 - $1,000,000	Moderate Reversible— Longer Hospitalization	Moderate legal issues, fines, or other penalties; potential of litigation	Moderate- or medium-term environmental effects; remediation required	Attention from multiple local media sources and/or NGO or community forum	Serious breach of regulation with investigation and potential fines
E	>$1,000,000	Major hospitalization and/or fatalities	Significant prosecution, fines, and/or serious litigation inlcuding class action	Serious long-term effects—major cleanup and reparation necessary; impairment of ecosystem	Repeated attention from national media or some selected international media	Major breach of regulation; significant fines or suspension of business

Using the consequence table as an example, start by setting up a scoring method for the risks. Rate the likelihood of a risk from, say, 1 to 5, with 1 being low and 5 being high. This score should encompass a minimum of 3 categories, although it works best with 8 to 15 categories. Assign each category a qualitative rating, a quantitative rating, or a combined rating of the likelihood of a risk materializing.

The simplest forms of this table seek a consensus with regard to any particular ranking. For instance, if you put five people into a room, the descriptions in the table would allow them to easily agree that any specific risk carries the same ranking. More advanced forms use a scoring method to "add up" and weight characteristics that contribute to severity to arrive at a ranking.

The translation of these tables is fairly straightforward. When you tell someone within your company that you are addressing a 1A risk, they will come to understand that you mean you are addressing a low-probability, low-severity situation.

> ### Risk Factors
>
> Common convention holds that risk likelihood tables rank with numerals and risk consequence tables rank with letters. It's useful to apply different conventions for each table, as you can later combine them without confusion. Typically, the higher the number and letter, the higher the risk. There are exceptions to this, however, so always read risk tables carefully.

Working the Comparisons

Risk tables anchor related concepts between business lines and risk managers. You can use a likelihood or consequence table to communicate upward and downward through the organization. These tables also allow you to focus on important items—the materiality of the risks in your company.

Determining *materiality* is the process of determining the greatest areas of material risk to your business, or the areas that could most seriously affect your business. Now that you have a method for identifying and ranking risks, you can address materiality in more specific terms and even define it for your organization. Since every organization is different, there are no hard-and-fast rules. What is material to one organization may not apply to another, for many reasons.

Best Bets

Make sure that you refresh your risk likelihood and severity ratings routinely. Review the ratings you have assigned each risk and see what may have changed. Ratings should be refreshed as often as the types of risks dictate. A quarterly review should cover most types of risks, although some types of risks, such as market risks, should be monitored as often as monthly. However, every risk should be reviewed at least once a year.

Now you can decide what creates or constitutes a material risk to your organization. Start by excluding minor, immaterial risks. Choose a level on your likelihood and consequence table as a threshold for what you deem to be minor and not material—say, anything below a 2 on your risk likelihood table or below a B on your consequence table. That doesn't mean you can stop tracking these minor risks, however. Today's 2B could rapidly become a 10C or, worse, a 10F! You want to keep an eye on these minor risks in case conditions change and one becomes a threat.

Another effective forecasting tool at your disposal is the risk register. A risk register is simply a record of all your risks. It is an incredibly handy tool for managing all sorts of risks, but particularly strategic and operational risks. These two types of risks can be much harder to discretely measure and quantify. Qualitative information is often your best way of tracking these risks, and the risk register delivers that material.

A risk register is also a great tool for managing project-based risks. You can list the project risks and track them as they affect different stages of a project over time. When you spot potential project problems, you can address them before they become an issue and derail the project.

A risk register should include the following information:

- A description of each risk

- The date you noticed the risk

- The date you target to address the risk

- A risk ranking (use the likelihood and consequence tables)

- An explanation of the risk ranking (why it is ranked as such)

- A brief statement of what is at stake if the risk materializes

After you've created your risk register, be sure to also evaluate any possible points of contagion as a result of these risks materializing. Finally, list what mitigation measures have been put in place and when.

It is useful to provide comments about these risks in your follow-up work. Ask yourself this battery of questions:

Has the risks' ranking changed? If so, when?

To what level did they rise? Or fall?

Who made that decision?

Is the mitigation effective?

Did it contribute to the change in the rating?

Has the risk been eliminated entirely? Why?

Best Bets

Once you have a complete risk register, you can draw from it to create a list of the "top ten risks" your company faces. This list is very useful for presenting information on risks to management. Most folks at these oversight levels are keenly interested in this type of analysis because of its simplicity. A top-ten risk list reveals the key threats to the organization so top officials can take steps to prevent or dissipate them. Some organizations track these relentlessly.

Implementation

Now that you are familiar with some basic forecasting tools, it's time to start thinking about how you are going to implement them.

Keep in mind that if you have a qualitative assessment tool, its descriptions need to be very clear and well understood. Otherwise, you may get two people ranking the same risk differently. This is especially a problem if you have different people across the organization ranking risks for each business within that organization. One person could rank a risk as a "4" in one business while another person gives the same risk a "6" in another business (allowing for differences in the businesses themselves). If you were to consolidate these rankings, you could have a real mess trying to sort out which risks were more important than others. That would lead to further uncertainty over which risks merit investment for mitigation or other forms of management.

What Are the Odds?

An adjunct to the likelihood table is the concept of risk rating or score—the risk scorecard. A scorecard is a set of information that allows you to attach a numerical score to a risk. The scorecard is usually built using statistical techniques that link information about a risk to the probability of a loss. In the case of credit, it might be information about someone's credit history, education, profession, employment status, and salary. There may be other factors that provide an indication of the borrower's creditworthiness and therefore their probability of default on a loan. This is how credit scores are derived, for example.

Scorecards are assembled in a number of contexts to achieve a more accurate view of the probability of risks than the first measurement provided. The primary use of these highly specific scorecards is to assess credit risk management. They are used to obtain a rating or score for customers trying to obtain a loan. However, risk managers use them for all sorts of other applications as well.

These high-efficiency tables are used most often with recurring risks that have repeating characteristics, such as customer payments and loans, warehouse damage, process breakdowns or failures, and customer service issues.

To gather data for your scorecard, identify a series of characteristics or variables that you can observe about a customer or a risk. If you issue credit to commercial customers, you would score specific characteristics of their companies, such as the strength of their balance sheets, debt load, and payment behavior. The next step is to link those characteristics to the likelihood of default. For a retail customer, you might consider payment behavior, total debt load, and overall credit history. You can obtain this type of information through credit rating agencies.

Red Flags

Risk scoring or rating works well with financial risks and certain operational risks, but not so well with strategic risks, since strategic risks are different every time.

To create a risk scorecard, start by developing a more detailed version of your likelihood table. Make it so detailed that it provides a true prediction of the exact likelihood of an event. You want to rank risks numerically (from lowest to highest likelihood) and accurately predict that likelihood.

How to Establish Likelihood

To rank risks according to their likelihood, it helps to think about how credit reporting agencies rate consumer credit. Credit agencies compile information about consumer debt and payment history and process the information using a standard formula to generate a credit score, which is an indication of a consumer's likelihood of defaulting on a loan. Banks and other creditors then use this score to rank potential borrowers relative to other borrowers.

Risk managers sometimes try to use similar ratings or scores for operational risk, but it is almost impossible to get a real fix on true losses and true likelihoods. These scorecards are even more difficult to validate and backtest. Nevertheless, they are helpful in establishing a rank ordering and in broadly sizing the risks.

If you don't want to build scorecards yourself, a few companies provide this service. You can buy the scorecards for both consumer and corporate credit.

Working with the Odds

Typically, a scorecard or rating provides you with a number (such as 1 to 10, in the case of corporate credit ratings, or 450 to 800, in the case of retail credit scores). How do you use that number to gauge the specific probability of an event? First, map the score or rating to an actual probability number. Purchased scorecards often come with some way to do this. These are called *odds*.

When you obtain your scorecard, you will receive the odds associated with each score. The odds represent the number of "bads versus goods." Mathematically, this is exactly what it sounds like: it is the ratio of bad outcomes to good outcomes. That is, the number of times you observed a risk event materializing (a loss) relative to the number of times that that risk event did not occur for each score or rating.

def•i•ni•tion

Odds are just another way of expressing probability or likelihood. In risk management, odds measure the likelihood of an event occurring versus the likelihood of that event not occurring.

This number can be mathematically transposed to a "probability of event" number. The probability of event is the likelihood of that event occurring among *all* events. Thus, it is the number of loss events or risks that materialized into loss ("bads") divided by the total number of observed risks or potential loss events that did not materialize ("goods"). So if you have 100 borrowers with a particular score or rating and 10 of them default, the "odds" are 10:90, or 1:9. That's a 1-to-9 chance that a borrower will default. If you want to convert that into a probability, divide the total bads (defaults) by the total number of borrowers. Thus, 10 defaults/100 borrowers = 10/100 = .1. The equation is as follows:

If the odds are a:b, then probability is a/(a+b)

Rank Ordering Risks

In the end, you will want to establish a probability or likelihood of event for each score on your scorecard. If you are setting up a risk scorecard yourself, establish scores so that they relate to likelihood in an exponential form from lowest to highest. That means that a risk grade of 2 is roughly twice as risky as a risk grade of 1, and a risk grade of 3 is nearly twice as risky as risk grade 2, and so on.

A Simpler Approach

If you're not ready to delve into the rather sophisticated math necessary to create precise risk scorecards, try creating a simple rating method instead. To do so, take the following steps:

1. Rank your risks from lowest to highest.

2. Measure or establish their likelihood using any of the approaches described in this chapter, even if they are a bit of a guess or somewhat qualitative.

3. Estimate the risk score or rating by looking at which risks are roughly twice those of the previous.

4. Link the questions on the scorecard to the risks in each rating. All risks that are associated with the same probability and lower are assigned the same risk grade.

This is easier to do when probability numbers are smaller and when risks are associated with numerical probabilities. But the idea works for more qualitative information as well.

Your highest risk grades should be associated with a very high likelihood of occurrence—i.e., a risk will likely materialize into a loss event (at least if you do nothing to stop it). Conversely, very low risk events may never materialize. They receive the lowest scores, associated with very low probability numbers.

Analyzing What Happened

Risk analysis involves more than just studying the likelihood of events. To obtain a complete picture, you must also analyze the specific losses of actual risk events as well as the causes of those events. In other words, sometimes it's very useful to look to the past to help predict the future. This is particularly applicable in the case of financial and operational risks, where there is a reasonable possibility that similar sorts of events could happen again. As with likelihood or probability of loss, it is important to develop a rating system for these sorts of events that focuses on the severity of the event. That way, you can repeatedly identify the effect before it occurs.

For each risk of a particular type, there are three main components to analyzing severity:

◆ Understanding the types of activities or characteristics that drive inherent differences in the severity of a risk (the same risk) when it materializes. What makes the same loss event larger or smaller? What events lead to losses?

◆ Understanding if and how the exposure to loss could change when it material-izes. Are there ways that larger or smaller amounts of money could be lost? How did the event occur?

◆ Understanding how much is actually lost overall. How much did it hurt?

When analyzing severity, move the process forward by examining these three compo-nents. Be sure you understand the characteristics that lead to differences in severity for the same sort of risk event. Then match those characteristics to the severity itself.

Events That Lead to Losses

As you've seen, much of risk management concerns the past; in particular, analyzing past events and using the information to forestall or prevent future incidents. This starts with an analysis of the similarities in your loss events *before* they happened. Can you identify certain characteristics that consistently lead to higher losses? To help tease out this type of information, ask yourself the following questions when analyzing past risk events:

Are losses on one product type higher than another? A more valuable product will naturally result in a greater loss if inventory is damaged. Or if you provide credit on that product to your customer and the customer doesn't pay it back, then the loss will likely be higher for that one item.

Is one type of raw material more valuable than another? Higher-valued material will naturally lead to higher dollar losses if the material is defective or the process itself creates a defect when using that material.

Do you require some form of collateral from your customers? More collat-eral will likely lead to lower losses.

Are there risks that could affect certain production areas? If so, are there more people or more valuable equipment that could be affected?

At what stage in the production cycle do these risks occur? Is it earlier in the process? Or later, when the product is nearly complete and is relatively more valuable (more investment in labor, processing time, and materials)?

These questions help you evaluate whether the same general type of risk could gener-ate a larger or smaller risk if it materialized. Even if the likelihood of a certain type of risk is the same, its severity could be different depending on what characteristics are present. Be sure to list all of the differences. They determine one of the key dimensions in your severity score.

How Did Events Occur?

When analyzing past losses to forecast future risks, you want to determine if there is any way that your exposure to the loss could increase or decrease beyond the inherent drivers identified previously. Quite simply, it is about ensuring that the estimate of future loss is scaled appropriately for whatever new quantity may be affected.

A simple example helps illustrate this point. Suppose you experienced product loss in the past due to a warehouse disaster. You lost $100,000 worth of products when a leaky pipe damaged your entire inventory of cell phones. Now pause to consider how much greater your exposure would have been if you had $200,000 worth of cell phones in the warehouse. Same product, but a higher risk exposure because of an increase in the number of products.

Another example is credit. If you allow a customer to buy more goods on credit, you increase your exposure to default.

Best Bets _____

Sometimes your exposure and other factors that drive severity are related. You can find any relationships by asking three simple questions:

◆ What is the exposure?

◆ Are there ways that it can increase and decrease?

◆ Is exposure independent of the recovery situation or not?

How Much Did It Hurt?

This question hits the core of severity analysis. Regardless of how you and your company arrived at this point, you must be able to accurately identify how much you lost.

To do this, first identify the exact point in time that the loss occurred. This is often much harder than it sounds, because in many cases losses tend to take place over an extended period. They don't just happen in an instant and then stop, never to be heard from again. Events are more like trailheads with paths fanning in all directions, rather than a single, well-worn trail. Question is, which path will a particular event take? There are many possible answers, many possible paths. Rather than wracking your brain trying to figure out those possibilities, try to view your analysis as a process or time-dependent activity that has a beginning, a middle, and an end.

Interestingly, losses associated with a risk event may not even become apparent until long after the event has happened. So you may need to be diligent about understanding exactly when the loss began. It may have begun months before you noticed it. A bit of forensic investigation is required.

Dealing with Recurring Events

Although recurring risk events can be a real nuisance to a business, from a forecasting perspective they do have advantages over one-time events. The main advantage is that you can analyze how they play out over multiple instances. Recurring risk events are very common in financial risks, where more than one customer will default on a loan, for instance.

When you look for the origin point of a recurring loss, try to find a position that is common to all losses of its type. Then, map the event. Look at each step of how the event unfolded and ask yourself the following questions:

How much was lost at each of those steps?

How much was recovered at each of those steps?

What mitigants prevented more loss?

What costs were incurred at each step?

How long did each step take?

Record your answers. When you are finished, move on to the next set of questions:

Is the event still playing out?

Are you still waiting for insurance money to come back?

Are you still resolving the outcome with a regulator, the police, a compliance organization, or any outside organization?

Are you dealing with the media or special interest groups?

Are you waiting for your customer to pay back his or her money?

Are you waiting for your supplier to provide the next shipment of material?

Are you in litigation?

Has your workforce recovered?

Did you have to hire someone to clean up the mess? Is that person or organization still working on it?

Has your market share suffered as a result? How long will it take you to be sure?

What has happened to your reputation as a result?

How do your stakeholders now perceive you? Has anything changed?

Focusing on the Aftermath

Many of the activities addressed in the preceding questions take a very long time to work through the organization. One of the biggest mistakes companies make in post-event analysis is ignoring the ongoing activities involved in the aftermath of a risk event. Many events are far more expensive than they appear on the surface when you consider all of the fallout from the event. It sometimes takes companies years to recover from risk events; yet, they report a loss that is only the size of the immediate event.

This sort of thing happens all the time in banking. Consider the true story of a bank that had a market loss of about $350 million in its trading portfolio. It was a fairly large bank, so the loss wasn't so big in the grand scheme of things. However, the loss was due to fraud committed by two traders who had found a glitch in the bank's security systems. As a result of the fraud, the bank received a multiyear regulatory penalty (cash fines and limited trading abilities), international bad press, and increased regulatory scrutiny. As a consequence of these repercussions, the bank found it very difficult to hire quality people, faced numerous rounds of auditors and other post-event analysis consultants, experienced several changes in management, was forced to pay higher insurance premiums, and suffered a host of minor issues.

The bank recorded a loss of about $100 million on the basis that it retrieved much of the original money lost. However, the real costs played out over the next three years and were considerably larger. In addition to direct losses and costs, the bank also suffered a large opportunity cost—its limited trading penalties translated into millions in lost business. The bank also lost customers because of its tarnished reputation.

Once you have determined a total estimated loss, review the items that you discovered were the drivers. Is this total loss higher or lower because of the product, the type of customer, the part of the product line, or some other factor? Once you figure out the drivers, determine what aspects of the process are dependent on the characteristics identified in the first batch of questions and which are independent. Verify that they would have happened in the same way and at the same costs.

Red Flags

When you incur an opportunity cost, you lose money, reputation, or positioning from the inability to seize an opportunity or complete a major task or project that you could have done previously. For a variety of reasons, you cannot (or choose not to) take that action now.

Leading and Lagging Indicators

Tracking *indicators* is particularly useful when done in conjunction with the forecasting tools described in this chapter.

The two primary types of indicators are as follows:

♦ *Leading indicators* are pieces of information that help spot an increase in likelihood or severity before it shows up in the actual risk measures. The event may not have even been identified formally as a risk yet!

♦ *Lagging indicators* are pieces of information that help to confirm that an event is likely to occur or will occur in a particular way. They usually react more slowly to changes in the environment than leading indicators, but they are often useful for describing trends.

def•i•ni•tion

Indicators assist with predicting future performance or likelihood of a risk event.

In terms of risk management, leading indicators signal that a risk has occurred or that there is an increased likelihood of a risk event. For example, home price depreciation may be a leading indicator for an increase in credit risk. Retail customers who use their house for security may receive less for it; therefore, recovery based on selling those homes as collateral will drop. Housing starts may be a leading indicator that the construction industry will dip. If many of your customers are contractors, they might have more difficulty paying you.

Lagging indicators often come from your own risk measures. For example, if you see that severity or likelihood estimates are increasing, then your overall risk profile is increasing. Lagging indicators may also take the form of unusual metrics spotted in the process control charts discussed earlier.

What Are They Good For?

Leading and lagging indicators are tracked for one major reason: they make our risk measures more predictive. If you don't use indicators, your risk measures could become stale.

Applying indicators to your forecasting enables you to stay on top of current trends and update your estimates when necessary. Risk managers use leading indicators to …

- ◆ Adjust likelihood and severity estimates (like the information, analysis, and assumptions we put into our risk scores, ratings, and other models).

- ◆ Use them more dynamically within those models and scorecards to actively help predict risks.

Using the previous example, if you are tracking the probability and severity of a credit loss, then you can adjust that severity upward if you see that housing prices have depreciated. For instance, you might increase your expectation of severity upward by 10 percent for every 10 percent decrease in housing prices. Or you may be able to build a home price depreciation index directly into the model for measuring severity by adjusting the recovery portion of the equation upward or downward in line with movements in the index.

Lagging indicators are used to analyze the movements within the scorecards and ratings in order to see if the risks have changed.

Applying Indicators

Leading indicators reveal when risks in the overall environment are changing. They also signal when your risk measures should be reviewed.

Risk managers often build their leading indicators directly into their risk measures. For instance, in a risk scorecard, leading indicators would be listed among the factors that drive the score. So if you are building a scorecard to predict the default of a customer to whom you have extended credit, you might include a factor that relates downturns in the economy, or in the economy of that customer's industry in particular, to the propensity of the customer defaulting. Risk factors can be built directly into the score, or the score can be adjusted up or down in association with the effect of the indicator.

Your own scorecards often provide the best means of determining lagging indicators. If a score increases from a low rating to a higher rating, then you can ascertain that risks have increased. The actual events may not have transpired yet, but the risks of them occurring have increased. If you are reviewing a severity score, the severity may increase. Thus, the overall impact of the risk may be worse when it occurs.

The Least You Need to Know

◆ Compare risks using risk matrices, likelihood tables, and consequence tables.

◆ Record and keep track of your risks by developing a risk register.

◆ Use scorecards to rank risk and to develop more accurate measures of likelihood and severity.

◆ When analyzing the severity of a past risk, be sure to consider all aspects of the loss, including the costs involved long after the event.

◆ Use leading and lagging indicators to help predict trends, enhance likelihood and severity measures, and trigger reviews.

Chapter 10

Impact!

In This Chapter

♦ Measuring expected and unexpected losses

♦ Analyzing groups of risks

♦ Using earnings volatility

♦ Performing stress tests

♦ Measuring risk versus return

What happens at the moment of impact—at the precise time that a risk event takes place? What happens to the present and future course of your company when a risk event, or series of events, disrupts your operations? Even more crucial questions: How well did you plan financially for such an event? Did you base your estimated damages (and reserves) on the predictable, expected loss? Or the unpredictable, unexpected loss?

Expected Loss

Expected loss applies only to a risk in which you expect to lose some money on average. Sure, you might make money on these risks, but the risks in these areas end up costing you some money, too. Because of the very nature of risk, many risks carry some expected loss—but not all. Operational risks usually generate expected losses, as do credit risks. Many market risks and strategic risks, however, have an average loss of zero —or near zero. In other words, we don't expect to lose money on those ventures unless something goes very wrong.

It is important to keep in mind that expected loss is *not* your true risk. This probably sounds counterintuitive, since the discussion concerns losses. Risk people view expected loss as an anticipated loss rate. (Keep in mind that expected loss is another name for the mean loss, which is also called the average loss.) You can count on incurring this loss in whatever business activity you are measuring. It is predictable and manageable, and so it is not where the real risk lies.

Measure It Up

The calculation for expected loss is quite simple. In Chapter 8 you were introduced to the concepts of probability (PE, a percentage), severity (S, also a percentage), and total loss exposure (usually an absolute number). To arrive at your expected loss (EL), simply multiply these three items together:

$$PE \text{ (\%)} \times E \times S \text{ (\%)} = EL$$

Risk Factors
More advanced measures of expected loss further adapt the core measurement so that it is more "forward looking." In those cases, companies try to anticipate future loss rates rather than arriving at estimates based on past information. You can create this forward-looking approach by trying to build in information that links to economic trends. These models can be quite a bit more sophisticated than the simple calculations included in this chapter.

Expected loss may also be described as a percentage, rather than a numeral. In that case, you multiply the probability percentage (PE) and the percent severity (%S) to arrive at your expected loss percentage:

$$PE \times \%S = \%EL$$

Figuring in Expected Loss

Expected loss can be applied to many different areas. It can be measured for segments of risk, sectors within your portfolio or business, or for your entire business. You can also measure it for each segment of your business and then add up each of those segments. The result is the entire mean loss rate of your business—in other words, your total expected loss.

Anything that does not have a certain outcome can be assigned a probability of occurring. You can also identify the possible range of effects and analyze these against each of their likelihoods of occurring. In this manner, you can analyze items that do not explicitly end up in loss but carry uncertainty; strategic risk is a great example. While you may not necessarily expect a loss, you are likely to produce a range of potential outcomes, each with its own assignable probability.

Unexpected Loss

Unexpected loss (UL) is the standard deviation of a company's losses. This is any company's true risk—the segment of risk that is harder to plan for and to forecast. It is arguably the most important concept to grasp in the field of risk management. You'll find that the concept shows up in many situations to define risk, even outside of risk management. In finance, when people talk about portfolio risk, they are talking about UL.

UL is measured as a deviation. Sometimes the deviation is low; sometimes it is high. At other times, though, it will be something completely different—unexpected.

Picture a business in a volatile industry—say, a minor league baseball franchise. When the franchise measures its risks, it will likely factor in its possible revenue swings based on a low average attendance for the last five seasons and a high average attendance for the same period. Woven into that calculation will be the present economic condition. Along with that comes sales from concessions, souvenirs, and other add-on items, which for obvious reasons are tied to attendance. These figures mark the high and low deviations, the average producing an expected loss number. What if the season is particularly rainy, however, and 10 games are rained out instead of the usual 3 or 4? Or, even worse, what if the team is predicted to win its division, and it instead finishes last? If these factors are not carefully incorporated into the high and low deviations, the rain-out and underperforming scenarios fall into the "something completely different" category—the unexpected losses.

Measure It Up

UL is measured as the standard deviation of losses. Standard deviation can be measured in a number of ways. The simplest is to simply observe the difference from the mean loss. That means that you take the difference between each observed outcome and the mean, square it, add up the squares for each outcome, and then take the square root of the whole thing.

The equation to determine UL, or standard deviation, works like this:

$$\sigma = \frac{\sqrt{(x_1 - \mu)^2 + (x_2 - \mu)^2 + ... + (x_N - \mu)^2}}{N}$$

Where:

σ is standard deviation (or risk)

x is the value of each of the losses that we have observed

μ is the mean

N is the total number of samples

Let's say the average or expected loss for any given minor league baseball season is $100,000 ($\mu$). But in the five seasons observed, the expected loss is $90,000, $110,000, $85,000, $115,000, and $100,000, respectively. These are the values (x). Take the difference between each of these observed values and the average to get –$10,000, $10,000, –$15,000, $15,000, and $0, respectively. Square each figure to get $100,000, $100,000, $225,000, $225,000, and $0, respectively. Now add them up and divide by five (N), which equals $130,000. Finally, take the square root, which leaves $11,400. That is the standard deviation or unexpected loss (σ).

There are other ways to model the unexpected loss. Some companies put a lot of effort into building complex computer models to examine the distributions of losses and potential losses, their sizes and shapes, and how this affects the measurement of unexpected loss.

Figuring in Unexpected Loss

As with expected loss, you can use unexpected loss to analyze individual risks, groups of risks, segments of portfolios, and entire businesses. However, there is one big difference: you can't simply add unexpected loss numbers. Because these figures are standard deviations, they are not strictly additive. Therefore, we need to bring in the *covariance*.

def•i•ni•tion

The **covariance** is a statistical measure of how much two variables change together. It is used in the process of adding up risks or, more specifically, adding up unexpected losses.

To arrive at a sum of the standard deviations, you add up the squares of each standard deviation, along with the covariance of the two risks.

This is the equation for adding up the standard deviations (or ULs) from two different risks, X and Y:

$$(\text{Standard Deviation})^2(X+Y) =$$
$$\text{weight}_{X^2} (\text{std dev})^2(X) + \text{weight}_{Y^2} (\text{std dev})^2(Y) + \text{weight}_X \text{ weight}_Y 2\text{cov}(X,Y)$$

Where:

Std dev is standard deviation

Weight = the relative amount (%) of any given asset or risk exposure relative to the total portfolio or group of risk exposures

$$cov = covariance = \frac{\Sigma(X - \mu)(Y - \upsilon)}{N}$$

υ is the mean of risk Y

μ is the mean of risk X

N is the total number in the sample

Let's head back to baseball's minor league. Suppose you own two minor league teams in different cities and you want to understand your total risk associated with owning the clubs. To do this, we just add up the unexpected losses, or standard deviations, of the two teams using the equation above. To start, you need the same information from both teams. On each of the same five years, the second team demonstrates expected losses of $20,000, $30,000, $10,000, $15,000, and $25,000. This results in a mean expected loss of $20,000 and a standard deviation of $7,071.

Now it's necessary to measure the covariance of the losses for these two teams. First, compute the difference between each observation and the mean for each of the respective teams. That results in respective annual figures of –$10,000, $10,000, –$15,000, $15,000 and $0 for the first team, and $0, $10,000, –$10,000, –$5,000 and $5,000 for the second team. Next, multiply each calculation for each year by that of the other team, and sum them up: the total should be $175 million. Divide by the number of observation sets—in this case, the five years. The covariance is $35 million.

This is what the scenario looks like in table form:

	Team 1 ($000's)		Team 2 ($000's)		Combined Teams (000's)
	X	(X-μ)	Y	(Y-v)	(X-μ)(Y-v)
Year 1	90	-10	20	0	0
Year 2	110	10	30	10	100,000
Year 3	85	-15	10	-10	150,000
Year 4	115	15	15	-5	-75,000
Year 5	100	0	25	5	0
Mean	100		20		Sum 175,000
Std Dev	11.4		7.1		Cov 35,000
Std Dev²	130,000		50,000		Std Dev 7.9

Now take the square of each of the standard deviations. The resulting figures are $130 million and $50 million, respectively. Multiply these amounts by the square of each team's portfolio weight. In this case, there are two teams, so we say that the contribution of each team is 50 percent, or .5; the square of .5 is .25. $130 million multiplied by .25 equals $32.5 million and $50 million multiplied by .25 is $12.5 million. Add these two sums together to yield $45 million, and then add that to twice the covariance times the weight squared. Multiplying the covariance ($35 million) by 2 equals $70 million, and multiplying that by .25 equals $17.5 million. Then, all we need to do is add this to $45 million. That yields a standard deviation squared of $62.5 million. To convert back to standard deviation, take the square root of $62.5 million to end up with $7,905.

Taking on the second team appears to be a good investment from a risk management perspective because it reduces the net unexpected loss (our true risk) and reduces the risk of owning the first team alone.

Measuring Groups of Risks

The technique just covered will certainly help you understand, strategically and numerically, how to analyze the expected and unexpected losses for single risks or risk events. However, you can also use this technique to think about analyzing *groups* of risks. You add up and compare the UL and EL for different risk groups.

Pretty simple, right? Well, this is risk, so there are a couple of wrinkles. Groups of risks also have a special characteristic—their correlation. Correlation measures how risks relate to one another. When some risks combine, they can actually offset each other and reduce relative net risk. The easiest association to make for correlation is with the interaction of prescription medicines. In some instances, the interaction is harmless or even beneficial to the person. In others, though, the interaction can flame up like two converging brush fires and create an even more dangerous risk. *How* the drugs interact, or how two risks correlate, often means the difference between high- and low-impact events.

Risk management professionals often think about groups of risks from two perspectives: first, how individual risks can add up to form groups of risks with similar behaviors (*bottom-up*) and second, how all risks behave together (*top-down*).

def•i•ni•tion

Bottom-up and **top-down** are ways in which companies evaluate the relationships and potential impacts of risks. The bottom-up approach takes each risk individually and looks at how they behave together in an additive fashion. The top-down method analyzes how the company is doing as a whole, and then tries to break that view into smaller and smaller segments.

Each term is very broadly applied to the approaches that risk managers use to analyze, measure, and manage risk. Each has its notable differences.

Bottom-Up Approaches

Bottom-up approaches involve measuring risks as individual risks or small groups of risks, then adding them up to get the total standard deviation for a portfolio, business, product line, or the entire company. This is done by using the equation for adding up unexpected losses you learned earlier in this chapter.

When analyzing risk for a company, be on the lookout for areas where there is a high degree of correlation between risks. Also look for areas where there are opportunities for diversification (the opposite of correlation, which was introduced in Chapter 8). Diversification is when correlations between risks or groups of risks are very low, or even negative. When this occurs, one risk or group of risks can offset the effect of another.

Another handy tool is to look at the correlation coefficient. It is calculated as follows:

$$\rho = \frac{cov(x, y)}{std\ dev_x\ std\ dev}$$

Where cov = covariance

Std dev = standard deviation

This uses the same concepts from the previous calculations to analyze the relationship between risks and groups of risks. It will yield a number between −1 and +1. Risks that are highly correlated will yield numbers that are close to +1. Risks that provide good opportunities for diversification will have correlation coefficients that are low, or even negative. In the baseball example, you can calculate the correlation coefficient between the two teams by dividing the covariance, $35 million, by the product of the two teams' standard deviations. This yields a correlation coefficient of .43. So there is correlation between the two teams, as one would expect in the case of two risks that have similar characteristics. However, the correlation is low enough that it still provides some diversification benefit because it reduces overall risk.

Best Bets

Try to identify areas of your company where risks are most similar and look at how you might be able to isolate the analysis in these areas. Or combine your total risk from two or more areas where identical or similar risks crop up. Include any risks associated with customers. These can often be segmented on many dimensions, such as industry, geography, and broad types of customers. Also review your risks by product line. In your finance department, you may find risks relating to the same financial factors, such as interest rate or currency exposures. These are the types of areas in which you will find fullest benefit of analyzing how risks combine.

Sometimes you may not have good correlation information. Correlations can be tough to work out even for the best risk managers. If you're in this boat, try this quick and dirty way to look at your groups of risk: Analyze the contribution of each unique group relative to the whole. Find out how much exposure or standard deviation comes from any particular industry, type of customer, product, division, or another segment you're measuring. It's ideal if you can do this analysis in terms of unexpected loss. If that proves impossible, looking at EL or exposure can be helpful. You're trying to spot concentrations, as well as how diversified your potential risks may be.

A Top-Down Approach

For the top-down approach to measuring risk, some companies create complex Monte Carlo models (described later in this chapter) or similarly complicated models. You can take a much simpler route, however, by using a technique called *earnings volatility analysis.*

With this approach, you can break apart different line items of the P&L in order to link different risk categories to different lines on the P&L. For example, the standard deviations of cost lines are often quite closely associated with operational risk. Different business lines may hold quite a lot

> **def•i•ni•tion**
>
> Earnings volatility analysis measures the volatility (standard deviation or unexpected loss) of a company's earnings over time.

of credit or market risk that can be isolated by reviewing their specific revenue lines. Strategic risks can often be spotted by looking closely at broader volume trends.

Most risks that are part of different risk classes may not be correlated much at all. Nevertheless, to be safe, add up the individual risks from each major risk class: financial + operational + strategic = a total view of risk. The reason? In day-to-day operations, you might find little correlation between risks or risk groups. However, when things go badly, the correlation becomes incredibly high. *That's* when you need to be safest. Whenever there is a major disaster or crisis, financial risks rise. Right along with that comes operational risk. One pulls the other. This often changes the competitive landscape, which, in turn, increases strategic risk as well.

The dominoes of every major financial crisis or major disaster come tumbling down in this manner. Consider a financial collapse on a grand scale. That event often exposes or creates weaknesses in operations, which increases operational risk. The rates of machine or human error increase, incidents of fraud increase, and so on. The flip side is true as well: if there is a natural disaster, for example, other operational risks often materialize as weaknesses become apparent. New financial risks also materialize: companies become financially stressed, markets ride a wild price yo-yo, or credit is choked.

Putting Them to Use

The types of measures presented in this section are used to inform the amount of overall mitigation required. They provide a baseline that allows a company to report its risks and monitor how they may be moving and changing over time as well as how much overall risk is being carried.

Take the initiative; use these measures. Consider building simple reports that disclose how much of each risk you carry in each segment of the business. Update those reports regularly.

Conducting Stress Tests

You undoubtedly heard a lot about stress tests in early 2009 when the U.S. government tested the strength of 19 key banks. Stress tests are an important part of analyzing risks. They can be used to test the quality of your risk models, project future conditions, and predict catastrophic conditions.

There are two basic levels on which stress tests are conducted:

♦ **The single model level**   An isolated risk or subsegment of risks is stressed.

♦ **The enterprise level**   This test provides a look at what could happen to the entire company (or all of the risks and risk groups in a company).

Key Approaches

Stress tests are conducted in a variety of ways, but there are three basic approaches:

Individual variable stresses. One specific aspect of a model is identified, usually a rate series or parameter of the model. It is "stressed" by increasing it to a much larger number than the current standard deviation.

Risk Factors
A good example of the individual variable stress test involves interest rates. Models for market risk or interest rate risk are commonly "stressed" by shifting interest rates up and down by several hundred basis points—that is, a couple of full percentage points. This produces an extreme risk scenario, which helps risk managers make plans to mitigate the damages.

Monte Carlo analysis. No, this isn't an evaluation of the crown jewel of European protectorates, though some might find it just as exotic. This method creates a random "draw" on a variable or groups of variables that are applied to the models. The key is to "stress" the portfolio, so you intentionally set up the draw from a range of already stressed variables. This will help you to understand a range of possibilities and how more than one stressed variable could converge in a risk event. The disadvantage of this approach is that it can generate a range of impossible examples if those items are not ruled out in advance.

Scenario analysis. These are specific financial and economic scenarios that are translated into numerical effects on rate series and economic conditions and then applied to the models. They can be either normal or very extreme scenarios. They can also be highly focused (as above, on individual rate series or risk factors) or used to address larger scenarios where more factors are taken into consideration. This can take on a wide range of forms—basically, whatever you can imagine!

Putting Them to Use

Stress tests are among the simplest risk measures to utilize. You don't need fancy models to conduct them. Instead, you need a little dark vision, the ability to think up some potential things that could happen. Then you simply create and evaluate those scenarios. Or you can just research some very bad things that have happened in the past and try those out on your own risk assumptions and measures.

When conducting stress tests, involve a broad range of people within your company, and maybe some from outside your company as well. It's a good idea to include senior management, boards, and investors. It's also useful to have people involved who don't carry a vested interest and who can think broadly about potential events.

There are two keys to this approach. First, at some point, make sure that you are trying truly severe scenarios. Often, companies don't ratchet up the potential financial severity enough in their stress testing. Similarly, folks often underestimate operational risks because they don't include the contagion effects. One company analyzed project risks and came up with a likelihood and a severity of what it could lose. When looking back on the company's real losses, however, the estimates—and what the company stressed—were lower than the company's actual losses under normal conditions.

Red Flags

Be sure to create extreme stress tests. Don't fall short as many companies do, particularly in the financial industry. Many companies there traditionally stress test interest rate shifts only to ±200 basis points (2 full percentage points). If you look at actual interest rate shifts, though, you will see that this test is inconclusive. The reason: in a given year, it's not uncommon for rates to shift 200 basis points. To get an effective gauge, stress test on a scale of 400 basis points, or even higher, to get a good idea of what extreme movements look like and what they could do.

Second, once you run these scenarios or stresses, act upon your findings. Many companies put a lot of energy and expense into conducting a stress test, and then they don't do a thing. They look at the numbers, say, "that's interesting," and keep doing business as usual. The key is to learn something from the data and to use it to create a healthier, stronger, and more secure business.

The following guidelines will help you use the results of your stress test to strengthen your company:

If this event happened to you. Would you still be able to support the level of implied loss with your current reserves or savings?

If you are modeling the entire distribution. Look at how the shape of the distribution might change. This can often tell you a lot about the more likely risks, as well as the less likely risks. Often the focus falls on the less likely end of the distribution—the tail. That's why people dismiss stress tests. Sometimes, though, there is a high probability of other risks that aren't at the tail. If those higher-probability risks get much bigger, then you may really need to worry.

How would you react? What would you do if a catastrophic or severe risk event happened to you? It's important to start thinking about the lessons learned and how you would act in the aftermath of an event. This will be discussed further in Part 4 of this book.

Converting Measures to Money

When measuring risk, the primary goal is to ensure that your risk estimates relate to cold hard cash. Money is the resource that matters most when considering risk measures. Fortunately, if you've been measuring risk using EL and UL (or VAR) or using some form of standard deviation–based method, you're nearly home. The best approaches for converting risks into cash are based on these techniques.

Traditionally, expected loss is expressed in terms of financials (dollars). Thus, it is used directly, since it is calculated as a measure of dollars likely to be lost.

For unexpected loss, or standard deviation, the number is usually converted into a measure of capital. This measure of risk-related capital is called *economic capital* or *capital at risk* (CAR).

Economic capital can be calculated using the capital multiplier approach or by establishing the *confidence interval*.

def•i•ni•tion

Economic capital or **capital at risk (CAR)** is the amount of money that could be lost in a more extreme risk situation. Conversely, it is viewed as the amount of money that a company needs to hold as a buffer to ensure that it can continue to maintain its obligations and conduct business as an ongoing concern.

The **confidence interval** reflects the overall riskiness of the company. It also allows risk measurement and risk mitigation people to establish a view on economic capital and buffers that relates to that confidence interval. A company's confidence interval is often derived from its target debt rating.

With the capital multiplier approach, you multiply the standard deviation by a number (the capital multiplier). That figure relates to the amount of capital a company requires to support most of the risk events it could encounter. The goal of a capital multiplier is to account for the shape of the distribution of losses and the relative safety factor (risk appetite) that the company is trying to achieve.

The confidence interval method is a bit more technical. It tries to directly measure the amount of risk that a company should cover by establishing a confidence interval for the distribution curve. If you have considered 95 percent of your risks and their potential range of outcomes, then you have a 95 percent confidence interval. Risk managers often think of confidence intervals in terms of the number of standard deviations, so there is a close relationship to the capital multiplier method. They also can use more sophisticated methods to analyze the shape of the distribution and to determine how big of a number is associated with the amount of risk covered by the confidence interval.

 Red Flags

Although the capital multiplier approach is easy and convenient, it assumes the distribution curve incurs little to no change. However, in reality, the distribution curve changes almost constantly in the course of business, which can change your capital multiplier. Such a shift can take you back to the drawing board if you don't consider it.

The process for determining the confidence interval that is right for your company is similar to that of the capital multiplier. Begin by making an assumption about the type and shape of the distribution curve, or use fancier methods of modeling the exact curve. The ultimate confidence interval is usually related to your desired degree of safety. It can also relate to your target or implied debt rating, whether or not you hold an actual debt rating. Remember that higher confidence intervals relate to higher levels of capital, as well as higher and safer degrees of risk coverage. For most companies these should be set above 99.9 percent—above "junk bond" status.

The best reason for choosing the confidence interval method over the capital multiplier method is that confidence intervals require companies to model the distribution curve itself. This makes it possible to account more precisely for the shape of the curve, and how that can change as the risk profiles change, which, in turn, changes the capital multiplier and the money involved.

There are more methods for computing economic capital. These are generally used by companies as they become more sophisticated in their analysis capabilities. These approaches involve understanding the precise shape of the distribution of risks and using more specific means to relate the absolute amount of capital required to their confidence in withstanding a severe financial loss. However, these approaches require explanations of statistics that are far too advanced to cover in this book. Sources for these models are available in Appendix E.

Analyzing Risk and Reward

Up to this point, the discussion of risk analysis has focused on measuring, forecasting, projecting, and otherwise trying to pin down a negative risk event. However, as you know, not all risk is negative. No one gets ahead, in business or in life, without taking risks. Therefore, it's time to look at the positive side of the equation—the rewards that come from taking risks that play out favorably or from building reward into a risky program (such as charging interest rates for consumer credit).

One of the best ways to use risk measures in a day-to-day setting is to get an understanding of how risk and reward are linked. This is done by comparing measures of risk with measures of return.

Key Approaches

There are two primary methods for analyzing risk and reward:

Return Measure or RAROC (Risk-adjusted return on capital). This method, which arrives at a percentage (or measure), begins by noting your net earnings after taxes. Subtract your expected loss (in dollars) from that figure. The difference is the risk-adjusted return. Next, divide that by the economic capital number calculated earlier. This gives you the total risk-adjusted return on capital. There are some minor variants to the RAROC name (such as *risk-adjusted return on risk-adjusted capital*, RARORAC, or *return on economic capital*, ROEC, and others, but they represent only minor variants—and sometimes are simply different names for the same thing!). Don't let them confuse you.

Risk Adjusted Return on Economic Capital	
Revenues	**$$$**
- Expenses	(xxx)
- **Expected loss**	**(xxx)**
- Taxes	(xxx)
Risk adjusted return	**xxx**
÷ **Economic Capital**	**$$$**
RAROC	**X%**

The risk-adjusted return on capital (RAROC) equation enables you to analyze risk and reward accurately.

Contribution measure or economic profit, this generates an absolute number, not a percentage. This measure also carries other monikers: NIACC (net income after cost of capital), SVA (shareholder value analysis), and EVA (economic value analysis) are the three most common. It seems that every accounting and consulting firm uses its own creative term for the contribution method, and here again, they are usually the same, or nearly the same, calculation. The basic equation is as follows:

Economic Profit = Risk-Adjusted Return – Cost of Capital × Economic Capital

This method is similar to the return measure. Start by using the same risk-adjusted return number as that calculated in the first step above. Subtract the cost of capital times the economic capital. Cost of capital is usually some sort of hurdle rate or minimum return that the company wants to use as a benchmark for what it receives on its products or it is literally the cost of raising capital. It may be what the company's investors require as their minimum return for their investment.

This measure is traditionally calculated over the term of a month, quarter, or year, but it can also be calculated over many months, quarters, or years. Make sure everyone in your company is using the same time period.

Putting Them to Use

The return and contribution measures are excellent for analyzing different product lines, business lines, or the relative risk of an entire company. You can even compare one business against another. These measures are often set as something risk and financial managers call "hurdle rates." That means a minimum RAROC is targeted for a specific measure, such as what you expect each business or product line to return.

Some companies use these measures in their remuneration schemes. They give a bonus to managers who can provide a better risk-adjusted return or economic profit than targeted and to those who make sure their business areas reach that goal level. (See Chapter 19 for more on rewarding employees.) These measures also serve as the core framework from which to create pricing models that take risk costs into consideration.

The Least You Need to Know

- ◆ How your business handles a risk event comes down to how well you can measure expected and unexpected loss.

- ◆ You can use expected and unexpected loss to measure individual risks as well as groups of risk.

- ◆ A stress test is a great way to measure a company's financial condition, as well as its risk models.

- ◆ Convert all of your risk measures to dollars and cents, so you can relate risk to your bottom line.

- ◆ Businesses become successful by taking risks, so consider risk versus return one of your key measures.

Part 4

Managing and Mitigating Risk

Congratulations! You have made it through the all-important early stages of determining the risk to your business. You've probably even uncovered specific risks that you didn't know existed previously, let alone had a specific name, risk group, and measurement model.

Now for the next big question: What do you do with all of those identified risks, their measures, and the assessments of those measures? You pin your ears back and move into the "management" aspect of risk management. Risk management is an ongoing process that involves constant action and supervision. It's time to let your management skills shine.

Chapter 11

Treating Risk

In This Chapter

- ◆ Deciding which risks to consider first
- ◆ Determining which methods you will use
- ◆ Knowing when to transfer risk
- ◆ Limiting key risks

This is the chapter you've been waiting for: what to do about your risks. Now that you have identified, measured, and analyzed current and potential risks to your company, it's time to take a key, and most likely familiar, action: management.

Unlike managing a business, however, there are only a few unique methods for managing risk. This is a good place to repeat an often-misunderstood fact: *risk management is not exclusive of your normal business operations.* Consequently, many of the methods for managing risk intertwine with day-to-day operations and management approaches. As a strong business manager, you might already be taking many of the right steps.

In that case, why bother with an added management layer? Because much of risk management is about understanding where there are gaps in your existing strategy and analyzing whether the steps you are taking are sufficient.

Initial Considerations

As you begin to manage and mitigate your risks, you must consider a few major factors. First, your approach to managing risk should be based on a comprehensive understanding of the risks involved; this understanding comes from an appropriate level of risk analysis. It is particularly important to identify the causes of your risks as distinguished from their symptoms.

Second, your strategy should focus on all of your company's risks rather than on isolated issues. Having a complete risk strategy and knowing how to manage that strategy is important to ensure that critical dependencies and linkages are not compromised. For this reason, development of your overall strategy should be a top-down process, driven jointly by the need to achieve business objectives and the need to control uncertainty to a greater extent.

Best Bets _____

It will usually not be cost-effective—or even desirable—to implement all possible risk management and mitigation approaches. Instead, you must choose, prioritize, and implement the most appropriate combination of approaches. When doing so, consider factors such as costs and benefits, effectiveness, and other criteria of relevance to the organization. Legal, social, political, and economic considerations may need to be taken into account as well.

This is the point where you might say, "I need some input." It is wise to be flexible and consult broadly about risk management approaches with stakeholders, peers, and specialists. Many options need to be acceptable to stakeholders and others involved in implementation if they are to be effective and sustainable. Keep in mind, however, that the more people you involve, the more time you'll spend putting together a plan that's satisfying to everyone and that also meets your budget.

Methods for Treating Risk

People often think about risk as a mountain of problems standing between them and success. However, risk is more like an iceberg, in that the 10 percent of risk that is visible disguises a colossal potential to harm your business lurking beneath the surface. The urge is to steer completely clear of the risk if possible, as the risk can seriously rock the boat and even sink it. Although it's true that risk can lead to disastrous results, it's vital to temper the urge to avoid risk at all costs with the fact that taking calculated risks equates to making money. Approaching risk with appropriate planning invites a truly positive way to handle it.

Sometimes, however, it's impossible to avoid hitting the iceberg. Your smoothly sailing business suddenly hits chunks of ice in the form of obstacles that disrupt operations. When those risks come together, you're staring into a colossal iceberg—a major risk event. It's important to already have a plan of action in place so that you can respond quickly and efficiently.

The four broad categories of risk management are as follows:

♦ Avoid it

♦ Transfer it

♦ Reduce its likelihood

♦ Reduce its impact

The following sections explore these risk management strategies in detail.

 Red Flags

When it comes to determining which of the four categories of risk management to combine to address serious risks, remember that each category comes with a cost. While it may seem like a good idea to apply them all, doing so may not make financial sense.

Avoid It

You're facing the iceberg. You want to completely change your course to avoid the possibility of any contact with it. This is a natural response for people who are averse to risk. Why jaywalk across a busy road when you can cross at the traffic light? Or better yet, take the overhead walkway?

In business, the reality is quite different. Sometimes, the right decision is to play it safe. Sometimes, though, the best decision is to move forward into the path of the iceberg, hoping you'll be able to skirt its edges without suffering any damage.

Risk is a necessary part of growth. Avoiding risk completely will prevent you from growing your business. It may even lead to business shrinkage. If you operated in a truly risk-free zone, you would never hire new people, never develop new products or evolve existing ones, and never invest in a new storefront or equipment. In short, you would be missing opportunities for growth. So instead of avoiding risk altogether, recognize which risks should be avoided and which should be handled in one of the three other ways.

Transfer It

Although it's not always recognized as a form of risk management, risk transfer is one of the most common methods for handling risk. When you transfer risk, you move activities that are considered currently or potentially risky to another company. You can also transfer the consequence of a risk to another party or company. The three most common ways to transfer risk are outsourcing, insurance, and derivatives.

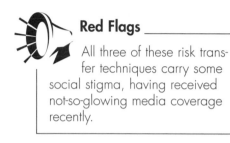

Red Flags

All three of these risk transfer techniques carry some social stigma, having received not-so-glowing media coverage recently.

Outsourcing. When you transfer risky activities to another company or specialist, you are outsourcing. Outsourcing is a dirty word to some because it is associated with moving operations and technology overseas to places like India, China, and the Philippines. Yet businesses and people "outsource" every time they see a doctor or lawyer or hire outside specialists to accomplish a specific task or function. You may know outsourcing by another, seemingly friendlier, term: contracting. Obviously, it makes sense to seek outside help when the cost to hire someone full-time would be exorbitant.

Adopt this approach with risk management. Contract out every time you identify an activity that is not a core component of your business model or in which you are not specialized and do not want to be specialized. Transfer your risk through outsourcing.

Insurance. The other forms of risk transfer are more financially oriented. They begin with insurance, when we pay a premium for insurers to cover the cost of an event should it occur. Insurance presents an interesting irony: it is a risk-reducing instrument, yet insurers operate on risk, effectively betting that an event won't happen or cost more than the premiums they have received. A year of uneventful activity and good weather is every insurer's dream. However, a year of wildfires burning in California, hurricanes swamping the Gulf Coast, floods covering the northern Plains, and tornadoes ripping through the Midwest and South—and their enormous damage price tags—underscores the downside of the risk insurers take.

For that reason, and by the nature of their specialty, insurers are expert risk managers. They use the same techniques described in the measurement section of this book (and other far more specialized tools) to determine the likelihood and impact of potential events. This enables them to set their compensation—premium payments—at a level that they believe can safely cover their bets.

Derivatives and hedging. Another form of risk transfer is hedging and the use of *derivatives*. Basically, these allow people or businesses to transfer different types of cash flows, and the risks surrounding those cash flows, to another party—a fund manager or financial institution—in order to obtain a different outcome.

def•i•ni•tion

Derivatives are financial contracts, or financial instruments, whose values are derived from the underlying value of something else, such as a monetary or real estate asset, commercial real estate, a stock, interest, an exchange rate or consumer price index, or weather conditions. The main types of derivatives are forwards, futures, options, and swaps.

Reduce the Likelihood

Every time you hire an outside service or professional to manage a risk or provide a service at which you are not expert, you are reducing the likelihood of risk. Companies pay premiums to reduce or avoid incidents that may be associated with their inability to manage the risk of the specialty service. The goal is to try to identify risks, or specific instances of risk within a risk class, and reduce their potential of occurring—even though you know that some risk events *will* occur.

The essence of this form of mitigation is to reduce the likelihood of higher-risk events. While a group of potential risks may look similar, some will hold higher impact potential than others. A perfect example is consumer credit management, which tries to identify and refuse higher-risk customers before they can create a domino effect when they default on payments. Likewise, your mission is to reduce the higher-impact risks by seeking them out and reducing their likelihood from the start.

Many business operational risks must be mitigated by reducing the likelihood of occurrence. The reason: not all operational risks can be avoided, nor all risk events prevented. That's part of the life of any assembly line or production facility. The goal is to identify potential trouble spots, such as the machine that might be failing and could cause you to lose product, create a safety hazard, or otherwise disrupt operations. In other words, the impact could be large.

Best Bets

People—your employees—are classified under operational risk. By fully and properly training your employees and finding backups for specific jobs when necessary, you create a system that reduces the chance of something going wrong and a risk materializing.

However, by ensuring that the machine is in tip-top condition, by planning regular maintenance, and by running it through a procedural check every time you turn it on or change a setting or a die, you reduce the possibility of the machine failing.

Reduce the Impact

The fourth and final category of risk management is impact reduction. It's the category of management no owner, executive, or manager wants to face, because it means a risk event has already occurred or is imminent. The good news is that there are many ways to reduce the impact of risk events. First, however, you must bite the bullet and accept that a risk event is occurring or about to occur. Then you can focus your attention on the back side, or the aftermath, of that event.

Risk Factors

Impact reduction assumes a risk event has materialized and there is nothing a business can do about some of its aspects. This makes impact reduction unique among risk management tools. Likely, there will be damage, costs associated with that damage, and related risks that will be triggered through concentration or contagion.

Even if you manage to negotiate the best insurance policy in the world and are covered for all of the net outlay, there are related events you'll want to try to reduce the impact of. These include the time it takes to receive insurance money and the amount of reputation risk or stakeholder risk you may experience as a result of the event.

There are several ways to approach impact reduction. Buffers and reserves, contingency plans, and even insurance fall into this category.

Choosing the Right Methods for Your Risks

Rarely will you need to use all four risk management techniques for a particular risk. That leads to the obvious next question: which technique should you employ for a given risk? While there is no specific right or wrong answer, there are some time-tested questions and guidelines that can help you decide.

What kind of risk are you trying to mitigate? Are there traditional methods (see the next section) that may work better for the application than other methods?

Do you have the correct problem statement? Are you treating the cause rather than the symptom? What risk or risks are you trying to address?

Are the risks the same type—or of more than one type? Do you need to consider different types of treatment strategies if you are facing multiple types of risk?

After you've answered these questions, conduct an analysis to make sure that the right risks and issues have been identified. Prescribe the most appropriate type of mitigation. Certain traditional mitigation methods work better for corresponding types of risk. We discuss some of these in greater detail in other chapters. A brief overview follows.

Evaluating Options

Choosing the right risk management and mitigation tools for your particular risk management issue is a matter of careful evaluation.

To start with, conduct a cost-benefit analysis. Ideally, make it both quantitative and qualitative, since each set of findings may be equally important. These findings may play out over multiple time periods. In these evaluations, take both direct and indirect benefits and costs into account. The direct and indirect benefits may have varying levels of uncertainty and need to be evaluated as separate issues. These may have different probability distribution curves. There may also be drivers such as social expectations and legal and regulatory issues. Those requirements and expectations may weigh heavily in your choice of options.

Another thing to consider: some approaches may not be considered satisfactory to the company. This happens occasionally when a mitigation approach has been tried before and failed. (The reason for failure may not even be rational; maybe the project manager became ill and the initiative never took off.) A conflict of corporate values can also create disagreement over approaches. A good example is the use of financial derivatives. Many organizations shun this technique or don't have the financial capabilities to support it.

Risk Factors
In the end, not all risks can or should be actively managed. Some risks are too costly, too unlikely, or too small to address. In these cases, the cost of managing these risks may well exceed the cost of the risk events themselves.

Residual Risk

When treatment options have been identified and implemented, the risks that remain behind are called residual risks. It is important that stakeholders and decision-makers be aware of their nature and extent. The residual risk should be documented and routinely monitored and reviewed—just like any other risk.

Cost-Benefit Analysis

One of the most important pieces of information in the mitigation and management of risk is a cost-benefit analysis. You will be evaluating both hard and soft categories—impacts measurable in dollars as well as impacts that are more difficult to quantify—to determine and rank the importance and size of your risks relative to one another. Quantifiable cost-benefit analysis involves adding up the costs and the benefits and comparing the two. This is often done as a ratio of costs to benefits. It is a form of return equation.

Red Flags

Keep in mind that some regulations require risk management regardless of its cost-effectiveness. Sometimes, however, regulation provides some leeway when the cost outweighs the returns. Document the case thoroughly.

If the return (or benefit) of an option is greater than its cost (or another predetermined figure), then the option is worth pursuing.

An ideal approach to cost-benefit analysis and implementation is as follows:

1. List all types of costs and benefits.

2. Group costs and benefits into hard and soft categories.

3. Calculate a quantitative measure for hard costs and benefits.

4. Rank soft costs and benefits against one another. Use techniques presented earlier, such as consequence tables or the risk matrix.

5. Present both the hard and soft cost-benefit analysis results together. Try to rank them against one another. Add the effects of both direct and indirect costs and benefits.

6. Consider if the costs and benefits will be realized over the next year, or if it may take longer.

Another complication lies in the potential uncertainty in the values assigned to costs and benefits. You will want to establish what the variance is for each cost-benefit assumption and establish a distribution of results, as described in Chapter 8. A probability weighting can also be employed on each line item. More sophisticated assessments, particularly when big money is at stake, often include a Monte Carlo analysis (discussed in Chapter 10) to factor in the variance around every line item.

Choosing a Cost-Benefit Option

Choosing the right cost-benefit option isn't always a straightforward process. It is often the case that there is no single best option or that the optimum solution is prohibitively expensive. Some options may have incremental benefit, depending on how much is spent on the implementation. Or a company may consider trading off between an implementation's benefit and cost.

Other realistic options include the following:

- ◆ A satisfactory (but not optimum) solution

- ◆ The most cost-effective solution

- ◆ The accepted, industry-standard practice

- ◆ The best achievable result (given your current technology)

- ◆ The absolute minimum

Believe it or not, doing little or nothing is often a real option, particularly if the solution is being applied for regulatory compliance purposes.

If you want to see how costs and benefits will be realized over a year or longer, you may need to employ a net present value analysis. This analysis examines the costs and benefits for each year that the solution takes effect. Next, it "discounts" the effect, which takes into account cash flows that occur over multiple points in time. Those cash flows are "discounted" by a percentage rate that takes into account the minimum value of the cash flow or alternative investment. This method will allow you to take into account the time value of money.

 Red Flags

When you discount the effect of your cost-benefit analysis, be sure to factor appropriate estimates of the cost and variances associated with risk into your figure. Don't just increase your discount rate. This confuses the calculations and often leads to incorrect assumptions being baked into the analysis, leading to incorrect results!

Putting the Plan in Place

Finally, the plan must be implemented and managed. This will usually include the following steps:

- Identify responsibilities

- Develop schedules, budgets, and performance measures

- Continue the review process until the project is complete

- Manage communication with all stakeholders

- Document, document, document!

Be sure to include a mechanism for assessing and monitoring the effectiveness of the solution.

The Least You Need to Know

- Risks seldom manifest in isolation. Include all known risk groups in your overall risk management strategy.

- Extend the analysis of your risks into the future to identify and explore treatment options that serve you best.

- Carefully evaluate your risk treatment plan. Choose an approach and measures that work specifically for your needs.

- Put your treatment plan into motion and oversee it as though you were managing a project.

Chapter 12

Reducing the Likelihood of Risk Events

In This Chapter

- ◆ How to reduce risk exposure
- ◆ Setting risk limits
- ◆ Building controls
- ◆ Outsourcing risks

In sports, everyone knows you can't win 'em all. Same goes for business: you can't prevent all risks. However, through careful planning, measuring, and analyzing, you can reduce the likelihood of risk events. This is both a preferred and vital method for managing risk, because it prevents many risks from ever materializing. Consequently, it reduces your exposure to other risks and tamps down virulent outbreaks of concentrated risks, contagion, and triggered risks, such as stakeholder and reputation troubles. You can increase the bang for your risk management buck by employing the same risk reduction methods to tackle groups of risk.

If reducing the likelihood of risk events was the easiest method to use, companies would deploy it all the time and never see a risk materialize.

Unfortunately, it is among the most difficult solutions to implement well. That's because it's often difficult to prioritize which risks to reduce, and it's a potentially very expensive endeavor. In addition, a company is often incapable of preventing all risks, or even a reasonable portion of them. Furthermore, many organizations struggle with the value of prevention, as they either doubt the likelihood of risk arising or underestimate the future impact of that risk. Because the benefits are hard to fully appreciate, the cost justification can be a challenge.

There are numerous risk prevention and reduction methods. In this chapter, we focus the spotlight on the most common and successful approaches.

Limiting Your Exposure to Risks

What do you do when faced with a mountain of projects, paperwork, or tasks, or, for that matter, a real mountain? Chances are, you size up the overall challenge, decide on the most important steps to take, break down those steps, and take them one at a time. By doing so, you reduce the likelihood of the entire mountain collapsing on you, and you limit your exposure to risk. And although you may not be able to avoid the pile of responsibilities, you can certainly reduce its size—and thus make the mountain feel smaller and easier to climb.

Risk reduction works in much the same way. The first step to take when faced with a pile of risks is to reduce your exposure to it. This approach is very common, particularly when dealing with external parties, such as customers and suppliers. It can also be used internally, such as when a company extends credit to customers. In this case, a business can reduce the likelihood of risk by limiting the amount of credit it provides, whether by deciding on a set credit limit for all customers or creating different limits for different customers based upon their creditworthiness.

Best Bets

If you receive 100 percent of your product, materials, or services from a single supplier, try to reduce your exposure to that supplier from 100 percent to, say, 30 percent by introducing two additional suppliers for the same product, material, or service.

A more abstract form of the same concept involves key man risk. A business can reduce its exposure to key man risk by either finding additional people to support the same job (maybe as apprentices or backups, at least initially) or by splitting up the job and distributing the critical responsibilities among several people. In this way, the overall exposure of running critical tasks through a single person is reduced.

Understanding Risk Limits

How do you understand and set risk limits? At first glance, it seems like a bit of skillful riverboat gambling. You can enforce *hard risk limits, soft risk limits,* a guess, or a precise number. How these limits are approached, met, or exceeded depends on the kind of risk you are trying to reduce and how much precision counts.

Imagine a customer breaks a financial limit on a loan. This might be acceptable once (soft limit), but if the behavior continues, it can add up very quickly and create big problems. If a business provides credit for hundreds of customers and begins to let customers creep over their $20,000 credit limits, its exposure to credit risk can grow very quickly. If not kept in check, the exposure can become very big and material—possibly big enough to decimate the business.

Then there is precision. Is it important to put a precise number (a hard limit) on

def•i•ni•tion

Hard risk limits and soft risk limits denote whether your threshold of acceptable risk is merely suggested (soft) or set in stone (hard). Would you fire someone over the risk? Would you care if your key man had backup—or not? The answer is based more on your level of comfort than any predetermined limits.

risk? Yes, if the competition puts pressure on those limits. You want to know almost exactly how much you are willing to risk so you can be sure that you are providing the maximum you and the customer can withstand. In the preceding example, maybe the competition extends a $25,000 credit limit to its customers. Can your business possibly push its boundary to $30,000? Or maybe provide up to $60,000 for your better customers? That would really sock it to the competition. But so does the opposite—when you limit your customers' credit, you leave it wide open for your competitors to boost their limits and deal with the accompanying stressed cash reserves and defaulting customers. That would also mean trouble for your competitors. When you work to understand risk limits, you will need to address the following specific aspects of financial and operational risk.

Financial risk limits. Financial risk limits create the allowable ceiling for expected loss, capital, or both. These are usually applied to credit or lending situations and for control of budgets and spending. They also come into play for trading or structural financial risks, such as the interest rate or amount of liquidity risk a company is willing to carry. In these latter cases, though, the steps to reduce and monitor exposure must consider much longer periods, across which a company can measure and manage remediation.

Operational risk limits. Operational risk limits are often both hard and soft. Soft limits or guidelines accompany measures such as numbers of suppliers or people who can support key activities. Hard limits are established to cap such things as the number of cycles a piece of equipment can run before it is shut down for maintenance or overhaul. A company might even keep strong data that correlates the number of runs before a machine is overhauled and the increase in defects. That would definitely quantify the exposure a company can afford.

Building Risk Exposure Limits

In risk, as in life or business, limits can be very arbitrary or very precise. They can either be strongly enforced or serve as points of guidance. Now for the tough questions: How do you know whether to set hard or soft limits for specific operations, financial programs, or other potential sources of risk? How do you go about it? Here are a few suggestions.

Decide the importance of having a firm view of total exposure. Will it lead to a guideline or something you want to strictly control?

Is precision required? Is there a competitive issue at stake? Will there be a material difference in your strategic position as a result of a higher or lower limit? Will there be a direct consequence? Financial limits often fall into this category. Decisions around credit, pricing, and financial management (hedging, budgets, etc.) are good examples.

Can you develop a direct link between the possibility of a risk materializing and the element you are monitoring? Generally, the more closely linked, the better. If you know how many cycles you can go because you have experimented with such monitoring before, then you have likely correlated the increase in any defects and can readily set hard limits.

Construct the limit. Make your limit the maximum exposure the company can withstand, minus a buffer, usually around 10 percent or so. If there is more than one area where limits will be created, consider using a *limit tree*. Common in banking and companies that extend considerable credit, limit trees set a total limit for the business and then sublimits for each sector or portfolio. This is often constructed for budgets and spending as well. Some limit trees also factor in diversification, since different "branches" will require their own limits. These "branch" limits need not add up to the total; you may want to create buffers in each location so they are lower than the total. When you use correlations to calculate the total, the limit tree's total could exceed the company's risk limit.

Take advantage of correlations between portfolios. When bringing two or more portfolios together, individual limits will likely add up to more than the allowable total limit. In these cases, use risk measures like those in Chapter 10 for adding up standard deviations. To do that, take the correlation coefficient between each portfolio and apply that to the risk in each. Suppose we place a $40,000 limit on one region and $30,000 on a different region. To understand the total limit for the two regions combined, simply apply the correlation between the two regions (in this case .8; with 1 being perfect correlation, these two regions are highly correlated). The total limit for the two regions would be roughly $66,500. Notice that it is less than what it would be if the two limits had been added up directly.

def•i•ni•tion _____

> **Limit trees** are risk limits that start at a central top limit (sometimes referred to as a "house" limit) and break down as "branches" across a company's departments, divisions, or possibly portfolios or product lines.

Build policies and procedures around the limit. State the limit, the rules for approaching it, and *consequences* and procedures of overextending or breaching it. Clearly delineate any limit that is used to drive day-to-day operations.

Consider soliciting feedback from related personnel and stakeholders. This is important to do before finalizing the limit. Also, test the limit in a *pilot program*.

Develop a training and communications program. This is important to ensure complete understanding and consistency of enforcement as you roll out the limit for routine use.

def•i•ni•tion _____

> A **pilot program** is basically a test or experiment. It usually takes place in the course of business operations, over a sufficient period of time. It obtains results comparable to the standard operation and is generally conducted on a product, region, branch, or other focused area of the business.

Triggers and Controls

Triggers and controls are similar to risk exposure limits. They are created to support and better enforce known limits. They may be less directly linked to risks, serve as the start of a chain of activities, or both. Think of them as a process of managing risk exposure rather than a numerical limit or threshold.

Types of Triggers and Controls

There are several types of triggers and controls. As with many things in risk management, they can be very simple and easy to implement, or they can cross into the twilight zone of complexity. The two biggest sets of triggers and controls for businesses are financial/economic and operational.

Financial and economic triggers and controls involve watching trends (such as leading and lagging indicators) or other signals within the operation that provide an indication of mounting risk. They can also be used to review risks or take additional action. Examples include home price depreciation or the employment index, housing starts, and missed or late credit payments. All can signal economic weaknesses that could trigger financial risks, particularly credit risk. In market risk, look at market fluctuations, as market volatility is a big trigger. In fact, it is synonymous with risk.

Best Bets

Create triggers within your risk measurements. A trigger could be a warning level built in ahead of a limit or even an increase in a risk measure itself. When risk rises, these triggers will prompt a series of actions. You might start cost reductions based on financial triggers, raise capital based on early capital triggers, or beef up recovery operations for credit losses if you see increases in credit risk signals.

Operational triggers are often connected to individual triggers set for each process or equipment output. This trigger often appears as a product characteristic or equipment setting. A useful technique is statistical process control, a very common and easy-to-implement approach to monitoring operations. Pick a factor to monitor—perhaps a key metric of the operation, such as a machine's output, or a measurement from product specifications or service levels—then monitor and record it. Measures that fall significantly above or below the average are signals to make changes in the machine settings.

Using Triggers and Controls

There are a few simple, effective steps for using triggers and controls in your business, starting now. They include identifying key metrics, observing and recording the behavior or the activity driving the metric, and analyzing the average and standard deviation for the variables being observed.

To put it another way: What is normal? What is abnormal? Find out. Utilize an X-bar chart to employ a series of simple rules for knowing if something is behaving normally or abnormally. Identify how many instances of behavior fall within each band above and below the mean. You can then take actions based on where you are on the chart. This is a simple, powerfully effective approach. There are variations for drilling deeper; resources for more sophisticated analysis are provided in Appendix E.

Sometimes it becomes necessary to take multiple samples at each interval. When you have that information, you can also plot the range of the samples to see if there is any abnormality in each set being sampled. This is called an R chart. The X-bar and R chart are often used together to assign numerical values to abnormalities (a method known as X-bar/R chart or Shewhart chart, after the man who invented them). For instance, a broken machine will show up as an abnormal pattern of points on the chart. Like other control charts, the X-bar/R chart helps determine if variations in measurements are caused by standard deviations that cannot be acted upon, also known as "common causes," or by larger "special causes" that can be acted upon and remediated.

Finally, document, train, communicate, and test. All of your trigger and control measures need to be accompanied by the correct documentation, training, communication, and even testing (particularly for certain sorts of operational applications) before being rolled out.

"Outsourcing" Your Risks

Outsourcing is all about getting someone outside of your company to perform a function in return for a fee. It is no different than hiring out accounting or legal tasks. Your outsourced project could be small—hiring a publicist to write press releases, for instance—or it could be very large—yanking out your IT systems and hiring an outside company for all IT service. In both cases, you transfer risk by paying a specialist to take on the job and its accompanying risk.

Thinking About Outsourcing

When contemplating outsourcing or contracting, consider both direct costs and benefits of the contractual arrangement and uncertainties in those costs and benefits. Also think about new risks that may arise from working with the outside contractor. Often legislation will determine whether or how risks may be shared.

Red Flags _____

The first rule of outsourcing any project or function is to establish specific wording in the contract document. It sounds simple, and it often is. However, if the contract isn't explicitly worded and every possible detail covered, an outsourcing arrangement can lead to a change in the nature of a risk or the emergence of new risks.

To be sure you identify all of the risks, make a cost-benefit analysis of outsourcing them (see Chapter 11 for details). Factor into your cost-benefit analysis the development of new risks and the uncertainty they may inject into your overall risk profile. Remember that outsourcing is not just about saving operating costs. This is a serious misperception that companies often have when they consider outsourcing. Outsourcing rarely saves operating costs. What it can do, however, is allow you to place functions or key tasks in the hands of specialists at the *same* cost as it would require for you to do them. You can transfer risks and improve the end results with no increase in costs.

Finally, consider the type of financial structure that you set up for your outsourcing partner. Set up the correct incentives and focus on outputs, rather than inputs. For instance, rather than lacing incentives or minimums on how many hours people spend on a task (or how many people are assigned to a task), focus on the quality of the work or how quickly it is completed.

Risks That Can Be Outsourced

How do you decide which operational risks to outsource? When considering outsourcing, first determine which aspects of your current business are core or fundamental functions or proprietary areas. Everything *not* in those categories is up for grabs among outside contractors.

New or growing companies find outsourcing to be invaluable, as it saves immensely on the costs of hiring new employees (salaries, benefits, pension plans, etc.). Anything you don't have the time or expertise to build and that is not critical to your daily operations can be outsourced.

Consider outsourcing the following key items to transfer and/or reduce risk:

◆ Accounting and related financial back-office activities

◆ Auditing service

- ◆ Legal services
- ◆ IT operations
- ◆ Payment processing
- ◆ Credit processing
- ◆ Credit checking
- ◆ Human resources administration
- ◆ Document production

Best Bets

A number of companies help small to mid-size businesses by providing consolidated business services, such as legal, accounting, finance, IT support, human resources administration, and so on. There are even companies that perform reviews of your operation to help you assess your needs.

Working with Your People

Experts and owners can talk about risk types, measures, and mitigation all day long. However, as with almost everything else in business, working with risk comes down to one asset over all others: your people. Your management and employee teams are your greatest assets and often provide the best way to prevent risks. A number of risks can be directly tied to people—and many other risks can be prevented through your people.

People-based risk management techniques can be broken into four major categories: workplace culture and environment, training and education, people-based controls, and incentives.

Workplace Culture and Environment

Every company wants a positive workplace that is safe and bolstered by reasonable-to-ideal working conditions. Within reason, the more positive the environment, the more productive and creative people are likely to be. Also, happy workers mean fewer grievances and mistakes.

A great example of this is Skywalker Ranch, the former headquarters of Lucasfilm, which iconic producer George Lucas built in 1979 with his earnings from *Star Wars*. Lucas, a driven man if ever one existed (he shot *American Graffiti* in 30 days and nights, fueling himself with candy bars and Cokes!), knew he would work his people hard as they made some of the biggest blockbusters in history. He sensed that the burnout rate would be high—a huge risk, in that he could lose one talented person after another. So he created a workplace environment that sparked creativity and productivity while also providing opportunities for rest and reflection. Skywalker Ranch is set among 800 acres of Northern California redwoods, live oaks, meadows, and hills. Every office window points out at nature—a garden, hillside, stand of wildflowers, blossom-covered trellis, grove, or pond. Walking trails and softball and soccer fields dot the property. The 10,000-volume library is a Victorian building with an adjacent glassed-in patio. Whose creative juices wouldn't flow in such a setting? Who wouldn't be driven to produce great work?

Very few business owners ever attain the financial ability to buy 800 acres and turn it into the quintessential alter-studio to the Hollywood system. However, the point is clear: workplace environment can directly impact people risk—for good or bad.

Training and Education

Training and education about risks or other workplace capabilities helps to reduce errors, improve quality, and increase focus on risk-related matters. Some form of training should be conducted regularly in order to ensure the workforce is aware of new developments or programs as they work toward continuous improvement. Ongoing training also helps you create redundancy of vital skills among employees, which can reduce or eliminate key man risk.

People-Based Controls

People-based controls are exactly what they sound like. These involve putting controls in place that are managed by people. They include such steps as documenting standard operating procedures and ensuring that people follow them by using a checklist or sign-off form. You can also use the checklist to routinely check equipment settings.

Incentives

Many companies consider using risk-based incentives to align objectives and focus on reducing risk or seeking better returns relative to risk. They can help ensure that everyone is working toward the same objectives.

Incentives are highly effective, but if you err in any way, they can create a huge mess. Think of incentives as a wildfire spreading through the organization. A controlled burn can be a good thing, but if it spreads in the wrong direction, look out! Having said that, a good start is to include risk metrics in your incentive scheme.

Red Flags

Be sure any operation-based incentives are clearly measured and tied to actual risk reduction. Sometimes an incentive can send the wrong message by overcompensating. People will respond by not taking any risks. They might also go the other way and allow risk events to reach their thresholds, when common sense suggests lowering these risks. Extreme circumstances on either end of the spectrum can easily result from incentive programs. Use metrics that balance risk with return and growth.

The easiest metric to use is a risk-adjusted return measure (see Chapter 8). Try to incentivize people on the powerful combination of both risk and return (as well as growth). When pay is linked to risk, return, and growth, it sends a clear message about what is important. A simpler approach is to ensure that operations run within the risk limits, although these incentives are often a bit blunt and limited in what they can do.

Checklists

Put your people to work to reduce risk likelihood with the simplest tool in the land—the checklist. An incredibly powerful tool, even the checklist needs to be managed. Ensure that the steps in the checklist are clear and reviewed by your employees regularly. Establish a simple procedure that makes it clear at what intervals or triggers to use a checklist. Require sign-offs and ask questions on a form that employees must fill out. That way, they can't sign it without answering the questions. For really critical items, require a second-party check.

As always, communication and training are key. Emphasize to your staff *why* you are requiring a checklist. Reinforce the reasons for it and create a thought process that requires response. Keep your checklists fresh and updated. Change them up periodically so they don't become stale, causing people to check off items without paying any attention. Create real consequences for people if they don't follow procedures. This intertwines incentives with simple tools.

The Least You Need to Know

- No company can prevent *all* risks.
- Reduce your risk exposure when you are faced with a mountain of risks or economic changes strain your reserves.

- Use risk exposure limits to safeguard your cash flow and reduce risk.

- Build triggers and controls to signal the potential for emerging or rising risks.

- The greatest assets in your business—your employees—also serve as the best tools for reducing and preventing risk.

Reducing the Impact

In This Chapter

◆ Identifying ways to reduce impact

◆ Deciding on an appropriate contingency plan

◆ Rolling out the plans

◆ Creating buffers and reserves

Sometimes risks just can't be avoided—or they are detected after it is too late to prevent them. When that happens, action must be swift, decisive, and effective. This brings into play the fourth set of methods for risk management and mitigation: reducing the impact.

Impact reduction techniques are most often used in one of two situations. They are deployed when a risk is so common, and so difficult or unattractive to fully prevent, that some management on the back end needs to be installed. They are also used when a risk is rarely realized but so significant when it does occur that plans must be in place to handle it. Like every other method discussed thus far, impact reduction techniques and strategies can be used in conjunction with other risk management and mitigation methods. For instance, you might employ a prevention technique first, followed by a method to address the impact after something does occur.

Risk managers use a few common types of management methods for reducing impact. They include contingency plans, buffers and reserves, diversification, hedging, and insurance.

Contingency Plans

Contingency plans are simply plans that have been prepared in advance. They go into effect as the result of a trigger that indicates a serious problem or the occurrence of a risk event. There are many types of contingency plans. They can be constructed for any aspect of your organization where you feel there is significant risk. An example of a contingency plan that everyone remembers from their school years is the fire drill (the school version, not the business version).

While contingency plans are fairly simple to create, they must meet two criteria to be effective. First, the plan must be complete in advance. The goal is to accurately second-guess the actual dynamics of the event when it occurs. If you have never before experienced the event being anticipated, it might be tricky to build a complete, well-constructed plan for the situation. Second, everyone involved must know the plan and their respective roles within it.

Both of these requirements mean that contingency plans must be routinely reviewed. You must routinely conduct communication, education, and training, particularly if your company is in flux and you are dealing with new people who need to know about the plan.

There are three major specialty forms of contingency plans (besides our old friend the fire drill): cash crisis liquidity plans, business continuity plans, and disaster recovery plans.

Cash Crisis Liquidity Plan

The cash crisis liquidity plan is put in action when a company finds itself in a deep cash crisis. Unfortunately, this happens all too often in small businesses. A company does not have enough money to meet key obligations (such as loans), which could shut the company down or force it to change hands. A contingency plan includes the following key elements:

- Potential sources of rapid cash that the company can tap, such as lines of credit, limited investors, your banker, and even government resources

- Sources to call (and in what order), including those inside and outside the company who control critical processes and decisions

- Operations or actions that need to be shut down (or initiated)

Best Bets _____

> Companies at risk of defaulting on their loans often avoid their bankers. What they don't realize is that most bankers will try almost anything to work out an arrangement before calling the loan and defaulting it. They would rather restructure a loan by entering the process early and helping the company manage payments. By biting the bullet and contacting your bank at the first sign of trouble, you can create a win-win for your company and your bank.

Business Continuity Plan

The business continuity plan (BCP) is one of the most common types of contingency plan. In particular, it is one of the most common methods of mitigating operational risks. You're shooting for one thing above all others: keeping your business running in the event of a disruption. The BCP's purpose is to recover and restore functions that have been partially or completely interrupted, and to do so within a predetermined time after a disruption. This is part of an organizational learning effort that helps reduce operational risk as well as reputation and stakeholder risks.

Best Bets _____

> Your business continuity plan and other contingency plans need to be refreshed regularly. Doing so ensures that participants don't forget their roles, new people can learn the plan, and the plan gets updated when business processes are upgraded or changed.

Disaster Recovery Plan

Disaster recovery plans (DRs) move into effect after full disasters occur. Their main objective is to establish the most basic capabilities and resources. You hear about DRs when damage is extensive or catastrophic; therefore, when a DR must kick into effect, you're likely looking at significant downtime, if not worse.

Risk Factors

Disaster recovery plans and business continuity plans work together and often overlap, which sometimes makes it difficult to distinguish between them. The main difference to remember is this: BCPs establish responses to situations as they occur, to limit the damage and ensure the business is up and running as quickly as possible. DRs go into effect after full disasters occur. The DR's objective is focused on restoring basic capabilities and resources, such as power, water, and clear roads.

DRs work hand-in-hand with BCPs, since the greatest goal of any business-related disaster recovery plan is to get the business up and running. Because of that, several other types of contingency plans are used in conjunction with BCPs and DRs (or derive from them). The most commonly used are crisis and emergency plans and—for an entirely different type of damage control—media and communications management plans.

Here are three tips for working through the snags of your business continuity, disaster recovery, and/or cash crisis liquidity plans.

Solicit feedback. Welcome input from people of all levels. Experience may be lurking in unexpected places. You might have auxiliary police or volunteer firefighters in your midst; their additional training is vital for some scenarios. Or a front-line machinist may know what could happen if a piece of equipment seizes up.

Conduct experiments. Conduct controlled tests or experiments. Recovery times and mitigation factors can be improved, particularly for high-value operations segments.

Use experts. BCP and DR specialists possess a wealth of standard recovery and event path information. Consider employing one of them to help with the plan. This is particularly true in IT matters.

Key Considerations

When do you trigger the company's cash crisis liquidity, business continuity, or disaster recovery plan? Hopefully, never! Unfortunately, however, many businesses will at some point need to use one of these plans.

The good news is that that dark moment can turn quickly to sunshine if you understand when to trigger one of these plans and take swift action. Your ability to identify triggers or signals, and your willingness to move instantly if required, are part of both the upfront analysis and the ultimate success of your plan.

Fast action can be an important component of making a BCP/DR (or any other contingency plan) successful. When you think of the alternative—an unmitigated disaster—it might create extra incentive to develop training programs. Everyone needs to know their role, what they are required to do, and when they need to do it. Ensure that each critical person has appropriate education and training. Even non-critical personnel may need some practice and basic understanding of the plan, depending on the type of operation and the scenarios that most concern you. Rehearse these scenarios! Also, don't forget the senior executives. They may not be on the production floor all day, but they will likely have critical roles to play.

Finally, make sure the plan is good enough to handle a worst-case scenario or to give your company the best chance of remaining operational. Just because you have a plan doesn't mean that you are totally covered. That is where you can mix elements of your BCP and other contingency plans to create the best possible course of action.

Putting Them to Use

There are four areas to contemplate and possibly act upon when preparing to implement your contingency plan.

Testing. Think about what aspects of your plan are the most critical to understand perfectly and build a test plan. This could be as simple as a walk-through of your operations or as sophisticated as a computer simulation. You can also conduct controlled shutdowns and start-ups.

Roll out. One of the most crucial aspects of contingency planning is the way in which it is rolled out to the team. Manage all stakeholders through the roll-out, ensure that everyone's roles are clear, then train, educate, rehearse, and solicit feedback.

Building a crisis management team. If the concern is strong enough, designate a crisis or business continuity management team to lead the recovery effort. These may even be two different teams with specific focuses. People on this team may have specialty skills and/or leadership responsibilities, and they are likely to need special training or rehearsal.

Keeping them up-to-date. Finally, keep the plans up-to-date. Over the course of any year, an organization changes in obvious and subtle ways. So does the type or degree of business in most cases. When meaningful changes occur, the BCP must change. Consider a quick annual review and look for triggers for a more comprehensive review or rewrite. These may include the purchase of a new business or critical piece of machinery, expansion to new products, the creation of a new department, or the addition of new service offerings.

Best Bets

In addition to periodically updating your written contingency plans, be sure to update the people involved with carrying out the plans as well. Employees leave and must be replaced by new people, and existing employees' roles evolve, both facts that need to be reflected in contingency plans.

Buffers and Reserves

Time to switch to the all-important financial side of risk management. Buffers and reserves team to form an extremely common tool in financial risk management, so common that banks and insurance companies are generally regulated in this area. They are required to hold specific amounts of reserves and capital (buffers). Buffers and reserves are often used in operational risk management as well.

The buffer and reserve approach is common in a number of other industries where short-term losses happen occasionally or even frequently. For instance, they are used when there is a high probability of loss, such as in the energy business, where substantial risk surrounds price shifts on commodities.

How They Work

Buffers and reserves are conceptually similar in their "rainy day" approach to risk management. Companies set aside reserves for the losses they anticipate—for *expected losses*. They are treated as an expense, because they are losses that will most likely materialize. Buffers consist of money put aside to support *unexpected losses*. There are also physical buffers to deal with operational risks, such as reserve power generators. These are the real risks of the business activity. This money is set aside from a company's capital base.

def•i•ni•tion

Expected losses and **unexpected losses** are the epicenter of risk management strategy. Expected losses are losses that a business anticipates. Unexpected losses happen suddenly, without warning. They can severely disrupt, damage, or devastate businesses that don't plan for them. Companies manage their risk exposure by setting aside funds for both types of losses.

For this reason, reserves are used whenever losses are an inherent part of doing business. This often happens when financial risks are present, such as when a company extends credit to customers. Reserves may be used when embarking on a highly risky strategy; when, for instance, it is necessary to lose money initially in order to make money down the line. Reserves may also be used in other scenarios where a loss is highly likely, such as when implementing a regulatory requirement that is likely to create losses. Reserves, however, are fairly finite and "sure." They have a starting and ending period. The money will be returned to the business at some specific point in time (or used to offset the real losses).

Capital, the buffer for true risk, has more general applications and can be used for any risk. Capital may have a finite nature, but it may be carried indefinitely to support the changing nature of risk in the business over time. Some of the methods for sizing the specific amounts will be discussed in Chapter 15.

From an accounting perspective, buffers and reserves show up in different locations in financial statements. For this reason, it is important to work with your accountants when you implement them.

Implementing Buffers and Reserves

The first step of implementing buffers and reserves might be the quickest action of any in risk management. After calculating the necessary reserves and capital, transfer the money into its appropriate form, either cash or a highly liquid asset such as a Treasury bill.

Next comes the ever-crucial second step: updating buffer and reserve amounts regularly to take into account changing risks and market conditions. This process can stretch deeply enough to link the amount directly to each risk. For example, if you lend money to a new customer, identify how much reserve is needed to support that single loan. Add it to the contingency fund until the loan is repaid. If the customer does not repay the loan, then you have a reserve to support your cash requirements. The reserve effectively offsets the loss.

Buffer and reserve plans also need to be updated regularly to account for changing risks. Some risks increase and decrease regularly, especially in businesses where risk is the primary activity or a key part of the business model. Such companies would include any firm that lends money, trades commodities or other exchange-traded

Risk Factors
Reserves are typically increased or decreased in direct proportion to the risks—or risk potential—a company develops or reduces.

instruments, or provides insurance. These risks can move around as your business grows. Sometimes they are so volatile that they fluctuate with market ups and downs and thus move dramatically within the same day! In such cases, the numbers often need to be recalculated just as frequently.

Also consider the accuracy and type of your measurement approaches. If you are using risk measures to work out how much money you need to keep in a safe, inaccurate measurements can be costly.

 Red Flags

The measures and models for buffers and reserves, as for many other aspects of risk management, tend to be fairly technical and scare off many people in management. Imagine how it feels to be told you need to hold considerable capital or extra cash that can't be used until a rainy day—and the amount depends upon the answers that spit out of the model! Make sure you or your team is educated in the approach to the problem and that your models are clear. In order to sway any skeptics to the approach, remind them that the models can be used to support other aspects of the company's risk management program—or maybe even its business strategy!

Many industries are required by regulations to use these sorts of approaches. Regardless, it is important to ensure that the approaches and assumptions are well documented. At the very least, your accountant will need to understand how you calculated the particular amounts of reserves and capital that are reflected in your accounts. He doesn't set the amounts. Rather, he makes sure they can be justified by accounting standards.

Finally, the buffers and reserves should be accompanied by a policy. The policy should describe when and how the reserves and capital should be used and how they will be released in the event of a risk materializing. The policy should also recognize the accounting treatment required. The policy is particularly useful when reserves and buffers become a routine part of risk management for your firm. That way, the business understands how to use them in the future and how to create a consistent management approach.

Hedging

Though normally practiced through financial instruments, *hedging* in risk management allows companies to offset exposure to risk with something likely to behave in an equal (or near equal) and opposite way. If the risk is fully offset, it's considered a "perfect hedge."

Hedging in business can be much more than a financial transaction. An example of something you might hedge is a contraction in demand for your product—particularly if it is held in inventory. Both insurance and diversification are forms of hedges.

def•i•ni•tion

Hedging refers to taking a position in one instrument or market that is designed to offset exposure to a position or obligation in another market. A typical hedge is a strategy designed to minimize exposure to business risks and financial risks.

Natural Hedges

Another key form of hedging is a natural hedge. A natural hedge is an investment that reduces the undesired risk by matching revenues and expenses. For example, an exporter to the United States faces a risk of the U.S. dollar changing value. He chooses to open a production facility in the U.S. market to match expected sales revenue with the cost structure. Another example is a company that opens a subsidiary in another country and borrows in the local currency to finance its operations. The local interest rate may be more than that in the home country of the company. However, by matching the debt payments to expected revenues in the local currency, the parent company has reduced its foreign currency exposure.

Many industries involve the purchase or production of commodities or cross-currency activities of some kind (where expenses are calculated in one currency and revenues in another). All use hedging. Or perhaps a business works with customers in many countries to sell or receive materials. Hedges may also be required where expenses are somehow matched to a fixed interest rate and revenue is denominated in a floating (moving) interest rate (or vice versa). A company may receive constant cash flows as the result of giving customers credit, but must repay a loan denominated in a floating rate.

Risks that can be covered by hedging are numerous and include the following:

◆ Commodities (where they are either produced or used as a key part of production)

◆ Currency

◆ Interest rates (usually the difference between fixed and floating rates)

◆ Equities

◆ Credit risk

How Hedging Works

Let's explore a commodity hedge to provide a deeper example of the way hedging works in risk. Farmers often use hedges on commodities (such as grain) to lock in a price for crops. Then they can plant and maintain their crops without worrying about uncertain prices when they go to harvest. They establish a price in the market at the time of planting and "lock it in." They run the risk that prices may be higher when they harvest, but they are protecting themselves should prices fall below their locked-in rate. Today's market price may be $10 per bushel, but on the commodities exchange, farmers can lock in a price of $9. Many farmers would rather live with a $1 per bushel "loss" and lock in the $9 price than wait a few months and run the risk of getting an even lower price.

When it's time to harvest, the crop may be worth $12. In this case, farmers would liquidate their positions by selling the futures they bought on the exchange. In this sense, the hedge acts like an insurance policy on price. The farmer has reduced his risk to the difference between the price he received on the exchange—the liquidation price—and the price he received in the market.

Here's how the math works. Say the season-opening market price for soybeans is $10 per bushel (or contract). A farmer plants with the expectation of generating 100 bushels—a gross proceed of $1,000. He decides to enter the futures market and buy a short position, or short, by agreeing to sell his 100 bushels of soybeans in the future at $9 per bushel. Note how he shorts the exact same amount as he plants. Before a single soybean pod appears, he has guaranteed that he will lose no more than $100.

At harvest, the cash market price sits at $12 per bushel—a $2 increase over the rate four months prior. The futures market is also trading at $12 per bushel. The farmer liquidates his commodity position and sells into the open market. He receives $1,200, a net profit of $300 over the original futures position. However, to liquidate the futures position, he had to pay $300 plus commission. This makes him largely net even (with a small loss on the commission costs of the hedge). The significance of his hedge would have been greater had the cash market price fallen from $10 to, say, $8 during growing season. After harvest, he would have either provided delivery of soybeans at the settlement date (rare) to collect his $9 per bushel, or closed out the position by buying a contract for 100 bushels at $8. Closing the position is necessary to offset the obligations of the two contracts in advance of the settlement date. Either way, he would have realized the difference. In effect, this is an insurance policy that shields him from the ups and downs of the market.

Diversification

Diversification is much like the natural hedge described earlier, but it takes place mostly within business walls. To understand how it works, think of the business as a portfolio of risks—much like a portfolio of stocks. In a stock portfolio, you would reduce net risk by buying different types of stocks. Each would carry slightly different risks and correlations with the others. This would reduce the net risk.

By diversifying, or taking on additional risk exposures through business or related changes or expansion, you can reduce the amount of *idiosyncratic* (or specific) *risk*. This is the risk unique to the asset, financial instrument, or any other distinct risk exposure. By combining more and more individual assets (or risk exposures), you can eventually develop a group with a net amount equal to the *nondiversifiable* risk.

Idiosyncratic risks are vital when you consider hedging based on diversification. Not all risks behave exactly equally in timing, likelihood, or overall impact. Some rise, while others fall. Some may increase or decrease a slight amount, while others may rise or fall a large amount. This is due to their relative correlations and overall contribution to the group of risks being combined.

There are several ways to diversify in risk management. They involve changing the company's risk profile, especially those risks that affect cash flow. This is done in any of the following ways.

def•i•ni•tion

Nondiversifiable risk, also called systemic risk, is the portion of the total risk amount that is not unique. It would be there regardless of the specific nature of the project, operation, or business. **Idiosyncratic risk** is risk that is unique to the project or operation. It is more difficult to measure and mitigate because of its maverick nature.

Product diversification. Producing different products for different markets (these may be industries or customer segments) or consumers. This provides some insulation from the economic behavior of any one market or group of consumers. Product diversification can be highly varied and range from minor variations to current products to drastically different product lines that may not have any resemblance.

Geographic diversification. Using different locations as well as local physical markets to help provide some insulation.

Channel diversification. Using different distribution channels to minimize risk and appeal to more customers, and to limit operational downsides.

Red Flags

Make sure that your product lines are not too divergent without a good strategic reason. Otherwise, diversifying introduces myriad new risks—some of which your risk management plan may not include.

Operations diversification. Locating manufacturing or other physical operations in multiple locations. This may take advantage of differences in workforces, union relations, cost structures, and even the risk of natural disasters or other *forces majeure*.

Other forms of diversification to consider include every step of the value chain, as well as every aspect of business operations and financial management.

Insurance

The final common hedging tool is one with which everyone is familiar, likely in a variety of ways: insurance. You are investing in a "hedge" (policy premium) against major losses. Few organizations have adequate internal financial resources to be able to cover the cost of major losses. Thus, they need to buy insurance. Insurance coverage may be available for damage to property and consequential costs (such as loss of revenue or increased operating costs) or for liability for the financial consequences of another party due to failure to discharge a legal obligation.

Not all major risks are insurable. For example, it is generally not possible to insure an organization's reputation, though there are some types of organizations in which losing the trust of stakeholders could be fatal.

Just like in other forms of risk measurement, insurers take likelihood and consequence into account when setting premiums, as well as existing controls. In some cases, insurers may insist on additional risk management or mitigation to reduce a risk. Conversely, they may agree to charge less if additional controls are implemented or if the insured party agrees to share the risk. That can be done by paying the first part of any loss to an agreed amount or excess (deductible).

It is usually a good investment to provide quality information about the risk being offered to the insurer. This helps reduce uncertainties and makes it more likely that the insurer will be prepared to offer cover on attractive terms. Insurance decisions are best taken in the context of other risk management activities to ensure that sound decisions are made about the extent of insurance required and to optimize the relationship between price, cover, and excess.

Key Considerations

Buying an insurance policy for risk management purposes is much like buying insurance for anything else. Given the crucial nature of this investment—the stability of your business in the event of a major risk event—the following few considerations are worth noting.

An insurance policy provides no more cover than the legal effect of the wording. Most policies will contain clauses excluding or limiting what is covered. If those exclusions create a large financial exposure, some other form of control may be needed.

An insurance policy is only as good as the insurer's financial ability to pay. Major financial rating agencies, such as Standard & Poor's and Moody's, provide information about the financial security of insurers. However, this is just a guide. Major insurance companies have failed or stood on the brink of demise despite positive rating information. (Can you say AIG?)

An insurance contract requires an explicit obligation of disclosure by both parties. An organization must not mislead its insurer. To do so can void the coverage. This obligation includes reporting losses to the insurer quickly.

Should a loss occur, an insured organization is expected to act as though uninsured. The company is counted on to take whatever steps necessary and reasonable to minimize the scale of loss. An example would be resecuring a property after a break-in. The company also should not admit liability before the insurer has been able to examine the issue.

These and other technicalities relating to insurance suggest that organizations should seek the advice of a professional before creating and implementing an insurance agreement.

What Should You Insure?

Many things can be insured: cars, homes, health, businesses, business equipment, lives, plane flights … the list goes on. In fact, if the market is legal and there is a buyer, any party or part of a transaction can be insured. Basically, the sky's the limit.

> **Risk Factors**
>
> The famed insurance company Lloyd's of London used to pride itself on the variety of subjects, objects, and people it insured. It seemed that Lloyd's insured anything. During the height of her pin-up years during World War II, Betty Grable insured her legs with Lloyd's for $1 million, which was a lot of money in those days. After all, she made her living from her legs. You'd have to say it was good risk management on her part!

Practically speaking, many forms of insurance should always be considered a standard part of doing business. These include accident, injury, and environmental damage. Other types of insurance may be common for your industry, such as medical insurance for the workforce (mandatory or expected under many circumstances) and coverage of key equipment or activities. You may even consider exploring insuring your more critical assets with a carrier like Lloyd's of London, even if your asset is nonstandard. Insurers use the same principles as other risk management practices to establish their pricing. If you understand your likelihood and impact as well as the ranges around those (the standard deviations), and your operations are well organized and well documented, you should be able to receive a fair premium price and coverage amount.

The Least You Need to Know

- Impact reduction steps limit risks that cannot or should not be prevented and so thwart serious but rarely seen risks.

- Prepare contingency plans in advance—and train your staff on their action steps.

- Make sure your contingency plan is good enough to handle a worst-case scenario.

- Set up buffers and reserves to offset expected and unexpected losses.

- Diversify a portion of your business, or consider similar tools such as hedges or insurance, to offset risk exposure.

Part 5

Deep Dive: Focused Solutions

The most important thing to remember as you move forward is that every business is unique—which makes its group of risks equally unique. Therefore, you'll want to tailor your solutions to meet your particular needs, especially when it comes to your most significant risks. Let's dive deep and get right to the heart of risk management: creating focused solutions for the special set of risks your company faces.

Chapter 14

Measuring and Managing Strategic Risk

In This Chapter

- ◆ Locating volatility in your business strategy
- ◆ Pinpointing your strategic risk problems
- ◆ Knowing the signals to watch for
- ◆ Determining your range of outcomes

Strategy is the cornerstone of every successful business. The strategy of a strong company is well-rooted and clear. If only working with strategic (or business) risk was so straightforward! As you've learned, it is one of the murkiest forms of risk. Strategic risks can fly in from any place at any time, and individual sources are hard to pin down. Recurring risks take on different forms each time they appear. In addition, "strategic risk" tends to serve as the catch-all for every form of risk that can't be directly measured or easily observed.

When dealing with strategic risk, companies need to be able to identify which parts of their business strategy will create volatility into the future.

You've seen how to identify strategic risk—broadly, anyway—but it is the toughest of all risks to forecast and to analyze in any given situation. Fortunately, there are ways to get it done.

Measuring and Analyzing Strategic Risk

To determine your level of strategic risk, take a two-pronged approach. First, analyze your specific strategies. Second, take into account your overall strategic risk in the company. To begin, break a specific strategy down to a more focused decision, and address the risks to cash flows in that context. The second approach, determining your overall level of specific risk, involves analyzing the monthly, quarterly, or yearly volatility of your company's return as a whole.

A few simple analysis and measurement approaches can help considerably when getting a feel for the materiality and criticality of your strategic risks.

Watch the Signals

Since there are two types of risk behaviors—systemic risk and idiosyncratic risk—it follows that there are two types of signals to watch. One is general trends that follow the industry, which should be watched for signs of systemic risk. The other is the effects of specific business decisions, which should be monitored for signs of idiosyncratic risk that could impact the company.

Each of these risks will generate different signals that need to be monitored. When looking for systemic risk, observe general signs of industry weakness. When monitoring idiosyncratic risk, check for specific reactions to a company's strategy decisions. Usually this involves a market response, but it could also be associated with suppliers. For instance, did a supplier's decision—or your decision involving a supplier—put someone out of business? Will it generate new price pressures?

Some signals could be well-telegraphed. Upcoming regulatory changes are a prime example. These are usually announced well in advance and could signal the need for a major investment on your part.

Build Awareness

You hold a number of options to help build awareness. You could track these signals with near mathematical precision. You could also get out the message by just being savvy to the environment.

Best Bets

Staying attuned to stakeholders is vital in your overall awareness of risk signals. This can be accomplished casually—by having a regular coffee catch-up with your local industry society president, for instance. You can also systematize it through a routine board or management team discussion. At that discussion, go over reports of your strategic risk.

Stay abreast of your competitors and their movements. What do their distribution channels look like? Their storefronts? What products and innovations are they developing? Similarly, where do you see the industry going? How will the needs of consumers evolve? How can you respond technologically to stay on the cutting edge?

You can also use scenario analysis (see Chapter 7) to build awareness. War-gaming and scenario development help key executives and board members build awareness, while also testing potential strategic effects. Develop high, medium, and low likelihood scenarios to get a feel for their relative outcomes, and then create a response plan.

Know Who's Watching

Now is the time to take a closer look at your stakeholders. You will want to identify key stakeholders for any major strategic initiative and for the company as a whole. Stakeholders become particularly important as they pertain directly to the way strategies play out. They may react to a risk from somewhere else in the company, enhance the success or failure of strategies, or even create new strategic risks themselves. Talk about a stakeholder triple whammy!

These stakeholders generally come from the following areas:

The community. Is there a town hall, city government, zoning committee—or individual key decision-maker from your local community—that has influence over your strategy or the broader nature of your success?

Special interest groups. These include environmental groups, health associations, and arts foundations.

Regulatory and compliance agencies. These agencies will create a new rule or material change to a rule that may wind up in your lap! Their changes are likely to affect your bottom line.

Industry groups or self-governing bodies. Many industries have societies that provide support or information to their members. These groups are very influential and have the ability to set standards and guidelines; they may even self-regulate or provide certifications.

Media. The media can influence your strategies greatly, and potentially make or break them. Learn how to work with the media effectively or, if necessary, avoid it. Use the "front-page test" (see Chapter 4) to see how various risks would play out in the media.

 Red Flags

> It is vital to understand how broad and immediate media has become, especially when it can affect your strategies. Through websites, blogs, e-mails, and social networking sites like LinkedIn, Twitter, and YouTube, anything you say or do can be posted worldwide within seconds. It is vital to the success of your strategies to keep all information close to the vest until you are ready to release it publicly.

Analysts. These include equity, fixed income, media, or specific industry group analysts. Their role is generally to provide focused commentary on your company for their constituency.

Consider Stakeholders

Whenever you think about implementing a new strategic initiative, be sure to consider each of the core and external stakeholders. Are any important enough to include in the discussions? How would they react? Would they react badly if they were surprised? Or is keeping them in the dark for a while necessary to launching the strategy?

Many companies are savvy about dealing with stakeholders, actively monitoring their relations with them. Some of them even summarize stakeholder relationships in a regular report or even a simple score or traffic light approach. A simple approach for this is a red, yellow, or green up or down arrow in a report with some commentary.

When All Else Fails

Often we find that the preceding approaches are useful, but not enough. If that happens, employ the residual risk measurement or residual risk analysis approach. Start by measuring the total earnings volatility of the firm. From that figure, subtract the parts attributed to financial and operational risks, allowing you to arrive at a total contribution for strategic/business risk.

As a broad measure of strategic risk, this approach isn't too bad. However, it has a few pitfalls. First of all, it reveals the contribution of volatility from the past, when you really need a view of future risk. With strategic risks, it is dangerous to assume the past will resemble the future. Also, it is very challenging to break this number down into its specific effects. Separating the systemic risks from the idiosyncratic risks is very tough; furthermore, understanding the contribution of specific types of strategic risk (such as their sources as a result of specific initiatives and decisions) is virtually impossible.

Red Flags

It is both tempting and very difficult to attempt a more forward-looking approach to analyzing strategic risk. Yet many companies find the need to take this step as a last resort. To do so, you will need to understand economic drivers, a complex science in itself. Then, you may need to build complex models. At best, the results from those models will be tenuous; at worst, they will be hard to defend. However, this process can provide a scale for strategic risk as it relates to other core risks the company will be facing.

As problematic or tenuous as they are, these last-resort measures still can give you a reasonable sense of what size and form mitigation needs to take. If you're lucky, you may also be able to pick out the effects of a few key strategic decisions and better understand what their impact may be in the future.

Managing and Mitigating Strategic Risk

It's tough to manage something that is inherently hard to identify and break down at a discrete level. Nevertheless, there are a couple of age-old techniques that can help. One is to build strategic risk into your plans and budgets, either for specific projects and initiatives or as part of your overall annual business plan and budget. The other is to add a buffer to your capital base.

What's in the Plan?

Direct planning for strategic risk is the most common way to address this type of risk. It is also the most straightforward approach, though it ranges from the extremely simple to highly complex modeling. In a simple approach, you would establish a range of possibilities for the outcomes of any plan or line item on your P&L or project budget.

You would also calculate a probability of occurrence for each of the established ranges. You would need to know probabilities at each end, and possibly points in between.

Suppose you are instituting a project to launch a new product. Inevitably, you will consider the response that the product will likely receive in the market, as well as how that response interfaces with price and overall profitability. At this interface, you will find most of the strategic risk.

With any luck, you have already conducted some market trials, gained perspective on the response rate from previous, similar products, or come across information on competitive products.

Range of Outcomes

From the preceding information, you may be able to establish a range of responses and the likelihood for each response occurring. This is called a range of outcomes. Now for some quick math. By multiplying the value of each outcome by the likelihood of this response, you can develop a *risk-weighted outcome* for each area of uncertainty.

def•i•ni•tion

Risk-weighted outcomes are strategic projections into which the likelihood of a particular risk (or set of risks) materializing has been factored. They enable the company to be more realistic in its overall range and to forecast a more likely outcome.

Having the full range of responses allows you to consider whether to beef up the budget or hold some capital aside in case of a problem. However, the most likely outcome is the figure that is built directly into the plan and budget. Set aside some capital against the high-end range as an internal insurance policy of sorts.

Your established range of outcomes will provide the opportunity to think about how you might want to mitigate or stop your risk. If the outcome falls within an acceptable range, you would move forward with the project. However, if there are other circumstances, you might wait or not proceed at all. This is the point where you may want to build triggers or signals in order to limit exposure within the initiative. If the marketplace changes, you may not want to proceed.

A perfect example of how a range of outcomes can impact strategic project decisions comes from oil drilling. Many small companies conduct oil drilling for small deposits.

These deposits are too small for big companies to chase and they tend to be more expensive, on a per-barrel basis, to extract. If oil drops below a specific price per barrel, it is not economical to drill in certain locations. Small oil companies face high strategic risk with any given project and need to know when to cut bait.

How to Buffer for Strategic Risk

Buffering for strategic risk utilizes the residual risk calculation described earlier in this chapter and applies that estimate to the overall capital approach. From this figure, you can derive a standard deviation associated with only strategic risks that your company has experienced in the past. Because you're buffering the company against loss, you don't need information from other companies that could dilute, pollute, or otherwise ruin your figures.

Suppose a company measures its earnings volatility and develops a standard deviation of earnings over the last few years. The standard deviation is $100. Previously, the company measured operational and financial risk and found their standard deviations to be $60 and $15, respectively, for a total of $75. Subtract $75 from $100 to arrive at the contribution of strategic risk to the company's overall risk: $25.

Now multiply the amount of the strategic risk—$25 in this case—by the capital multiplier that was described in Chapter 10. For the purposes of this exercise, it is $6. The amount of capital used for strategic risks is $150.

You can apply several other measures to extend that standard deviation to a level appropriate to support the company's risk appetite. Use the same confidence interval or a capital multiplier.

Now for another tricky part: with strategic risk, ensure that you are holding enough capital to support future risks. That's where range of outcomes can be so important. You might need to stress your assumptions to ensure that you sock away enough capital to feel sufficiently confident in the outcome. Do this by developing a series of scenarios and applying them to your historical levels of strategic risk. It is a one-question test: How would your cash flows (your P&L) have responded in each situation? This enables you to test the effect on the residual risk calculation and, in turn, the capital.

When you have identified an acceptable level for strategic risk and overall capital, review against actual capital levels. Now determine whether you are sufficiently capitalized for future risks. If not, look at ways to reduce the risk, scale back the initiative, or raise capital from investors.

Pitfalls in Managing Strategic Risks

At the measurement and assessment phases of managing strategic risk, there are several significant pitfalls to watch for. Any of these can cause damage that ranges from muddying your all-important residual risk calculation figures to threatening your business.

Don't Ignore It

It's easy to assume that strategic risk is just part of doing business and that you're stuck with it. You can still take steps to plan for and insure the company against its strategic risks. Don't ignore it.

Get Out of the Past

Anticipating strategic risk is all about looking into the future and making assumptions based on actual company and industry experience and information. Although this involves looking into the past, keep in mind that managing strategic risk is not about the past.

Be Aware of Changes in Complexity

Bear in mind that the core of your business changes all the time to keep up with competition and customer needs. So does the market in which you operate. Frequently, companies forget that relationships that once held true can shift, particularly as the business model changes.

Now, let's look at an overwhelmingly successful example. In 1973, American distance-running ace Steve Prefontaine and his coach, Bill Bowerman, came up with ideas for lightweight racing shoes with very specific tread designs. They ran the designs past a young shoe manufacturer, Phil Knight. For the next 15 years, his company, Nike, dominated sales in the world of running shoes, brushing aside competitors like Adidas, Puma, and others. It also drove much of the distance-running boom that captivated America during this time.

Beginning in the early to mid-1980s, the market shifted. Phil Knight figured out a range of outcomes for his business. He measured and analyzed the risks of expansion. He knew it could either be wildly successful or blow up in his face. Remember, strategic risk is often hit-or-miss. Then he made a strategic forecast, backed by the future of his company: that people would buy well-crafted athletic shoes from sports outside Nike's prior comfort zone if the right athlete endorsed them. Sure enough, in the late 1980s, Knight's strategy hit gold through the next great basketball superstar, Michael Jordan. Air Jordan basketball shoes came to define Nike as much as the company's roots in the distance-running boom.

Fast forward almost 20 years. Today, Nike is the model of combining good product, superstars, and the "shoe is you" approach to bring in customers from many sports and keep them brand loyal. Nike has pulled off a strategic rarity: becoming a conglomerate while maintaining its grassroots identity as a running shoe manufacturer.

Like Nike, be aware of how the complexity of your services or value proposition, industry, or market can change.

The Least You Need to Know

- Levels and types of volatility change regularly with strategic risk.

- When measuring strategic risk, look at the relationship between your industry and your business.

- The effects of strategic risk are extreme; they can either be devastating or minor.

- Work with risk-weighted outcomes to determine the potential impact of strategic risk on your business.

- Increase your awareness of how your market, industry, or customer can and will change.

Measuring and Managing Financial Risks

In This Chapter

◆ Calculating your exposure

◆ Working with credit and market risk

◆ Using buffers and reserves

◆ Avoiding pitfalls

Financial risk contains two absolute truths. First, it comes in all shapes and sizes. Second, unless you live completely off the grid (or planet), it eventually affects everyone—including you! If you buy merchandise on credit, sell items and provide credit, make loans, pay loans, buy or sell market instruments (like stocks), or generate revenue to cover costs, you incur financial risk. If your activities fall into two or more of these categories, you are probably dealing with significant financial risk.

Given the many ways to create financial risk, most companies carry it in some form. The good news is that finance is one of the most developed areas of risk management—and for good reason. Thousands of banks and financial institutions bet their existence on their ability to measure and manage financial risks. They send money out the door in the hands of customers and hope it will return with interest. Usually, it does. So these risk management methods tend to work pretty well.

Financial risk may be the most studied and treated form of risk, but it certainly harbors some special challenges! Whenever big dollars are at stake in such a direct way, people get all worked up. They want to understand the exact concerns so that they can manage their money and make sound mitigation decisions.

The beauty of dealing with financial risks is that they can be mitigated directly through other financial mechanisms.

Measuring and Analyzing Financial Risk

You have already been introduced to the primary concepts associated with credit and market risk. Credit risk concerns the potential default on an obligation, whether you are the creditor or debtor. Market risk arises from the normal course of doing business and the ups and downs of the overall market or industry.

Let's take a closer look at the special challenges posed by each risk and risk type.

What to Do About Credit Risk

To estimate your credit risk, employ the following three measures:

- *Probability of default (PD)* measures the probability over some point in time— usually one year— that the debtor or payer will default (not pay a contractual obligation after 90 days). The probability of default (PD) is a vital concept when analyzing credit risk. It determines how likely your debtor will be to default within a year. The traditional tool used for determining a PD is the credit rating or score.

- *Exposure at default (EAD)* shows your potential total dollar and asset exposure at the time of default. When a customer draws down a line of credit, that creates greater exposure for the extender of that credit line. Businesses use EAD when deciding whether or not to reset credit lines.

- *Loss given default (LGD)* is the same thing as *severity* (see Chapter 8). It's a measure of how severely your business will be affected by a specific loss.

To determine your expected loss due to financial risk, multiply your figures for probability of default, exposure at default, and loss given default, as follows:

PD × EAD × LGD = Expected loss

To determine your unexpected loss, calculate the standard deviation of your expected loss.

To determine your overall financial risk, add up each of the individual unexpected losses as you learned in Chapter 10. Each group or type of financial risk is accompanied by correlations. Correlations exist between individuals, regions/geographies, industries, and more. In doing so, you will see that there are many opportunities for diversification.

How do you measure this type of diversification and exposure? When there are many exposures, companies often use sophisticated models to manage these properties and analyze how they combine to generate the big beta distribution. They often employ a Monte Carlo analysis (see Chapter 10). A number of companies supply these sorts of models or variations of them.

What to Do About Market Risk

Recall that market risk can come from both traded financial instruments and structural financial risk. Structural financial risk, or nontraded market risk, comes from a business's cash flow requirements or liquidity risk. You don't need to be a bank or insurance company to hold such risk. Market risk can result from a mismatch in the way cash flow is structured, interest rate risk, and the way money moves in and out of your business.

Market risk distribution resembles a normal distribution more than credit risk does, particularly in the case of traded market risk (from trading financial instruments on an exchange). There is a roughly equal likelihood of achieving more or less of the target value than you expect. This also means that, unlike with credit risk, the tendency is not to have an expected average loss. Instead, the main concern associated with market risk is unexpected loss, or its market risk equivalent, *value-at-risk* (VAR).

 Best Bets

You don't have to be trading in the financial markets to incur market risk. It can arise from something as common to everyday business as your balance sheet—cash flows coming in and going out.

190   Part 5: Deep Dive: Focused Solutions

def•i•ni•tion

Value-at-risk (VAR) is a measurement method that models and yields a standard deviation of return. It generates a distribution by using numerous values, rates, or other market factors to test how the instruments will behave. It attempts to simulate the way markets behave. This is important because most market portfolios are very dynamic, with lots of market changes per day.

There are some interesting twists to consider when calculating market risk; they involve what are called *distribution tails*. Sometimes, a distribution has "fat tails" or little speed bumps on its ends. The fat tails result in bigger estimates of risk than we would naturally expect as part of a normal distribution. Sometimes they can be surprisingly large. These are the sorts of issues that cause big problems for banks (and other companies that have large trading portfolios). When you hear about a bank losing a boatload of money in a trading problem, you can be certain the distribution tail was overly fat. (These kinds of tail problems are normally associated with derivatives.)

Risk managers use different types of VAR models to assess market risk, depending on the types of instruments they are examining and the types of distributions common to them. Let's take a closer look at three models and how they can work for you.

Parametric VAR. This model assumes that the distribution is normal. Generally, the means and standard deviations of previous values will behave the same way in the future as they have in the past. Consequently, they can be applied directly to the instrument or set of instruments that you analyze. When analyzing a portfolio, historical correlations are generally used as well.

Historical simulation VAR. With historical simulation VAR, a historical rate series, such as interest rates or daily foreign currency exchange rates from the past year, is run through the financial instruments in your portfolio to see how newer instruments in different proportions in the portfolio would have behaved under past conditions. This involves saving historical rate series data, particularly that from periods of stress. Believe it or not, some market risk analysts collect rate series like some people collect baseball cards. You can imagine how valuable it would be for businesses to have access to rate series from certain periods of market behavior—the Mexican peso crisis, the Russian debt collapse, the U.S. subprime disaster in 2008, and so on.

Monte Carlo VAR. The Monte Carlo VAR is effectively a random number generator that creates a set of market rates. From that springs countless simulations. Investment banks sometimes use supercomputers to simulate all of the possibilities.

How do you decide which type of VAR model to use? It comes down to what sorts of instruments you have and whether you must adhere to any regulatory guidelines.

If you are going to trade derivatives of any kind, you need historical simulation and/ or Monte Carlo. These models can pick up the fat distribution tails and speed bumps mentioned earlier. Parametric VAR assumes that your distribution is perfectly normal and doesn't simulate real behavior in any specific way; therefore, it doesn't work very well for derivatives.

Most regulators want to see at least historical simulation models; some also encourage Monte Carlo simulations.

Each model has its downside. Historical simulation is rooted in past events, so unless you make up new rate series to run through these models (which can be done), you could miss out on new effects that might happen in the future. Monte Carlo can generate new effects, but it can be taxing on computer systems and sometimes makes incorrect assumptions about the distribution of the rates that it is generating.

In the end, many companies use all three types of models to test and compare assumptions and approaches.

Managing and Mitigating Financial Risks

You can reach into your risk management toolbox and use many of the techniques discussed thus far to manage financial risks. However, a few methods are used more commonly than others. In particular, limits are frequently deployed to manage both credit and market risk. Limits allow financial managers to restrict their exposure to any customer, industry, product, or instrument. Virtually any dimension of a transaction can carry a limit. These limits can be constructed as individual numbers or as tree structures that cascade down from a consolidated "house" limit to individual limits. Each branch or level in the tree represents a level of organizational hierarchy or a portfolio segment.

Limits come in many forms. The two most common types are exposure limits and stop-loss limits.

- *Exposure limits* reflect the total allowable exposure to any particular risk factor. They restrict the amount of lending or trading that you can conduct in association with a particular factor. Exposure limits also enable you to measure your diversification. The risk factors exposure limits are applied to may be any aspect of your business or portfolio that drives risk behavior—an industry, a single customer, or any large customer.

- *Stop-loss limits* attempt to control the total amount of losses your company can incur. They basically work by keeping a running count of losses, usually from the start of the year. Once the total limit is reached, production, lending, or trading typically stops and major remedial action is taken.

There are also other types of mitigation methods more particular to financial risk management. To review briefly, they include reserves, buffers, financial hedging, and portfolio diversification.

Using Reserves

In Chapter 10 you learned about expected loss and unexpected loss. To review, expected loss is the mean loss rate from an expected event. To manage expected losses, a company holds reserves for that amount of money. Unexpected loss is the standard deviation of the expected loss, and it is the true risk. To manage unexpected loss, capital (a buffer) is held in direct relation to the standard deviation and in line with the company's risk appetite.

When it comes to financial risks, buffers and reserves form one of the most common methods of risk mitigation, whether they are used separately or together. Reserves are used to provide coverage for the amount of loss expected each year; they cover expected loss. Reserves are treated as an expense in the P&L and are established as the exact amount of money identified in the expected loss calculation.

When the expected loss is calculated, the reserve money is set aside en masse, either in the corporate savings account (uninvested) or invested in highly liquid assets (such as Federal Treasury bills). As a specific loss materializes, the appropriate amount is released and used to offset the shortfall. This smoothes out earnings and supports any obligations that are dependent upon the at-risk financial instrument or cash flows.

Keep in mind that not all financial risks require reserves. In fact, you normally wouldn't construct a budget or make market trades by anticipating losses from the outset. Usually, you apply reserves in situations where you can expect a certain amount of loss. Among financial risks, these are predominantly credit risks. It is also possible to hold reserves for operational risks, although that is less common.

Using Buffers

Unlike reserves, buffers are applied to all types of risks, including situations in which reserves are already in place. When addressing financial risks, buffers are a key component of the risk manager's tool set. In regulated industries, buffers are often one of the chief requirements.

Buffers work directly in line with unexpected loss (or VAR)—the standard deviation of losses you have previously identified through your measurement models. They are set to be equal to your economic capital.

Let's go back to the capital multiplier method you learned in Chapter 10. Assuming a typical distribution, you can calculate the economic capital for a financial portfolio by using a capital multiplier is normally at least 5 or 6. This is because most companies' financial portfolios have a long tail, and it takes that many standard deviations to create sufficient confidence that the risks are well covered with capital.

In this case, for a typical credit portfolio, you would be covered for roughly 99.9 percent of your losses (at 5 times standard deviation) or 99.97 percent of your losses (at 6 times standard deviation).

Best Bets

The capital multiplier for financial risks increases the standard deviation to a level that accounts for the majority of risks that are likely to occur. The normal multiplier is at least 5 or 6. This number may look huge. However, if you consider that most companies expect to be able to get through even a major loss event with at least enough to cover basic financial obligations, this level of capital is required.

This approach to using economic capital to establish your buffers directly equates to the methodologies rating agencies use to provide business credit ratings. Companies like Fitch, Standard & Poor's, and Moody's use a similar approach when they consider the riskiness of a company. A capital multiplier of 5 roughly relates to a BBB rating, just above junk bond status.

Combining Buffers and Reserves

Buffers and reserves are used in combination most often for credit risk, but this strategy can be applied to other types of risks. The aim is to set aside money for both expected loss (reserves) and unexpected loss (capital or buffers). The process works exactly as described earlier in this chapter for reserves and capital. You set aside the amount computed for reserves plus the amount computed for capital. For accounting purposes, the reserves are considered part of your expense base and the capital is treated as part of your equity.

Red Flags _____

> Note that for some capital models, the capital number includes both expected loss and the adjusted unexpected loss number—in essence, both capital and reserves in one line. So always ask what the capital number includes to avoid double-counting the amount of money you need to set aside.

Financial Hedging

Chapter 13 introduced hedging as a risk management tool. Now it's time to get a bit more specific and look at the things that can be done with financial hedging.

Numerous investment items can be hedged through financial instruments, including foreign currency, equities, agricultural and metal commodities, interest rates, indexes, interest-earning assets (such as bonds and mortgages), credit, energy (oil, gas, and power; usually hedged as an index), freight, inflation, insurance, and even the weather.

When exploring the relationship between financial hedging and risk management, the following types of instruments are traditionally used. While they are mostly associated with larger financial firms or corporations, even small companies that have commodities or foreign currency exposure often partake in these instruments:

♦ **Futures**   A futures contract is a standardized contract to buy or sell a standard amount and quality of a specified commodity at a certain date in the future, at a market-determined price (the *futures price*).

♦ **Options**   An option is a contract between a buyer and a seller. It gives the buyer the right—but not the obligation—to buy or to sell a particular asset (the *underlying asset*) on a future date at an agreed-upon price. In return for granting the option, the seller collects a payment (*premium*) from the buyer. A *call* option gives the buyer the right to buy the underlying asset; a *put* option gives the buyer the right to sell the underlying asset.

♦ **Swaps**   Swaps are derivatives in which two separate parties with differing business interests agree to exchange one stream of cash flow against another stream. For example, companies might swap floating-rate obligations against fixed-rate obligations if they think that interest rates may be going up and they could get caught in a squeeze between their prices and the market rate on the loan.

♦ **Forwards**   A forward, or forward contract, is an agreement between two parties to buy or sell an asset at a specified future time.

Risk Factors
Hedge instruments can consist of almost anything that can be leveraged against a market rise or fall. When used properly for the purpose intended, most hedge instruments serve as great tools for mitigating risk. Some hedge instruments are constructed, however, mainly to make money as investments. As you might surmise from watching the news, some of these instruments can be spectacular failures (not so spectacular, of course, to those who paid for them)!

Futures, options, swaps, and forwards provide different ways for businesses to hedge assets and benefit from market conditions. However, most businesses do not have large and sophisticated finance teams that can spend their days looking for these opportunities. For the already-too-busy businessman, the primary sorts of hedging are likely to come in the way of currency, interest rate, or commodities.

Real Live Diversification

In financial risk management, it is vital to move beyond the tendency to seek temporary, fleeting, "flavor of the month" methods of diversification. For diversification to be effective, it must reduce your risk by creating more customers and more revenue streams using the same expense base.

The same holds true when diversifying a business portfolio. When preparing to diversify, start by reviewing your portfolio to understand exactly how much of any given financial instrument you should carry. As you review your portfolio, ask yourself the following questions:

◆ What segment(s) of the market are most appropriate for your business model?

◆ What are your current asset concentrations—and why?

◆ What are the correlations between each segment or instrument and every other segment or instrument? (See Chapter 10.)

◆ What volumes should you purchase or develop in each segment to obtain an optimal balance of risk and return?

◆ What is the likelihood of achieving that mix?

People who oversee funds, such as mutual fund managers, ask themselves similar questions on a daily basis. It's their job: they can buy and sell in and out of as many different financial instruments as they please (taking into consideration transaction costs and taxes). Take a look at the asset combination of most mutual funds. They consist of literally dozens or even hundreds of stocks, bonds, commodities, or indexes. In part, people invest in mutual funds because they trust the fund manager to pick the right stocks, in the right volumes, at the right time.

Best Bets _____

The goal of diversification is to target the types of risk you take on so that you can take advantage of their differences and proportionally reduce your combined risk.

You want a situation in which the combination of the two risks adds up to less than the cost of the two risks on their own. If each risk measures $100, and your combined risk is $180 (rather than $200), then the diversification created by the two risks saves $20 in total risk, and therefore results in some mitigation.

Pitfalls in Managing Financial Risk

One of the biggest issues in managing financial risk is the proliferation and ever-deepening complexity of models. However, uncorking the model genies can lead to a lot of information that is beyond the comprehension of mere mortals—and the vast majority of businessmen and women. There are often so many moving parts that it takes a large team of people—generally with Ph.D's—to manage the model. *Costly.* It often becomes challenging to explain the outputs, why the movements develop and occur in that manner. It is easy for management to lose confidence in the models. At that point, models cease to serve their primary purpose, which is helping to support the mitigation and monitoring of risk.

Conversely, many companies think they can avoid investment in models entirely by relying on credit rating agencies and other simple outside assessments of risk. This often leads to poor assumptions about the real behavior of risk. Be relentless about identifying and examining the behavior of specific financial instruments. Pay heed to the maxim, "If it looks too good to be true, it probably is." Your suspicions should increase if you see a situation where the risk is purported to be low, but returns are very high. Ensure that your calculations and models are based on reasonable assumptions, and that they are designed to reflect how the cash flows behave.

Red Flags

Beware of "low-risk, high-return" financial instruments. If something sounds too good to be true, it probably is. Certain asset-backed securities, which provide cash flows based on other cash flows from credit or lending assets, are a good example. Before the subprime crisis, many of these were rated AAA (highest quality; very low probability of loss). However, they provided returns of up to 20 percent—way too high for AAA-rated instruments, which generally return less than 5 percent. The underlying assets were not well analyzed, and there were very low-quality assets buried within the overall asset groups. When economic conditions turned, these low-quality assets defaulted. This drove the value of the securities—and those 20 percent returns—down to nearly nothing.

You can't avoid all risks, and even if you could it wouldn't be a good idea, because you would never grow your business or make money. For the same reasons, you can't mitigate all risks. And even if you could completely mitigate all risks, the cost of tackling each in totality would be prohibitive. With financial risk mitigation, for example, you would need to pay for the hedging instruments, as well as the people required to trade and monitor them. It might cost the organization as much—and maybe a lot more— to do the mitigation as it does to ride the risk.

The Least You Need to Know

♦ Financial risk affects every business.

♦ Specialized models are used for each type of financial risk. Understand which ones are appropriate for your business.

♦ Reserves are held for expected losses. Buffers are used to offset unexpected losses, which are the true risk.

♦ Resist the temptation to overmitigate financial risks. Doing so can be costly and may not be effective.

16

Measuring and Managing Operational Risks

In This Chapter

- ◆ Studying external risk events
- ◆ Capturing loss events
- ◆ Finding the root causes
- ◆ Building a business continuity plan

Operational risk is the oldest type of business risk. It has existed for as long as people have been running businesses. Think about the tremendous operational risk incurred by the London and East India trading companies as they ferried colonists and supplies from England to America in the seventeenth and eighteenth centuries. These trading companies, and others like them, would have continually red-lined any modern operational risk manager's scale of severity.

Recently, operational risk evolved into a formalized risk class. Risk specialists have been attempting to address operational risk using the same approaches and theories as other risk classes for only a relatively short time, which might explain why one of the greatest challenges of operational risk is measurement.

Measuring and Analyzing Operational Risk

A key issue in operational risk management is the difficulty associated with pinning down a likelihood and a severity, as well as using information from external events in a meaningful way. Because of that, the measurement of volatility in operational risk is the primary puzzle risk specialists seek to solve. However, they have developed a few good techniques you can use to put your operational risks into perspective.

> **Risk Factors**
>
> The measurement of operational risk is a relatively new concept. Risk management experts have only been seeking measurement methods in earnest since the mid-1990s, thanks in part to regulatory authorities in certain industries placing more attention on the concept.

What's the Score?

In Chapter 9 we introduced scorecards and consequence tables as basic risk management tools. These tools are particularly useful for gauging operational risk. Risk managers often adapt them to provide more specific information and increased value in understanding and tracking operational risks.

Begin by developing specific scorecards for each critical segment of operational risk, including all operational risk subcategories (e.g., people/organization, business process management) that affect you. If you are creating a scorecard with a special focus on people and organizational risks, for example, first develop a specific set of questions and indicators. These questions should signal the propensity of specific sorts of risks in your organization. When doing this, it is important to identify indicators as much as possible. Example: the number of vacant positions relative to total workforce or the percentage of vacancies. Another example is the attrition of workforce—are you losing people? At what rate? Do you have key man risk? In how many positions?

Next, try to link these answers to actual likelihood. If you don't have specific numbers, try to determine relative likelihood. Set up a scale:

Best Bets

When you develop score-cards, ask staff members within your operation to help fill them out. Have separate scorecards for each area of the organization—say, each product line or department.

- ◆ Very low

- ◆ Low

- ◆ Medium

- ◆ High

- ◆ Very high

Try to avoid lumping every risk about which you're uncertain into the "Medium" category. Be as specific as possible. In fact, many organizations avoid this middle category and use an even number of categories. This forces the ranking to reflect either slightly higher or slightly lower risks.

Likewise, create a consequence table (see Chapter 9) for each subcategory of operational risk and for each department in your company. Try to link these to specific financial impacts wherever possible.

Take It to the Team

As you've seen throughout this book, your own teams can be enormously useful in supporting analysis and solutions for operational risk. The teams can help develop scenarios, likelihood estimates, and consequence estimates.

There are several techniques for integrating individuals and teams into the risk management process. Work with different teams throughout the organization to identify key areas that could be sources of risk. Start by developing process flowcharts for each function. List all of your key items of equipment and the supporting teams. Identify the critical success factors or key steps to which your teams must adhere. Determine which of the process steps, pieces of equipment, and teams are most critical. Work through the likelihood of any failures in the processes. Rate the probability of each result (high, medium, low, or very low), or try to provide comparative probabilities. Try to phrase these comparisons or ratings in terms of how frequently an event could happen: once a month, once every three months, once a year, etc. This can help you obtain a more specific view of likelihood.

When you're finished, repeat the same process flowchart to analyze event consequences. Consider drawing external event data from other companies, or simply work through an event flow with experienced team members. When you do this, try to determine roughly how long an event might take to play out, how much product could be lost, and so on.

Sound like a lot of work? It is, but once you have gone through the exercise, it is much easier to refresh it and update it in the future. This approach generally leads to valuable data about where your true risks lie and what they could really mean. It also gives you data you can feed into the other basic measurements that support your analysis of mitigation cost-benefit trade-offs.

Using Loss Event Capture

Another valuable technique for measuring and analyzing operational risk is loss event capture. As the name suggests, the object is to record all of the losses that have occurred in the organization.

 Red Flags _____

If you've gotten this far in the risk management process and haven't set up loss categories for operational risk, use Chapter 6 as a reference and set them up. Without loss categories, any variety of "other" causes can make it very difficult to properly analyze your loss from a specific risk event. Many organizations find that fairly granular loss categories are helpful for this purpose.

To fully capture each loss event and generate the information you need, follow these steps:

1. Set up a minimum loss threshold. This is the lowest amount or type of loss that you are interested in collecting. Organizations use many different levels for this. Just make sure that the level you choose makes sense for your company. If it's too high, you might miss a systemic problem. If it's too low, you could easily be chasing shadows.

2. Go back through your records. For starters, see how many of your past losses you can capture.

3. As you move forward, capture losses as they occur.

4. Review the list of losses routinely. Does it match up with your operating expenses? Does it appear that your losses are being adequately captured?

5. Finally, analyze the list of losses. Are there any events that appear routinely? What are the largest individual losses? What groups of losses are costing you the most? Is there a consistent source?

Build a simple checklist or spreadsheet that includes the following basic information about each loss event:

- ❑ Size of loss
- ❑ Category
- ❑ Where in organization loss occurred
- ❑ How it happened
- ❑ Follow-up
- ❑ Result of follow-up
- ❑ Type of mitigation in place
- ❑ Result of mitigation
- ❑ Equipment involved (if any)
- ❑ Individual(s) or team(s) involved

Root Cause Analysis

By now you should realize how important it is to analyze risk events after they have occurred. Doing so provides a means of understanding what happened and helps expose critical information about how to prevent it from happening again. The information can also be used to gauge probability of such an event happening again and its severity should it occur.

One of the key methods for analyzing past risk events is *root cause analysis*. To reap the most benefits from this type of analysis, you need to start it as soon as possible after an event has occurred, so the data, information, and people's memories will be freshest.

In addition, to maximize root cause analysis, you must be inclusive. Everyone in your organization needs to feel that they can contribute to the investigation. Don't dismiss or discount ideas that may seem naive or come from a source who is not an expert. These seemingly worthless comments can often unlock a key piece of the puzzle.

def•i•ni•tion

Root cause analysis is a risk management procedure in which you track a complete chain of events back to discover what caused a risk event.

Begin by establishing a timeline for the risk event. Track every activity that led up to the event. Note each event and activity on the timeline.

Next, categorize the potential sources to investigate, which are known in risk management parlance as 4ME:

- **Materials.** Defective raw material, wrong material for job, lack of raw material.

- **Machine/equipment.** Incorrect tool selection, poor maintenance or design, poor equipment or tool placement, defective equipment or tool.

- **Environment.** Orderly workplace, job design or layout of work, surfaces poorly maintained, physical demands of the task, forces of nature

- **Management.** No or poor management involvement, inattention to task, task hazards not guarded properly, stress demands, lack of process, other causes (horseplay, inattention, etc.)

- **Methods.** No or poor procedures, practices different from written procedures, poor communication

- **Management systems.** Lack of training or education, poor employee involvement, poor recognition of hazards, previously identified hazards not eliminated

Display the specific categories and potential sources of the event on a chart, called a "fish bone" diagram. Treat each of the six core categories just described as one of the main "bones" on the "fish"—its spine, if you will. The subcategories below each primary category will fill out the "small bones" along the spine of the fish.

When conducting this analysis, ask "why" or "how" the event could have occurred under each source category. Use a technique called the "five whys," which involves asking the question "Why?" five times to drill down to the core truth, or root cause, of any particular matter.

For an example of the "five whys" in use, suppose that your car has broken down. Begin with the first, most basic, question:

"Why didn't my car start?" (1)

The first response: "The battery is dead."

Next: "Why is the battery dead?" (2)

Answer: "The alternator is not functioning."

The follow-up: "Why isn't the alternator functioning?" (3)

Answer: "The alternator belt has broken."

Next question: "Why has the alternator belt broken?" (4)

Answer: "It was beyond its useful service life."

Final question: "Why was it beyond its useful service life?" (5)

Answer: "I haven't been properly maintaining my car."

There you have it—the root cause.

These techniques not only help you get to the root cause more quickly, but they also help identify weaknesses throughout the operation. As you become skilled with root cause analysis, you may discover that it can serve as a means for developing probability, severity, and mitigation tactics for events that worry you but haven't yet occurred.

Managing and Mitigating Operational Risks

When managing and mitigating operational risk, you can leverage many of the methods you learned about in previous chapters. With operational risk, the key thing to keep in mind is that many methods are imperfect. They rely on a risk occurring before it can truly be managed, which inevitably leads to some likelihood of loss.

The two primary means of reducing the likelihood of an operational risk event are insurance and outsourcing/contracting. However, you can't insure everything, nor can you outsource everything.

The concept of controls also comes into play, particularly the X-bar chart (see Chapter 12). This is one of the simplest and most predominant approaches to prevention.

Be Prepared

The business continuity plan (BCP) is a key risk management contingency plan. Its overall uses were explored in Chapter 13. Where operational risk is concerned, though, the BCP is one of the most widely used methods of responding to an event as it materializes. The bottom line of a BCP: be prepared.

You can build a BCP for any type of operation, whether you sit at a desk or work in a manufacturing facility. At any given moment, something can fail. When that happens, your one and only objective is to get the failed or deficient machine, assembly line, computer, or operation up and running quickly. Ideally, you want to prevent the situation from getting worse while the event is occurring.

BCPs require just one big development and production effort, followed by occasional updating and upgrading. Simple BCPs take the form of a printed manual stored away in a safe place—usually away from the primary work location. It is critical to ensure that a BCP manual is realistic and easy to use during a crisis.

A simple business continuity plan should include the following key information:

- ❑ Contact information of crisis management staff
- ❑ Contact information of general staff
- ❑ Contact information of clients and vendors
- ❑ Location of offsite data backup and file storage
- ❑ Copies of insurance contracts
- ❑ Materials necessary for the company's survival

A more sophisticated BCP would include the preceding information in addition to the following items:

- ❑ Means to establish a secondary work site
- ❑ Technical requirements and readiness plans
- ❑ Regulatory reporting or notification requirements
- ❑ Work recovery measures
- ❑ Means to establish physical records
- ❑ Means to establish new supply chain
- ❑ Means to establish new production centers

There are five core phases in the development of a BCP, the last three of which are rolled into one related process. Think of them as sections of a book, standing on their own but completely integrated with the other four phases:

Analysis involves understanding potential threats, impact scenarios, and impact analysis. Your task is to comprehend types of threats, how they will likely occur, and what sort of impact they will make. It is also critical to establish a maximum amount of time to restore business functions and what level of recovery is acceptable—at least as a first step.

Solution design identifies the most cost-effective method to support the main requirements (or issues) identified during the impact analysis. The planner is concerned with the minimum amount of time and degree of recovery. The plan is often broken into time segments, such as first hour, first day, first week, first 30 days, 60 days, 90 days, or one year. The time segments used depend on the nature of the scenario. A power outage can wreak havoc, but power generally can be restored in hours, rather than days or months. The effect of a hurricane could be more devastating, particularly in certain geographical locations and in some industries. Solution design also considers other plans that might be required to accompany the BCP and disaster recovery plan, such as a media plan in certain situations.

Implementation, testing, and organizational roll-out ensure plan implementation without any major deviation. In this phase, planners make sure that the plan or its key elements are tested and members of the organization understand the plan and their roles. A training and education component ensures communication with stakeholders. In this phase, risk managers also determine if scenario rehearsals or drills are necessary (think "fire drills") and whether a disaster recovery or business continuity team needs to be created. Finally, all plans must be updated frequently.

Back to the Team Again

Your team or workforce is the best way to prevent or limit the likelihood of operational risk events and to minimize their impact once they do occur. Developing a workforce that can comfortably raise the warning flag helps ensure that risk events and their impacts don't deteriorate from bad to worse—or, ideally, don't happen at all. Because of the essential role of your workforce, it is especially important to ensure that your team members are well trained in their roles and well versed in the roles of those around them.

Training begins before the inception of a risk event, with information that helps the team spot trouble. Work with your team so each member learns to spot signs that may be building toward an event. Both root cause analysis and scenario analysis are excellent training tools. Choose a potential event that concerns you, and work through the process by conducting a root cause analysis in advance. Rehearse the BCPs that have been put in place.

Building Buffers

Buffers come into play in a huge, potentially lifesaving way for businesses that plan for operational risk. Since many of the methods for mitigating operational risk are indirect and rely on events having already occurred, it is vital to have buffers in place.

Some loss will likely occur, in which case the buffer helps to support the company through the initial aftermath.

There are two predominant ways to build buffers for operational risk:

◆ Set the buffer based on the size of your operations.

◆ Set the buffer based on your measured risk (economic capital) or standard deviation.

In the first case, review the size of your revenue base and multiply it by a factor—usually about 15 percent. This offers a pretty good basis for determining the amount of capital that you should set aside for operational risk.

The second method works much like the techniques mentioned in other chapters. If you haven't built a VAR model, a quick and dirty way to obtain a measure is to focus on the cost lines of your P&L and work up a standard deviation from there. To do this, collect the monthly cost figures from your P&L and calculate the standard deviation of those costs using the equation presented in Chapter 10. The resulting number should be fairly close to your operational risk figure. Finally, multiply that number by your capital multiplier, which for operational risk is usually at least 6.

The Least You Need to Know

◆ No two incidents of operational risk are exactly alike.

◆ Review the risk cases of other companies to gain a better understanding of your internal and external risks.

◆ Collect your own loss history to develop a basis for analysis.

◆ Use root cause analysis to drill down to the fundamental cause of a risk event.

◆ The best risk prevention measure you have in your company is your team.

Part 6

Integration

It's time to bring every measure and analysis to the table and integrate them into your daily business. The good news is that you do not need to create a new division, department, or spin-off company just to manage risk. To make risk mitigation and prevention work for your business, you need to weave them into the fabric of your existing operations and strategies. It's time to bring risk management home.

Inviting and Integrating Risk

In This Chapter

- ◆ Building in risk approaches
- ◆ Governance, organization, and culture
- ◆ Weaving risk into business processes
- ◆ Integrating new projects
- ◆ Achieving the right level of implementation

A key objective of risk management is to find the most beneficial management and mitigation methods for your business. You want to develop strategies and techniques that stick. In this and the following chapters, you will see how to make that happen by building risk management directly into your business. Ideally, you will build across many dimensions and develop participation in risk management throughout the organization, from the executive level down, and across all departments and functions. To succeed, your risk management processes must be accessible and routine.

Once you hone your risk management techniques, they become fabulous tools for making money. We're not talking about merely preventing losses, cutting budgets, or pinching pennies (although all of these things definitely help the bottom line). Now, it's time to be more proactive: to use risk to *make* money. If you learn to apply risk management to business processes, strategic decisions, and core product and pricing decisions, you can improve and optimize those decisions so that you make a lot more money than you would have otherwise!

Where to Build In Risk Approaches

Time to put risk to work to fatten your bottom line. Integrate risk management into all aspects of your company. Three of the most important areas in which to integrate are your *governance*, your organization, and your culture.

def•i•ni•tion

Governance is basically the "ensurance" mechanism in risk management. It comprises the "checks and balances" that review the measurements, mitigation methods, and risk monitoring results over a period of time. It also ensures that risk is aligned to the core objectives of the firm and that risk management implementation is appropriately balanced—trading off costs and impacts.

Governance

Someone must keep an eye on your risk management programs and status. Realistically, the impetus for managing risk comes from the top, because risk management is a supervisory task that requires regular decision-making. Governance becomes a key part of making sure that risk capabilities are implemented and developed as intended.

Transparency is key to governing. You want to develop a clear understanding of what you're measuring, how you're measuring it, and the outcomes and implications of your findings. You also want to oversee and evaluate how your risk management actions and decisions are being carried out.

Strong, progressive governance creates and sustains momentum. You'll know when you have momentum; there will be a seamless interchange between your business and risk management practices. You address new risks, implement the prevention and management approaches that you identified and agreed upon with other decision-makers, and ensure that the processes and risks are monitored. Momentum-based governance also supports a continuous improvement mindset, creating active and ongoing interest from the top. Of equal significance, it also gives everyone, especially senior management, a clear line of sight on what is going on within the framework of risks and the programs that are relying on their mitigation.

Organization

As it pertains to risk management, your organization is an enabler (in the positive sense). After all, how else do you implement risk management without your people? The old adage about people being a company's greatest asset certainly applies to risk management.

The culture you and your staff create will enable your risk management approaches to succeed. Your staff will implement the programs, help identify risks, and support (if not actually conduct) the measurement, mitigation, and monitoring of risks. They also are the means by which you establish a culture that embraces risk management capabilities and creates greater risk awareness.

When risk management implementation goes well, the organization can support the delivery of capabilities and the development of the right risk culture. This happens while the organization reduces its sources of risk and lessens its overall exposure. When implementation goes poorly, the exact opposite effect will result—a negative, often backstabbing culture that doesn't achieve its objectives. Your employees not only serve as the drivers of your risk management approaches, but they can also become a big potential component of operational risk.

Culture

Developing a *risk culture* is one of the most important things you can do to manage risk. The way in which key decision-makers view the relationship between risk and the company defines the tone and spirit of the culture. Like any culture, yours thrives only to the degree in which everyone contributes to its success, and every company has its own nuances when it comes to risk. Some organizations foster and do very well with high-risk cultures and activities (e.g., financial trading firms). This can be fine as long as you are aware of the consequences and what they mean with respect to your investment in risk management. Other organizations are inherently risk averse (e.g., regulators). By looking at a map of industry risks, you can determine where you stand. Being in an industry with high risks doesn't necessarily mean that you need to be more aggressive (some of the most successful companies are conservative players in high-risk industries), but it does help to understand the range of potential behaviors that you—or your competitors—may consider in order to be successful.

def•i•ni•tion

A **risk culture** is the combination of corporate policy, philosophy, attitude, and plan of action that determines how you approach risk and make decisions within your company. It also is a reflection of how you manage the signs of risk on a daily basis.

Consider the type of culture that you want to foster within your organization. Now consider how it pertains to risk. Does your culture foster a risk-aware environment? If not, should it? Next, consider how your team perceives risk.

You can go a long way by simply making people aware of risk and the issues that it presents. This alone can be one of the best risk mitigation methods.

Ten factors matter more than any others in the development of a risk culture. The level of urgency with which people understand and manage risk depends upon their views of these factors:

1. Randomness or intent of risk

2. Immediacy of effect

3. Risk knowledge by the person(s) exposed to the risk source

4. Technical knowledge

5. Control over the risk

6. Newness of risk

7. Style of risk: chronic or catastrophic. Do your risks occur one at a time? Or can they occur in large numbers?

8. Attitude toward risk. Have people become used to the risk and learned to live with it? Can they think about it reasonably and calmly, or do people dread it?

9. Severity of consequences

10. Trust (in the agency, persons, or approaches that manage the risk)

Risk Factors

Numerous studies have shown that most people do not perceive their own contributions to a situation as risky (as an example, most people rate themselves as better drivers than average). Yet, statistics suggest that 90 percent of all accidents are caused by human error. This likely goes for accidents within your company, too.

Overall, the bottom line comes down to two questions:

> What sort of culture do you want to foster in your organization?

> What are the consequences of fostering that culture when it comes to risk management?

Business Processes

Daily operations and processes are to your company what the heart and lungs are to your body: the driving force that makes it functional and successful. Consequently, this is one of the areas where the rubber really meets the road when it comes to applying risk management capabilities.

There are several ways in which working risk into your business processes makes a big difference:

You can manage risk when and where it happens. You can identify risks more quickly and prevent or mitigate them more effectively. If they do materialize, you can identify the root cause more efficiently. You support continuous improvement as an integral part of the risk management process.

Risk management becomes cheaper and more effective. When risk management becomes part of the business process itself, it is easier and less expensive to manage. It is also more effective.

Risk management information can be used to optimize processes. This can happen in many ways, which will be discussed in greater detail in Chapter 20. By building information about risk into your business processes and decisions, you optimize your processes. Consequently, you can make decisions more quickly, target customers more effectively, and price customers relative to the risk that they bring to your company.

Risk information can improve workforce management. You can build risk-adjusted return measures into your remuneration system and performance monitoring approaches. By doing so, you give people incentives to generate the sort of outcomes you seek—optimizing profit on a risk-adjusted basis.

New Projects

Your overall risk management approach is determined, and you have made the proper analyses and evaluations. The overall program is so thoroughly integrated into your business that daily risk management duties feel no different from any other tasks on your routine to-do list. Good for you! However, there is one area of business process that always changes, always poses new challenges, and therefore must always be addressed to ensure stability: new projects. In day-to-day management, the project environment is considered to be its own microcosm. You must use the entire risk management process but focus it narrowly on the execution of a single project.

Best Bets _____

When evaluating and approaching risk for project management, always identify risks at the start of the project. Measure them, determine your management strategies, then implement the strategies and monitor the risks throughout the life of the project.

Risk management can be applied to new projects in two ways: as part of strategic decision-making and as part of day-to-day project management. The aim of strategic decision-making is to understand the potential strategies and initiatives that support the long-term objectives of the company, both in terms of the return and growth they bring to the company and the risks they carry.

Applying risk management to new projects helps determine whether or not the company should move forward with the projects. It also helps stakeholders understand what needs to happen to improve the likelihood of strategic success. This can be as simple as building in some mitigation strategies, such as capital buffers. You could also try more sophisticated analyses, such as looking at different approaches and implementation paths and evaluating the trade-offs associated with these options from return, growth, and risk perspectives.

Choosing What's Right for Your Business

Companies that excel at risk management build risk approaches into all the areas discussed up to this point in this chapter. They also run the risk process and its techniques throughout the company to support strategic decisions, as well as manage day-to-day decisions and the business process. Consequently, their efforts support the management of projects.

There are different techniques and approaches for every type of risk and every aspect of business management, and there are different levels of difficulty and sophistication associated with each. Ultimately, the key is to understand the appropriate level of implementation for your business.

Striking the Balance

The key to implementing a sustainable, well-integrated risk management practice is to strike a balance. Find the right level of implementation and the right focus for its uses in your company, both across the whole enterprise and for individual departments or areas.

Red Flags _____

The specific balance of risk management implementation varies from company to company. Many make the mistake of thinking that they can balance their risks according to a general formula or general guidelines built on the case studies of other companies. Risk balance is unique to each company—and, in most instances, to specific projects within the company. You need the special risk recipe that works for your company, and your company alone, at this moment in time. And that balance can change quickly based on new risk exposures.

Every business must concern itself with continuous improvement. This is a recurring theme of risk management, as you've probably noticed. It is likely that whatever approach you decide on today will not be the right answer forever, regardless of its short-term success. Things change within your company and in your competitive environment. Your risk management approaches will need to change as well.

And risk professionals aren't just sitting still on the sidelines. They are constantly developing new techniques that make certain capabilities clearer and easier, as well as less expensive to implement.

Things to Consider

There are a few key things to keep in mind as you seek a sustainable risk balance for your company:

How big are you? How do you size up from a revenue standpoint your costs, headcount, number of products, or market share? There are many ways to measure size, but you probably know where you stand relative to your overall industry position. If you don't, make it a priority to find out. You can use many of the same questions you answered when identifying your risks (in Chapter 7) to determine how much and in what form to implement your solutions.

How fast are you growing? Growth begets risks. Your rate of growth can be a key factor in determining how much you want to focus on risk management.

How complex is your company? Do you have many products, geographies, complex processes, or delicate items that are difficult to produce?

What do you have at stake? You might be a tiny company with a single product, but if you hold people's lives in the balance, risk management becomes a big part of what you do. (At least it should!)

How many material risks do you have? What are they? Are they changing or growing?

What is the probability of those risks materializing? Is there a high probability? With which risks?

Can you count on a routine expected loss worth noting? Numbers over 5 percent of expected loss generally are worth noting. Even numbers as low as 2 percent, as long as they routinely and consistently register at this rate, may be worth considering, particularly if the unexpected loss can be considerable.

Have you conducted any risk management practices to date? How advanced would you say your firm's capabilities in risk management are? Would you say that your workforce is well versed in risk concepts? How about your risk culture? Do you have a strong awareness of risk and how to manage it in a way that integrates with how your company's employees think? Or with your company's philosophy?

How educated is your workforce at risk management? Do they understand the basic concepts? Do they have a formal sense of their risks and how they should be managed?

How well suited to change is your workforce? Is it comfortable adopting and implementing new ideas?

How stretched is the workforce? What is its capacity to manage new implementations? Can it handle an additional project—such as implementing a risk management program? Regardless of how open your workforce may be to making the change, does it have the physical capacity to do it?

Have you had any serious losses in the last three years? What have you done about mitigating them?

Do you have a regulator or inspector to whom you need to report? What types of requirements do they present? How are you viewed by them? Are you under any unusual scrutiny? Are there likely to be any major changes in those requirements?

Are you competitive in your industry? Are others taking on risk management capabilities as part of their competitive strategy?

By asking these questions and pondering their answers, you will develop a strong risk balance structure in the company. This might seem like an exhaustive process, but it will help to prevent and mitigate future problems that will truly be painful to you and your company.

The Least You Need to Know

◆ Effective risk management can lead to additional money-saving and money-making opportunities.

◆ Governance and workplace culture are core enablers of your risk process.

◆ Foster a risk-aware culture as a minimum starting point.

◆ Apply and integrate risk management measures into your projects, as well as your overall business processes.

◆ Develop risk implementation strategies based on the size and complexity of your company and your and your staff's experience with risk management tools and approaches.

Integrating Risk into Business Governance

In This Chapter

◆ Setting a governance framework

◆ Clarifying management's role

◆ Deciding who to include

◆ Preparing risk policies

◆ Shaping your risk culture

In the previous chapter, governance was introduced as an important part of any company's approach to risk management. But you might be surprised to learn that risk management can actually enhance your business's governance. You can build risk management right into the governance process, developing clear frameworks of its own. These frameworks will ensure that you identify, measure, monitor, and manage risks, as well as address the overall health of the framework. They also ensure that both structure and policy exist for any risk or workplace issue that might arise. Any type of governance framework exists to provide guidelines for company oversight; this is also true of risk management.

The way you structure your company's governance framework is vital to everything that follows. The framework creates transparency, sets the channels of communication, and drives expectations. A good framework sets the tone, goals, and values of the organization. It also clarifies all perceived, potential, and actual risk among these goals and values.

Before risk management can be integrated into your business governance, make sure a few core elements are part of your corporate culture. Obviously, risk management needs to be a central part of your goals and values. If you have a formal mission statement, your company's view of risk and risk management should be prominently featured as part of it. This may take the form of a risk appetite statement (see Chapter 21 for details). In addition, include risk management techniques in the company's policy for assessing strategies. Finally, develop policies to include the view of risk and to manage risk within the company.

Role of Management

When you consider setting up your risk governance framework, think about which of your company's senior managers will be leading risk management activities and which will be key receivers, or constituents, of risk management activities. All of these individuals are your core internal stakeholders.

When integrating and implementing risk in business governance, your core internal stakeholders have the following responsibilities:

- Ensuring that risks are appropriately identified and prioritized among each other and against other initiatives in the company

- Ensuring that risks are appropriately measured and monitored—today and on an ongoing basis

- Verifying that risk mitigation and management are put in place and that they meet the criteria spelled out in advance

- Ensuring that risks and the entire risk management framework are routinely reviewed and that appropriate policies and processes are in place and being adhered to

- Ensuring that the culture of the firm is supportive of risk management

Set the tone at the top, with your highest managers and stakeholders. Governance is their chief responsibility. They also have the general responsibility to ensure that key stakeholders are informed and that, in particular, the board is part of the process.

Committees

Committees take on all shapes and sizes and specific business functions. A 3-person committee can oversee a project or make a new hire, but it might take a board committee of 12 people or more to institute new policy. Every company has different names, functions, and objectives for its internal spin-off groups, but they all answer to one general description: committee.

When it comes to governance and risk management, many organizations set up a committee to address each key risk area. For instance, you might have specific committees for dealing with operational risk, market risk, and credit risk. Asset-liability management committees are often found in financial institutions where these risks are large and common. If your business is small, you might decide on a single committee to address all of your risk issues.

If you have a board, decide how these committees will report to it. Will there be a board risk committee? If so, what is the relationship between that board committee and company-level committees? These committees may also have several layers, particularly if your risks are more complex or your organization a bit larger. A subcommittee with certain specific issues may report to a larger or more senior committee. This is often the case when key risks lie within the subclasses of risk.

 Red Flags

> Committees need the authority to make or ratify decisions, but they cannot take responsibility away from the individuals who manage risk on a day-to-day basis. Many blow-ups arise because those responsible for individual transactions and managing operating decisions abdicate their risk responsibilities to a committee. The committee, in turn, runs the risk of creating "groupthink," where the individual voice is lost and everyone goes with the flow.

Committees can serve as an efficient means of disseminating key pieces of information and convening the right people to make decisions. The outcomes of committees can be readily documented and information further disseminated for the broader staff.

Independence

Independence is a key aspect of risk management. Sometimes risk decisions work at odds with business interests. If your risk managers are not able to think and act independently, your risk management program will never flourish.

A means must be created for arguments concerning risk to not only be heard, but also held in higher priority than business arguments. For instance, suppose you have previously decided that you will not lend money to a certain customer. One day, the customer walks into your company and says he will give you a major deal on a product or service *if* you lend him money. The risk-averse side of your business says no. Perhaps you've lent to that customer before and he didn't honor his obligation. In any case, you have a policy in place for dealing with this issue, and the policy dictates that you not lend the customer money. All the business proponents can see, however, is dollar signs. They urge the decision-makers to make an exception and lend the customer money.

An independent risk manager can run tough decisions like this against a few considerations:

What policies do you have in place? Will granting the loan work against the policy or limits and controls you have installed? What will the ramifications of breaking the policy be? (At the very least, it sends mixed signals to the workforce about the value of the policies and controls.)

Is it bad business? Often the risk side of any business argument is based on what a businessperson learned from the past—usually a tough, painful lesson. If the guy didn't pay you back in the past, then extending the loan is simply bad business.

What is the return on the deal relative to your risk? Does the risk versus return view balance itself? Is there sufficient return to cover the risk?

Who needs to be a part of the decision? After working through most of the preceding questions, if it's still not clear which direction to pursue, it might be time to think about the stakeholders involved and determine if any higher authorities need to participate. Is this a decision you need to take to your risk committee? Is it sufficiently big to share with your board? Are there external stakeholders (maybe regulators) with a view on the deal?

Make your policies clear. Adhere to them. Develop a clear channel for driving the discussion. This allows for an open and transparent method of resolution.

Best Bets

When working through these questions, bear in mind that the risk view needs to be heard independently at all times. Create a nonthreatening channel to bring up, escalate (if need be), and resolve these questions. If breaking a policy is not permissible, give your risk folks the authority to simply say no.

Stakeholder Management

As defined previously, stakeholders include any group or individual that participates in the company's success. Considering stakeholders as an input to the governance framework is a key to successful risk management.

Most companies view the following groups as their core stakeholders (in order of importance):

- Customers
- Employees
- Suppliers
- Board of directors
- Investors
- Analysts (stock analysts, credit analysts, etc.)
- Business partners
- Unions
- Government (including regulators)
- Special interest groups
- Communities
- Media
- The public

Let's consider the role of some of your top stakeholders in integrating risk management into your business framework.

Customer Management

Customers are your most important stakeholders. Without them, your business would fail. So it's only natural that they are a source of risk to be monitored. Think about each stage of the customer life cycle with an eye to how you can apply risk management practices—including limits and controls, scorecards, and other techniques—to customer management. Manage both risks and delivery. *Know your customer.* Continuously provide quality goods and services to entice your customers to return.

def•i•ni•tion

Know your customer (KYC) is a concept tied to the behaviors and needs of the individual. In the risk world, KYC works by actively seeking and spotting key risks, such as poor credit, theft, fraud, embezzlement, misappropriation, or money laundering. In some industries, it is even regulated. Look for customer payment and transaction behaviors. This usually happens "under the radar." Make everyone aware of the danger signals.

Manage your customer relationships from both a profit and risk standpoint, beginning with your first interaction with a customer. From a customer's first purchase, you can determine what she buys, how she pays, and, if credit is extended, if she pays on time.

When you manage customers well, your efforts and reputation will often effect (positively!) how other groups perceive the company. Regulators, special interest groups, and the community at large often take their cues from customer perceptions—and sometimes vice versa. So it is important to keep an eye on these groups and ensure that your risk management policies appropriately manage these interests.

Employee Management

An ideal way to build strong risk management is to bring in the right people, with appropriate skills and cultural profile, and retain them. Sounds simple, right? If only it were that easy.

It's essential to find employees with the right values to support your own risk/return profile and goals. If your company is trying to take more calculated risks but you only hire people who are risk averse, you aren't doing anyone any favors. Much of your risk management work can be undertaken by your workforce, but equally, much risk management can be leveraged through your workforce.

Be sure to offer ongoing risk management training. And as an incentive, offer rewards or promotions based on your workforce's ability to exhibit appropriate values and generate the right mix of outputs on a risk-adjusted basis. Focus your attention on recruitment and screening, training and education, and retention and promotion.

Board and Advisory Group Management

Companies use boards in various ways when including them in a risk management program. Many companies set up a board risk committee, a subcommittee to the board. It is separate from the audit committee and other committees. The risk committee discusses risks and makes or ratifies key decisions about measurement, mitigation, and investment.

Some boards even become involved in reviewing risk models. Board members are a very useful bunch when it comes to determining stress scenarios to explore. They often possess a much wider view of the environment than many employees because of their involvement in other businesses. They also frequently serve as a communications conduit to media, industry affiliations, thought leaders, regulators, and analysts. Because of that, they need to understand all of your strategies and approaches, as well as the risks associated with them.

Your Policy Framework

Your policies are one of your company's best risk management tools. Once the business grows to more than one person (though even "lone wolves" need guidelines), policies—from those at the organization level on down to product-specific policies—become useful. They set operational boundaries and expectations for any given process or function.

Best Bets

Good policies have the following key characteristics:

- They are written in clear and concise language.
- Their authority is unquestioned and represents a consistent and logical framework.
- They are readily available to anyone at any time.

A good framework to use to review your policies and controls is that of ISO 9001. Many organizations even adopt a model risk policy. This policy governs how the organization's models for measuring risk will be maintained.

ISO 9001 is a set of standards for ensuring quality management systems of all types, not just information technology systems. It helps to ensure that formalized business processes are being applied. ISO 9001 broadly requires a set of procedures that cover all key business processes; monitoring processes to ensure they are effective; keeping adequate records; checking output for defects (with appropriate corrective action); regularly reviewing individual processes; and facilitating continuous improvement.

Reviewing Company Policies

Although people often confuse policies with procedures, there is a difference between them. A *policy* sets the broad rules by which an organization operates. A *procedure* provides the approach to implement a policy. You will rarely need to change policies once they are established, as they stand above and beyond the specific tools and processes in place. However, procedures need to be updated frequently to reflect new methods, tools, and developments, including new products and business lines.

Best Bets

Your company should include a risk appetite statement in its policies. The risk appetite statement typically describes the organization's overall tolerance for risk, as well as its tolerance for specific types of risk. (There's more on this in Chapter 21.)

Building Risk into Policies

Where should you consider building risk management rules into your policies? The answer is simple and overarching: where policies exist. Key points to consider:

Product development. Are there actions you won't take? What types of products or services will you refuse to consider? What are the limitations on design, investment, and so on?

Product regulations. Do regulations exist that limit what you can offer, how it's priced, or how it can be provided to the customer?

Product validations. What validations are required before your products launch? Do any involve outside agency requirements, health, or safety? What sort of reputation risk could be generated if the product doesn't work?

Purchasing. What criteria do you require your suppliers to meet? How will you ensure that your suppliers routinely meet requirements for products you purchase? Do you have any restrictions on types of suppliers? How will you verify that the products you receive meet requirements?

Products and services. Do you have controls for the production and delivery of your products and services? How will you verify the output of process steps? Do you identify and track your products?

Monitoring and measurement. How do you monitor and measure your products, services, or interim production? (This category includes your risk management measures and monitoring tools, as well.) How do you ensure the validity of measures?

Maintenance. Do you have policies for the way your company maintains equipment, systems, or models? Are they the right tools for the job? Do you have a formal process for equipment and system maintenance in place? How do you calibrate your equipment and tools? Are they managed on a schedule?

Managing Policy Implementation

Don't forget that you need to manage the implementation process on your policies as well. They should undergo a review period with all relevant stakeholders. In many cases, a second review period may be necessary after receiving initial feedback.

On the personnel side, identify staff who need to review the policy, and seek their formal approval or sign-off. If you are implementing procedures at the same time, make sure that the procedure clearly references the policy.

Meshing Risk Culture and Your Business Values

Building a culture that emphasizes risk awareness is often the most valuable action you can take to manage risk. The spirit, philosophy, and attitude of a business culture constitute one of the few business frameworks that can carry you forward, no matter your level of risk management sophistication and maturity. Such a strong culture also carries the company through difficult challenges, regardless of the types of risks you face.

Setting up a risk culture is all about creating awareness and respect. The objectives to meet to establish a risk-aware environment are as follows:

- Getting the workforce to proactively identify risks

- Making the workforce keenly aware of the risks that lie within their responsibilities

- Giving workers an understanding of risk consequences and their role in mitigating them

- Inviting people to feel comfortable about communicating throughout the organization regarding risks that require others' attention

This leads to the second component of creating a positive risk culture: respect. In virtually every major risk blow-up that includes a severe financial or operational shock, respect (or lack of it) lies at the heart of the problem. Frequently, coalitions form that resist risk management in favor of seeking the great rewards associated with high-risk behaviors. These coalitions create a sense of "groupthink" that promotes disrespect for rules or people who are trying to manage risk.

When these incidents happen, risk management and those associated with it are often dismissed within the organization. They are not the cool kids. What happens next is almost as easy to script as a blockbuster movie: disaster strikes.

What Sets Great Apart from Good?

Organizations that manage risk well share characteristics, and those characteristics aren't fancy models and systems. Invariably, companies that manage risk successfully have developed highly risk-aware and informed cultures.

How do they create such cultures? For starters, they set the tone from the top and send a clear signal to the organization (big or small): *"Risk management is important."* They demonstrate strong involvement, commitment, and knowledge at the senior management level. This is crucial, because sometimes tough executive decisions are required. What happens if a top-selling product also happens to involve the most risk? Or if the top salesperson is the one generating the most risks by selling most of his products on credit?

When creating a risk-aware culture, a good place to start is by setting a budget for risk. Commit to that budget and its implementation. This takes some guts, because your expense might equal (and thus be a trade-off to) very tempting investments in new products or other necessary aspects of ongoing business management.

Also, ask questions about risk measures and models. Make sure that senior management understands them at least broadly. Managers should understand the assumptions behind the models, the basics of how they have been constructed, and what the information contained in them implies.

Senior management can set the tone for a risk-aware culture by asking the right questions, including the following:

♦ What risks are emerging?

♦ Do you have the proper controls in place?

♦ Are you well prepared for an event?

♦ Do you have the right people with the right skills?

♦ Are you tracking and measuring your risks with the right tools?

♦ Are you achieving the desired return relative to the risks?

Attitudes about training and education separate great organizations from others. An organization that ensures that everyone holds at least a basic understanding of risk management is generally successful. This starts on day one; enforcement sets the tone for the way things will be run. However, this understanding must be ongoing. Give your workers refresher courses. Those at the top should develop a basic competence to understand what is going on within their organizations. Those assigned more specific responsibilities around risk management should also receive ongoing education. Even though they are experts today, they may not be so astute tomorrow—unless they are encouraged to continually educate themselves on new developments and scenarios.

Culture vs. Investment

When the rubber hits the road, organizations with a strong risk culture typically experience fewer risk events. They sustain fewer actual losses and fewer swings (unexpected losses) in their loss profiles. They also require less investment to reach that point. A strong corporate culture equals lower net cost. A weak or high-risk culture leads to a higher net cost.

That's because businesses with less risk-aware cultures must rely more on mechanics and formal risk mitigation to manage risks. In turn, they need to invest in better measurement capabilities and monitoring capabilities—all of which carve valuable dollars from other, sexier areas such as product development, reinvestment, and profit-taking.

And without a strong risk management culture, even these investment initiatives are no guarantee of success. Employees or management in less risk-aware cultures (or worse, risk-denigrating cultures—talk about high-risk!) may take shortcuts or try to evade the risk controls that are in place. This leads to an even higher likelihood of losses and blow-ups.

Business Blow-Ups: Case Studies

Sometimes, the mighty fall. Successful businesses "suddenly" fail because of a breakdown around policy, values, or governance. Whether the business is big or small, the themes are similar: people become dismissive of risk and the tools in place to avoid and mitigate it. Risk management personnel are often treated as hindrances to the task of making money fast. The last thing a floor trader wants to see is a risk manager setting controls or trading limits on him. Likewise, the production line of a fast-selling product needs to keep up with demand. Why bother with checklists or control forms?

Years ago, when Bankers Trust collapsed, the company was already struggling with reputation risk. It was already known as a company that ran questionable risk practices, opting for aggressive investment positions. Yet, Bankers Trust didn't collapse because of the $288 million in settled lawsuits. It collapsed because the bank ignored its own risk models that warned of dire consequences from further investments in Russian bonds. Rather than heed the warning, Bankers Trust *increased* its investment in these bonds. This happened despite the fact the chief risk officer sent red flags all the way up to the CEO and board level. Their response? *Keep buying Russian bonds.* The culture at Bankers Trust was so risk-seeking that it took down the company.

Another example comes from the Barings Bank collapse of the mid-1990s, one of the most infamous collapses prior to the 2008 banking crisis. Rather than exploit low-risk opportunities, trader Nick Leeson took a far more aggressive approach. He assumed much riskier positions by buying and selling different amounts of contracts on the Singapore and Osaka exchanges or by buying and selling contracts for different types of derivatives. A lax senior management then handed him the reins for both the trading and back office functions. As Leeson's losses mounted, he increased his bets. The final blow came in the form of an earthquake in Japan, which caused the Nikkei index to drop sharply. Leeson's losses increased rapidly, plummeting the bank more than $1 billion into the red. This was too much for the bank to sustain; in March 1995, the Dutch bank ING purchased Barings for just one pound—about a dollar and a half.

Here's the rub. Many of Barings management suspected that Leeson was running these positions, *positions that violated their own risk policy.* While they may not have foreseen the full implications, they were aware of large and potentially high-risk exposures. The positions looked highly profitable, and senior management backed Leeson. When the company tanked, that same management pointed the finger at Leeson because he broke policy. Even though Leeson took the brunt of the punishment, the entire senior management team had a part to play in poor risk practices.

The Least You Need to Know

- Your company culture may give you your best bang for the buck when it comes to risk management.

- Always factor risk management and risk practices into your business policies.

- By knowing and managing your employees and customers, you can spot and govern risk before it hurts your company.

- Risk managers or consultants work best when they operate independently of the day-to-day business flow.

- Many business failures, blow-ups, and breakdowns revolve around governance and risk policy issues.

Chapter 19

Integrating Risk into Your Organization

In This Chapter

- ◆ Creating your risk organization
- ◆ Setting up the four lines of defense
- ◆ Enlisting help
- ◆ Using incentives

Call this the "power to the people" chapter: you have the power to deter and manage risk. Your team of employees or key outside contractors serves as your best risk deterrent and biggest ally in risk management. This team is best positioned to spot potential or existing risks. Company lawyers, internal auditors, and human resources people form another stern line of defense against many forms of risk. Also, you can employ a variety of methods to bring people from throughout the company into the risk process.

Still, a risk organization is about more than just the people. It constitutes the specific roles in your company that measure, manage, and monitor risk. These roles may be adjunct to other duties, or they may be specific, dedicated roles—or a combination of both.

There are important formal concepts to contemplate when thinking about creating a risk organization. It begins when you consider what roles to build into your company.

Building the Framework

The type of risk organization you build depends on the kind of business you have and your ongoing activities. Most companies that work in financial services, that conduct regular trading activities, or that engage in highly risky activities (such as airlines) have formalized risk management teams. For other companies, size usually dictates how formalized the risk management function is. But no matter your company's size, if it operates in a highly regulated industry, you will want someone in a formal risk management role.

Risk Factors

When more formalized roles are in place, companies often dedicate teams to each of their major risk classes. They may also assign groups to different aspects of risk management, such as measurement, policy-making, management, and mitigation. Smaller organizations sometimes use one team with individual roles for each of these activities. The individual assignments can also consist of handling each different class of risks.

The information on forming a risk organization in this chapter applies to any business, whether or not you have a formal function fully dedicated to risk management.

Risk Management Is Everyone's Business

Risk management is everyone's business. This is emphasized for a reason: it is one of the most important sentences in this book.

How do you involve everyone? Simple: make risk management an explicit part of each person's job description. Everyone doesn't need to sit down and measure each risk, but everyone should be aware of the risks associated with your business and how they might manifest. Teach employees how to identify mounting risks and, just as importantly, how to communicate information. Make sure they know who your key risk management people are—and to talk with them. Make them broadly aware of the management and mitigation tools within their control.

Four Lines of Defense

Despite its sporting connotation, *four lines of defense* applies to risk just as well as it does to football and soccer. In risk management, the expression refers to a common organizational model.

Part of the premise associated with this model is that companies cannot effectively manage risk by compartmentalizing it. This holds true even if they choose to have a formal in-house risk management or compliance function. It takes a whole company working together to manage risks in a successful, cost-efficient manner. This takes on added significance when viewing the ever-soaring cost of compliance with varying regulations and other types of requirements.

Also, by including a total company view of organizational roles and responsibilities, risk approaches become better embedded in a company's operations and culture. This begins at the early stages of strategy formulation and product development and continues through the product and customer life cycles. This enables the formal risk or compliance organization to serve an advisory role in deepening capabilities, particularly where risks are most prevalent. The compliance organization is the formal team responsible for managing and monitoring compliance with existing regulations and other formal rules and requirements.

def•i•ni•tion

The **four lines of defense** are the basic areas for managing risk within a company: business management (front line), risk and compliance management, auditing, and senior management and board. The model assumes that risk is everyone's business. Each employee takes on a slightly different function, depending on his or her specific location within the organization.

The Front Line: Business Management and Risk

The front line serves as the first line of defense. It consists of business management functions, particularly those dealing with developing, producing, and selling products. They are best positioned to keep an eye on risks, understand what decisions to make (or not make), know which customers and products to focus on, and maintain production and systems. They turn away many day-to-day risks. The front line works within a framework supported by risk management or compliance teams.

Best Bets _____

The front line framework works best if it includes someone designated to provide guidance on controls and limits. That person or group should not be specifically part of the business function, as the job will be conducted best when it can operate independently of business decisions.

Senior managers are an integral part of any front line. Since they oversee key functions and business lines, it makes sense to task them with the day-to-day responsibility for managing risks. They convert strategy into actions, identifying and assessing risks and risk responses. The process works when they guide the implementation of the risk management process within their spheres of responsibility. They should also strive to make their approaches consistent with the company's risk tolerances.

Senior managers usually assign responsibilities for risk procedures to lower-level managers, who attach them to specific functions. This helps senior staff develop the particular risk procedures that address their objectives. Such procedures could include things like how raw materials are purchased or how new customers are accepted. The supervisors of these functions also make recommendations on related control activities and monitor their effectiveness. Your job is to give each manager authority and accountability for these activities. Make sure the manager is accountable to the next higher level, with the CEO ultimately accountable to the board.

Running Alongside: Compliance Management

The risk and compliance team runs the risk management process, and it steps forward to provide the next line of defense. This group does not have to be large, nor does it need to be staffed by dedicated personnel. However, the team must have a clear mandate and authority to make risk management decisions.

This group provides support and guidance regarding identification and day-to-day management of risks to other groups in the company. The group may also offer focused special support in the analysis of strategic initiatives.

When companies handle risk management in-house, they usually choose a director with strong analytical capabilities. They usually include the title "chief risk officer" (CRO), or something along those lines. If you have a manufacturing company, the role may fall to one of the senior production or process engineers. If the majority of your risks are financial, choose a financial expert for this role. Some companies assign the job to another senior officer, such as the chief financial officer, general counsel, chief auditor, or chief compliance officer. Some organizations even make the risk management role part of the strategy function, viewing it as an important component of how the company evolves and builds its core business. Others find that the job requires a full-time commitment. It even may be important enough to warrant reporting to the CEO or directly to the board.

Best Bets

Make your risk management function as independent of business decision-making as possible. Risk managers should not feel that success in their careers or their remuneration is tied to increasing production or sales. The compliance individual must be uncompromised and have the authority to say "no" when it comes to certain business decisions. The person or team might also step in to overrule or problem-solve decisions that might otherwise put the company at serious risk. This requires that the CRO possess authority, often by virtue of experience and seniority, and be able to report directly to the CEO or board.

Many companies start compliance efforts by giving their CRO and risk management team a policeman's role. Although policing is fairly effective in establishing safeguards, the *partnership model* is much more efficient. And employees don't appreciate being policed! With the partnership model, the CRO or risk team partners with departments of the business. Their goal: to reduce risk and comply with company policies.

Ultimately, the CRO is responsible for day-to-day risk management. That includes identifying risks, ensuring that they are assessed and monitored, and overseeing the implementation of risk treatments. He or she makes sure that information about risks is reported throughout the organization. The CRO also ensures that the organization's risk appetite is defined and maintained. The CRO coordinates and facilitates the risk management process, working with other managers to establish an effective risk management framework and approach. The CRO's duties are as follows:

def·i·ni·tion

A **partnership model** describes the interaction between two teams within an organization. In risk management, the risk team partners with the other teams within a company. The model allows the risk or compliance team not only to safeguard the organization, but also to work with various divisions or departments to optimize their capabilities.

♦ Establishing risk management policies, defining roles and responsibilities, and participating in setting goals for implementation of risk management capabilities

♦ Framing accountability and authority for risk management in the business units or departments

- Ensuring that the company develops a basis of risk management competence and knowledge, including an appropriate level of related technical expertise within the company

- Aligning risk management responses with the company's risk tolerance

- Ensuring the integration of risk management into business planning and other management activities

- Creating a common risk management language that includes common measures around likelihood, impact, expected loss, and unexpected loss

- Overseeing the development of specific risk tolerances and controls for different business activities

- Establishing (or ensuring the establishment of) reporting approaches, including quantitative and qualitative information and thresholds

- Overseeing the monitoring of the risk management process

- Ensuring that there is appropriate reporting to senior management, the CEO, and the board, as well as recommending actions as needed

This role comes with a big challenge. Although the CRO is responsible for risk management implementation and decisions, line managers must still assume primary responsibility for managing risk within their areas. After all, they usually generate most of the risk.

The Backstop: Audit

The internal audit department (if you have one) serves as the third line of defense in risk management. It plays a key role in evaluating the effectiveness of the risk management process. Auditors consider risk management process and control review a natural part of their role. As a matter of fact, these responsibilities are explicitly stated by all of the bodies that govern auditing standards.

It is important to note that auditors do not—and should not—hold primary responsibility for establishing and maintaining a risk management framework. That is the responsibility of the CEO and CRO.

The internal audit function ranges from assessing quality and efficiency to pure compliance. The auditor's specific role is to review the effectiveness of the risk management process and recommend improvements in reporting, assessment and controls, and efficiency of operations. Auditors also play a key role in ensuring compliance with laws, regulations, and contracts. Auditors can be a great support to risk managers when they work in partnership to establish greater efficiencies and continuous improvement.

Red Flags

Auditors focus their attention on the quality of financial statements. The information presented within those statements should provide a fair view of the company's financial position. While poor risk management may not affect the statement of today's financial position, it can make an audit more expensive and the auditor's job of verifying the information more difficult. In all likelihood, that next financial statement won't look so rosy.

If you don't have an internal audit department, you can use external auditors. The external auditor provides a completely unbiased view of the condition of the company's financial statements.

Be clear in your expectations of the auditor. Find out to what extent the auditor will review control systems. Make sure he or she knows that you want clear, unbiased commentary on control systems.

Setting the Tone: Senior Management and Board

Senior management and the board of directors constitute the final line of defense. Ultimate responsibility for the risk management process lies with them. The board and senior management ensure that the risk management process is implemented and conducted in line with the firm's values and requirements. They ensure that the company-wide implementation of risk management is effective.

Senior management and the board also have a critical oversight role in risk management. It includes …

- Deciding and ensuring the extent to which risk management is implemented across and down the organization.

- Setting the company's risk appetite.

- Reviewing the company's risk portfolio and comparing it to the company's risk appetite.

- Determining how the company will respond to its most significant risks.

The board and senior management lead and participate in many key decisions and adjunct activities that create or utilize risk and risk management thought processes. They set strategy, create high-level objectives, and determine resource allocation in the broader sense. However, there are some subtle differences between board and senior management responsibilities. Management is directly responsible for these activities, while the board provides the oversight.

The responsibility buck stops with the CEO. The regulator's loud knuckles will rap on the CEO's door first. The CEO has ultimate responsibility for appropriately managing risk. That includes ensuring that the right culture and environment for managing risk exist. The tone is set from the top.

The specific responsibilities of the CEO with regard to risk management are …

- Providing leadership and direction to senior managers.

- Meeting periodically with senior managers responsible for key functions and business lines to review how they are managing risk.

- Understanding the risks inherent in the operation.

- Understanding the risk measurement, monitoring, and mitigation techniques being used, as well as the status of any ongoing efforts.

Together, the CEO and senior management establish the principles, values, and major operating policies that form the basis of the company's risk management framework. They also establish the risk appetite and culture, and they ensure that key policies are appropriately communicated.

Typically, a risk committee forms as a subcommittee of the board. If your organization is small, risk management might entail a regular, scheduled discussion at board meetings.

Who Are Your Risk Managers?

Specific risk management roles and responsibilities cascade from the board and CEO.

Many of the staff perform risk management roles in their respective areas. Staff functions such as human resources, compliance, and legal all have important supporting roles in designing or shaping effective risk management capabilities.

Human Resources

Human resources has a twofold role in risk management:

◆ To implement and manage initiatives that relate to the broader culture and capabilities of the organization

◆ To support the hiring of specific personnel

The human resources department implements training and cultural awareness programs and change management. The department also designs and implements the company's code of conduct and addresses related policy issues.

The department is also integral in the identification and development of the business's leadership, including succession planning. The criteria for selecting the company's future leaders should include candidates' personal values and how they use those values in their jobs. This includes their attitudes about risk management and risk versus return.

Legal

Do you have a legal department or an in-house attorney? If so, you enjoy an obvious built-in form of risk management. The legal function ensures that contracts are made and followed, that the company is kept abreast of new laws and regulations that may affect operating policies, that customer disclosure requirements are followed, and more. The legal folks often interact with (or are) the compliance officers who provide critical information on whether planned transactions or protocols conform to legal and ethical requirements. They track the company's adherence to those requirements as well.

Make the legal department a key component of your communication plan. Consider how to include legal in your reporting and monitoring framework for risk management. It may become a key part of the identification of risks and the management of risk mitigation.

Strategic Planning

Many organizations tie risk management to the strategic planning process. They use it for broad initiative planning, as well as for yearly strategy and budgeting discussions. For many organizations, strategic planning is key to establishing a view of the mix of products and the identification of new products, acquisitions, new channels, etc. All of these decisions can deeply affect the mix of risks within the firm.

Conversely, risk information can help inform and optimize strategic decisions. With risk information, you may be able to target your mix of products and make maximum use of the inherent diversification that they provide. You can analyze channels or different customer segments for the relative risk that they present.

Therefore, strategic planning and risk management go hand in hand, each informing the other. Some organizations build risk management directly into the strategic planning team. Regardless of whether you do so, make sure you include risk management in the strategic planning process, and vice versa.

Finance/Accounting

Finance folks are often significant participants in risk management in a number of ways:

- Their broad, company-wide reach often makes them aware of the plans of all different functions.

- They are generally involved in budgeting and planning.

- They track and analyze performance.

- They may track or manage reporting and certain compliance requirements.

- They are responsible for the company's hedging and market activities.

- They are typically responsible for the company's funding activities.

- They interface with investors and the board.

- They interface with equity and credit analysts.

- They are responsible for the company's financial reporting and for designing, implementing, and monitoring the company's external financial reporting requirements.

- They are key to setting the company tone regarding ethical conduct.

Risk Factors

The chief financial officer heads up the finance function. The CFO is typically at the table when objectives are established, strategies are set, risks are analyzed, and decisions are made. More broadly, the CFO is strongly influential in equity (capital), and therefore on how buffers dependent on reserves and equity are implemented. The CFO is also responsible for preventing and detecting fraudulent reporting.

The finance department is one of the chief recipients of risk information and recommendations. The department uses this material to implement risk mitigation methods through reserves, buffers, hedges, or budgeting arrangements. Finance typically manages the performance reporting framework and any risk-adjusted return measures that will be used. The department, represented by the CFO, is a vital stakeholder, an intimate accomplice in the implementation of risk management. However, finance can also take major risks through its management of treasury and market decisions.

Many organizations have traditionally placed the responsibilities of the CRO with the CFO as a dual role or with the CRO reporting to the CFO. In recent years, this has been frowned upon by regulatory agencies, which greatly prefer a separation between risk management and risk-taking activities. In addition, the risk manager's role is expanding for many companies, particularly in industries facing greater requirements from regulators and industry bodies.

For example, it is viewed as very poor form (and even disallowed in some countries) for the CFO of a bank also to assume responsibility for risk management (or even have the CRO report to him). This is because the CFO is responsible for financial risks from a business sense. Often, trading and treasury management reports to the CFO, so his organization is the direct instigator of certain sorts of risks. Having him manage both risk management and risk-taking activities is viewed as a conflict of interest.

Nevertheless, it is important to make the CFO an integral player in risk management activities. Develop a specific and well-articulated view regarding risk management roles and the finance function—and how they will work together.

Managing Risk Through Employee Compensation

Virtually every study espouses the importance of linking compensation to performance through incentives, such as commissions, bonuses, stock options, and extended paid vacations. Most studies also describe the dangers involved in incorrectly linking performance and incentives.

The same is true of risk. In fact, risk management plays an integral role in creating the appropriate balance between objectives and incentives.

In general, most companies have two basic interests: to be profitable and to grow. The question you need to answer is how much growth and profitability you want relative to risk. The answer involves striking a balance that works with your risk appetite.

Set up a culture that rewards behaviors supporting a balance of risk with return. This is vital. Reward the balance directly and explicitly. Use incentives based on risk-adjusted performance measures introduced in Chapter 10.

Using Incentives

The concept of incentives is simple. The company wishes to provide individual, team, or company-wide rewards for meeting or exceeding returns on a risk-adjusted basis. Do this by establishing targets and thresholds based on the risk-adjusted return measures you've already learned.

There are three short and sweet rules of thumb for awarding incentives:

- Keep the metric simple.

- Be aware of what the measure implies.

- Be consistent.

Some organizations try to use multiperiod measures (measures that forecast over multiple years) or measures that are perfect from an accounting perspective but confusing from anyone else's. Multiperiod measures are great for certain forms of decision-making and pricing models, but lousy for performance measurement. They always sound like a good idea, but they become exceedingly complex to implement. Start with a one-year measure (length of the performance period). If multiperiod approaches still make sense, then try one once you've ironed out the bugs of the one-year approach. Seek a measure that people can readily understand and implement in their daily decision-making. If they can't figure it out, then they can't act on it.

The same concerns apply for a measure with numerous accounting adjustments. It is often tempting to take this approach, because it can align to whatever the accountants report. You can also compare your performance to other companies, and possibly even to competitors. If you choose this approach, consider it a separate exercise. Don't mix it with your performance framework. The act of adjusting accounting figures on the performance metric is confusing and frustrating. Managers simply don't know where they stand until the accountants are finished with the measurements.

It is easy to adjust the performance metric so it benefits the company. In your performance targets, include a growth objective side-by-side with the return objective. You can also use an economic profit term (or something like it), which is contribution-based—measured in dollars, not percentages. Generally speaking, a contribution-based method is often better than a return method, for this very reason.

Make sure that the measures align with corporate objectives and targets. Implement them in the same way across all functions and business lines.

Another strategy: Think about the performance objectives holistically. What are the company's major objectives in risk and in other areas? Have you covered each in some form in your performance framework?

> **Red Flags**
>
> What's wrong with reducing risk or not taking any risk to improve a measure? Plenty. You can shrink the number of company transactions and focus on a very few high-return deals. Unless that's specifically your objective, it can drive the company into a death spiral.

Linking Performance to Incentives

Since you don't want to overwhelm your workforce, pick your top few objectives—no more than five—and focus everyone on those goals. Link their performance to your incentives. These can take the form of minimum expectations in order to achieve a salary raise or bonus. If the target is more serious, increase your expectations—and your rewards. Also create consequences for poor performance or noncompliance with risk policies and controls. It is important to send a strong message that risk is serious!

The Least You Need to Know

- Make sure everyone in the company understands his or her role in risk management.

- Establish your "four lines of defense": business management, risk and compliance, audit, and senior management and the board.

- Consider your key support personnel part of the broader risk management team.

- Develop incentives or bonuses for staff who support your prescribed risk targets and objectives.

Building Risk into the Business Process

In This Chapter

- ◆ Building your business rhythm
- ◆ Budgeting risk
- ◆ Monitoring risk
- ◆ Benefiting from risk versus reward
- ◆ Reporting on risk

Now it's time to funnel everything you have learned about risk management into your business process. This is arguably the most important aspect of risk management, because most risks emerge from within the everyday business flow. The processes that create your flow, or rhythm, become the points of greatest opportunity to prevent or mitigate actual risks—and to make risk management part of the everyday environment. This is also where your opportunity to make money is greatest.

By reading the next few chapters and applying the points raised, you can gain a strong business advantage over your competitors—and greatly enhance your bottom line.

Three Keys to Integration

Integrating risk management into your business processes works in three distinct dimensions:

◆ It builds risk into the yearly management planning, budgeting, and monitoring cycle. Most companies use this overarching cycle to some degree.

◆ It drives risk into day-to-day processes—the business operations.

◆ It enhances development of a monitoring and reporting framework.

Develop a Business Rhythm

Most companies run on some sort of annual cycle. This cycle defines the company's *business rhythm*. It may be finance-driven, beginning at the start of the financial year and moving into development of strategic planning and budgeting. There may be hard checks when interim financial statements are due or an investor or board review is pending. These reviews often take place quarterly. The whole cycle ends with consolidating the financial position and developing the yearly financial statements.

def•i•ni•tion

Business rhythm is the cycle of activities that revolve around financial management and monitoring. Usually the cycle is annual. It often starts with strategic planning and budgeting and budget allocations, then progresses through the year with routine checks of the plan. It ends with the production of yearly financial statements and the review of performance measures and objectives.

Much of the company falls in line with plans, budgets, and reporting targets in some form or another. The company should do the same with risk. Embed the consideration of risk in planning, budgeting and reporting; they should integrate with the existing cycles. Even the smallest companies operate on a cycle like this, although it may be a less formal process. If your business includes any sort of shareholders, investors, or board members, then you utilize a business rhythm, even if it's lean. At the very least, you probably create plans, set a budget, and track it on some level. That, too, is a business rhythm.

The more routine or formalized your business rhythm, the more it tends to drive many of the company's activities. Most businesses align with this rhythm to implement projects and new products and achieve return targets. The rhythm also drives hiring and firing decisions to a degree, along with bonus and salary adjustments and possibly formal personnel reviews. As a company grows, the rhythm becomes one of meeting goals, objectives, and checkpoints in preparation for end-of-year financial statements and board meetings.

Including Risk in Your Business Plans

Good business rhythm starts with smart business plans. While a business plan discussion may not seem relevant to risk management, it actually is vital to planning for risk.

Hopefully, you developed a business plan at some point and have refreshed it regularly—or at least rethought its basics.

Your business plan should be reviewed annually. At a minimum, it should include the following elements:

◆ Strategic direction of the company

◆ Core initiatives to support those objectives

◆ Initiatives to be met over the next year

The company business plan also provides a basis for the financial plan by laying out the following information:

◆ Growth expectations

◆ Cost expectations to support growth

◆ Initiatives requiring investment

◆ New markets and key new customers or suppliers that may require special financial arrangements

◆ Any requirements for new investment money

◆ Any requirements for debt or bank loans

The business plan creates a broad, and hopefully specific, view of what the balance sheet and P&L will look like at the end of the year. It also spells out financial activities that must occur to support it.

When you build risk into your business plan, include answers to the following questions:

Is risk information included in the company's strategic planning?

Have you considered how your plans affect risk?

Will new initiatives carry different or more risks?

Could they reduce risk?

How do the new initiatives measure up on a risk versus return basis?

Will any of the plans require new or additional mitigation?

How will you monitor risks as you implement the new plans?

Will you require new investment to support this?

Will you require more capital for buffers or reserves?

Have you discussed risk in your strategic planning with senior management and the board?

Incorporating the Risk Appetite Statement

When integrating risk into your business plan, make sure to review your risk appetite (see Chapter 21). Your risk appetite should be considered yearly. As you look at the issue, ask yourself the following questions:

Has your risk appetite changed since last year?

Will any plans or initiatives require you to reconsider your risk appetite?

How will the thresholds identified in the risk appetite be affected?

Should these thresholds change to reflect company growth or changes in the inherent risk profile?

Who needs to participate in decisions that may arise from this process?

Budgeting Risk

The best organizations project the growth and mix of their businesses and then apply risk measures. They do so in order to understand changes in expected loss and unexpected loss and how diversification can affect the overall risks. These steps enable the company to estimate what sort of reserves, buffers (capital), and other forms of mitigation will be required, all of which fall into the budgeting process.

Ask yourself the following questions about your budget:

Have you developed an explicit budget for risk management?

Does it allow for continuous improvement?

Does it consider the changing profile of company risks and growth?

A quick tip: the core risk budget usually needs to increase if the company is growing.

 Best Bets _____

When developing a budget, it is important to think about a few key things in order to adequately include risk management. Consider the type of business you'll be doing over the next year (your mix of product sales) and how this might affect your risks. Next, forecast how much growth you will experience in the next year, overall and in particular sectors. Factor in how much mitigation you will require to manage the mix of risks and the growth of risk. Finally, determine which new initiatives are required for risk management and how these might change your budgeted buffers and reserves.

Once you have pinned down the basics, make sure your budget includes general enhancements to the risk management process. It should contain necessary resources to address the growth and mix expected for the coming year. These areas can include new improvements to measurements, controls, and even personnel (education and hiring). Make sure your budget considers additional or new mitigation or risk management approaches to support your plan.

With this information in hand, you will be able to finalize your company budget. Determine how much you need for reserves, capital (equity), risk operations, and risk investments.

Driving Business Through Risk and Reward

It's time to revisit an old friend, a concept introduced in Chapter 10: your key risk-adjusted return measure (RAROC). Now comes the time to put that concept to work for the company. To do so, you will need to have a good idea about four things:

◆ Your risk-adjusted return, the net profit after accounting for reserves (expected loss)

◆ Your economic capital

- ◆ How to routinely measure and monitor risk-adjusted return and economic capital

- ◆ How to split this measure across all key business activities and locations

Consider the final item in the preceding list. In order to split up these measures, you will most likely want to practice *capital allocation*, assigning the budgeted economic capital to each core business or location. This will help you gain a sense of how much risk capital comes from each of your businesses, departments, and products.

def•i•ni•tion

Capital allocation is the assignment of economic capital across core business operations, separate businesses, or locations. It provides real capital to a department within a business to "hold" as a buffer or to manage. This includes any buffers for risk. Companies can then attribute risk capital to the aspects of the enterprise creating it.

Allocating Economic Capital

Determine how you want to split up capital within your company. This top-down process starts with a measure of your total risk in terms of economic capital and expected loss. Evaluate what that risk looks like for the company, then contemplate which segments need to be managed as separate groups. Look for sensible splits that describe the way you run your business; manage according to your risk-adjusted return. If you're small, little or no major separation will be required.

If you operate in more than one location (separate franchised locations, production facilities, or branches), manufacture more than one product, offer more than one service, or reach different types of customers that you want to monitor separately, all of these scenarios create potential opportunities to split the numbers in a meaningful way.

Best Bets

If you measure risk versus reward top-down or utilize combinations of top-down and bottom-up measures, but you haven't yet readied every type of risk you need to manage by business sector, find a way to break down the risks already measured. This can be done fairly simply by splitting up the exposures based on their sources from different business sectors. You may need to understand differences in the risks inherent in each sector, and adjust accordingly for probability and severity deviations as well. When you split up the risks from the top down, you'll need to account for the fact that they don't add up in the simple sense. Use the equations described in Chapter 10 to account for correlation.

When splitting economic capital, many companies follow their normal organization chart. Some even split it up further. If you have used a bottom-up measurement for achieving this, you probably already have a good sense of how the allocation breaks up across businesses or sectors. Keep that separation in mind and then adjust the amount to account for any changes that will occur over the next year.

Using RAROC vs. Economic Profit

Capital allocation can also be important in supplying critical inputs to our measures of risk-adjusted return: RAROC and Economic Profit. In Chapter 10, you learned about their value in assessing different product lines or business sectors. When capital is allocated to different business sectors and even customer segments, it can be applied to these risk-adjusted return measures in order to better understand where to make investment or how to price better. You can also use them to support incentives to your sales force, for better management of your customers, and your bottom line—relative to risk, of course. Now for an important nuance: when applied without foresight, RAROC can get you into trouble.

The problem is that when RAROC is used in remuneration, managers can shrink the book with micromanaging. Imagine that you have a group of products with different prices and risks. The RAROCs may all be different. So the idea would be to focus on the products with better RAROCs … right? The answer may not be so obvious. Your sales managers may completely stop selling the products with higher risk, lower RAROCs, in order to yield a better RAROC for the overall business, but this can reduce the overall sales of the company. Instead, an economic profit calculation would suggest that the revenue generated from those other products is better overall. Growth needs to be part of the equation. Remember that your measure should reflect a balance of revenue, cost, risk, *and* growth.

Forecasting Risks

Will your business growth or strategic initiatives change the profile of risk, and therefore economic capital and reserves, required to support each of your businesses, products, and locations? Make this adjustment by projecting how risk exposures will change from the beginning to the end of the year.

You also may require adjustments to the probability and severity if you believe that the overall risk profile will change as well. This also applies if economic conditions change to affect the probability and severity of risks.

Combine this data with your economic capital figures to determine what you will need at the end of the year for each split.

Try to establish overall expected loss and economic capital for each business sector that you monitor or populate. Then, build RAROC or economic profit measures for each of those sectors. Now look at how you'd like each sector to perform. Should it be doing better? How? Can revenue improve in that sector? Can you reduce risks (and therefore expected loss and economic capital)? Can you reduce costs?

Setting Performance Targets

To manage your sectors, set up targets or thresholds to beat or meet. These can be tied to any type of remuneration.

When you generate the measures, make sure that they are top-down, bottom-up, and horizontally consistent. They should be generated and split across sectors using the same sorts of assumptions.

Monitor your performance against set targets by organizing and running performance checks a few times during the year. That way, people understand where they stand.

Make sure that the measures are straightforward. Help your managers to see the links between their actions and the outcomes of the measures. The measures should focus on managing revenue, cost, risk, and growth/volume.

Benefits of Risk vs. Reward

The benefits of the risk versus reward approach are twofold: you align the interests of your employees with company objectives and you drive a view that optimizing risk versus reward is the best way forward. It's quite amazing, but once people see that you're serious about converting risk measures into money-making tools, they usually start to grasp the concepts. They even gain interest in improving the quality of the measures.

However, it is risk … which means there is a flip side. There are always cases in which someone doesn't "get religion" or finds a way to game the system. Clear consequences are the solution. Set minimums for acceptable behavior and expectations for adhering to limits and processes. Enforce them strictly; tie them to consequences. If necessary, make the consequences severe. Consider forgoing raises or bonuses or even dismissing employees.

Keep Your Finger on the Pulse

Many crazy glitches happen when no one is paying attention. It is imperative to establish a control framework that forces a regular check on the risks being taken and compares those to the limits that have been set.

In this process, you want to take the following actions:

♦ Establish a clear framework.

♦ Describe the framework simply.

♦ Build in clear monitoring expectations.

♦ Build in clear action steps for when limits are approached.

♦ Establish clear consequences for breaches of processes or controls.

Building Risk Controls into Business Processes

The most effective way to build risk controls into day-to-day activities is to consider present risks and identify the processes where they are generated. Determine the source of the risk, and manage at that point. Undertake your root cause analysis before a risk event occurs, if possible.

Building these controls is a pretty straightforward activity. The key is to incorporate checks and controls into the business process. Make them as seamless as possible. Also, make your checks and controls sensible and easy to manage. If the controls and limits are based on concepts like unexpected loss, they may not work in the sales organization despite their fundamental soundness. This is because the administrators may not have access to the measurements.

Best Bets

When you use indicators as guidelines for building risk controls, seek indicators that can be reasonably measured. They must also be efficient in terms of demands on time, effort, and resources. Confirm that the measurement process encourages or facilitates desirable behaviors and does not motivate the opposite (such as data fabrication). Finally, be sure that those involved understand the process and expected benefits. Give them input into the development of procedures. When finished, deliver the results in a straightforward report that fosters learning and improvement.

For that reason, it is important to consider what is being implemented, who will manage and monitor it, where checks and measures will originate (if used), and if measures can be translated into information that's useful to staff.

A Builder's Approach

Now that the ways and means of building risk into business processes have been covered, what about the best approach to take? Try something like this:

Identify the key sources of risk. (Hopefully, you've come this far already.)

Group the risks into categories of similar or identical locations. There may be several different types of risk festering in the same location. This is more common in divisions of your organization that handle customers, human resources, or production.

Consider the types of management and mitigation methods to use for each risk and group of risks in each category. Are there any similarities? Are there opportunities to combine these risks or groups into a broader risk management program for the sector?

Consider the business process. What needs to be changed or added in order to implement the mitigation? Are there new steps, such as a measurement or a check?

Generally, if you can identify a control or measure that can be managed early in the process, the likelihood of managing a risk before it further materializes is going to skyrocket. Limits and controls can be built into the process at key points of inception. That way, you can identify the challenge and make a quick decision on whether to take that risk.

A quick scenario helps to illustrate this point. Consider taking an order from a customer on credit. That order serves as the start of a potential risk or group of risks. However, it's fairly easy to gather information about the customer at the time of order. You can identify creditworthiness using scorecards, describe the products, and make sure the products hide no key issues that could result in a potential lawsuit. From there, you can establish the right contract terms that ensure timely payment and expectations from your company.

There's more. You can manage against several potential risks—all based upon the path you take with the customer. You can decide up front if you want to do business with that customer. Or you can set the terms. You might recognize that gaining this new customer or transaction will cause you to break one of your core limits. What price will you provide? Does the price cover anticipated risks? In some cases, you can even look at your performance measures and see whether the risk versus return results are in line with company expectations and targets.

Mitigation methods that can be built directly into the steps and flow of the business process are often the most successful. The challenge is that they may involve adding a new step to the process, which could cause disruptions and likely new requirements for training, education, and documentation.

Monitoring Exposures

Routinely monitor your risks. Try to understand how your risks change as you conduct business and further evolve when you take on new clients, add a division, begin a new product line, or acquire another company.

For each risk, ask yourself: "How often will these risks change?" Next, establish time-lines and methods for monitoring each risk. In your method, include the control and limits to be used as checkpoints.

If you possess measures such as expected loss and unexpected loss for each exposure, you can generally convert those figures into limits. Then you can rapidly check and compare exposures against the total amount of risk-related loss that the company can survive. Often it is easiest to list each exposure and check it against already established measures. Look for changes or trends in the exposures. Are they growing? Why? Is the company approaching a limit?

Monitoring Groups of Risk

Checking and monitoring groups of risk is similar to checking and monitoring individual risks, except that the additional characteristics require additional checks. Consider how your risk groups combine and how the correlations among risks will be addressed (if at all). Monitor by type of risk, originating business line or department, or product or service type. Also consider who will be responsible for this measuring and monitoring. This leads to a new concept: the *hierarchy of assurance*.

A typical hierarchy of assurance takes a predictable shape when depicting organized risk management. Business department employees take responsibility for monitoring individual risks and small groups of risks in their respective businesses or departments.

The **hierarchy of assurance** describes responsibilities for monitoring risk relative to seniority and location in the company, as well as the level of reporting that takes place relative to that position. This is similar to the four lines of defense concept addressed earlier in the book.

In larger companies, they may be assisted by a risk officer. As groups of risk "roll up" within an organization, line management and perhaps higher levels of management swing into action. They take responsibility for monitoring across their spans of control (again, generally aided by risk people). However, they are looking for broader conclusions about the movements of risks. They are also more concerned about the coverage and effectiveness of controls. The funnel narrows even further at the final review point—the audit. This area of focus will be fairly narrow and generally wrapped around compliance.

The hierarchy of assurance shows how the greatest level of responsibility for monitoring risks and groups of risks falls with the common workforce.

The Hierarchy Of Assurance

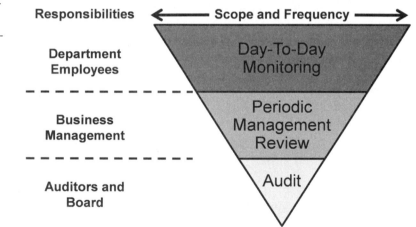

Responsibilities ←——— Scope and Frequency ———→

Department Employees — Day-To-Day Monitoring

Business Management — Periodic Management Review

Auditors and Board — Audit

Reporting

Reporting on risks probably ranks right up there with watching grass grow for many employees. There are at least a thousand more exciting ways to spend a moment, even at work.

However, reporting carries enormous importance and needs to be conducted with fullest skill and seriousness. In fact, a report won't be nearly as effective if it isn't done right, because no one will understand or pay attention to the results. Bear four things in mind when preparing reports: what to report, the audience for the report, high-impact information to report, and reporting frequency.

The Key Elements of a Report

Most risk reports have the following four major components:

♦ The key risks

♦ Why they are critical

♦ How they are changing over time

♦ What you are doing to stop or mitigate them

Try to limit your key risks to those that are truly vital. Can you tell a full story by talking about only the top ten risks? Can you get it down to the top five?

Keep the report physically brief. Even many large organizations order report writers to keep these statements to two pages. Nobody has enough time to review an exhaustive 60-page report on risk.

What are your risks? What do you need to act on right now? That should be the focus of the report.

Identify Your Audience

Consider your audience. If your organization contains more than one management tier, think carefully about who needs to know specific types of information, and at what level. As a rule of thumb, the higher you climb in an organization, the more important it is to limit the amount of information you include. This becomes increasingly challenging, because more risks usually appear as your reporting "rolls up" toward the top.

Risk Factors
Ever hear of the "rule of less than seven"? The human mind can remember fewer than seven items simultaneously (which is why phone numbers were originally built on seven-digit number series!). The mind also responds to items in odd-numbered clusters. When reporting risk processes, aim for three or five key points. That way, recipients are more likely to retain, and hopefully act upon, the key messages.

Always keep your focus on the top risks. Most likely, the CEO only cares about the top five for the entire organization. It's likely the maximum that the organization can handle at one time.

For multiple-site or multiple-department businesses, managers in different locations or departments will require different information, which may need to be tailored to them. What does the human resources department need to know? What does legal require? How is that different from what the head of a business department needs?

Don't generate too many reports; they take too much time and effort. But in certain cases where groups or risks are large, multiple reports are often worthwhile.

Create an Impact

Now that you have generated the risk report, how do you disseminate it to others? This requires more than simply submitting the document. Actually, you will be seeking a much more dynamic platform—one that creates impact. After all, you're reporting on risk processes, which many high-powered businesses would rather ignore than implement. Thus, you need to deliver the goods with as much impact as if you were pitching a business plan to investors or a proposal to prospective clients.

Create that impact by tightening up the material you have gathered. Make it very concise. You have identified the company's top risks; hopefully, you have also narrowed them down to the top five or so for each audience. You know the trends and explanations behind them. Now, see if you can condense that information into a report about two pages long! Or put it on an intranet with a *risk dashboard*. Keep it very brief and to the point. By doing so, you will make an immediate impact on your board members and senior management.

def•i•ni•tion

The **risk dashboard** is a reporting tool used by risk managers to see all information about risk in an easy, accessible format. Often, it consists of a website in which the risk manager can drill down into different layers of information. If your company has an intranet, then risk dashboards are perfect.

Be sure the report spotlights not only pure risks but also risks versus return. That way, you can gain perspective over the entire view of the key risks' relationship to your business. Don't forget to build in some good news as well, such as successfully implemented risk mitigation or an averted risk event. Make sure that risk is viewed positively, particularly when you are working toward a change in the company's culture and attitude toward risk.

Set a Schedule

Determine a schedule for generating risk reports and follow that schedule consistently. When determining the frequency with which you will issue reports, consider the following questions:

How often can you realistically update information on risks?

How meaningful is the update? How often do the types of risks move or change?

What sort of reviews or reporting cycles would generate the need for a report?

Most companies prepare monthly or quarterly reports. If you carry more financial risks, then your reporting frequency would increase, perhaps becoming monthly. (Some risks move even faster, such as trading risks.) If you have more operational risks, then you might consider quarterly or semiannual reports. Strategic risks may require only semiannual or annual summaries.

Keep in mind that every business contains notable differences in operations, strategy, finances, and types of risk. Ultimately, the frequency of reporting will be determined by how often your risks change—and how they shift the company's overall landscape.

The Least You Need to Know

- ◆ When you build risk into your business processes, you improve those processes *and* create money-making opportunities.

- ◆ Budget for risks directly as part of your planning exercises. Include risks in budgets for projects and business processes.

- ◆ Set up regular monitoring of risks in your business processes.

- ◆ Reward your employees with incentives and bonuses for managing risks and hitting targets based on risk versus return. (Not only return.)

- ◆ Regularly report on key risks. Make your risk summary reports *brief* action statements—no more than two pages.

Chapter 21

Your Risk Appetite

In This Chapter

- Identifying the right risk level for you
- Creating your risk appetite statement
- Deciding on risk and return targets
- Setting risk boundaries
- Managing within the risk appetite framework

Successful risk management is directly tied to a company's ability to gauge its risk appetite and work within its parameters.

The risk appetite serves as both a benchmark and a reminder of the company's overall willingness to take risk. Senior management and the board use this critical tool to set the organizational tone from the top. They articulate how much risk the company is willing to take, in what areas, and for what sort of return. The risk appetite statement also describes the types and degree of risk a company specifically wants to take and avoid.

The Broad Concepts

Your risk appetite encompasses the following broad concepts:

- **The overarching statement of risk appetite.** As a company, how hungry are you for risk?

- **How much risk you expect to carry.** What is the right amount of risk? Try to answer these questions in quantitative, numerical terms.

- **Your risk versus return profile.** What return will you seek for your risk? What mix of risk and return will you see across your products and services?

- **Your threshold for risk.** How will you control your threshold so you can manage within the company's set risk appetite?

Best Bets

If the company has a management team and a board of some sort, then it's incredibly useful to make the articulation of risk appetite a more formal process or at least a focused discussion (perhaps a whole day or a dedicated session) with one or both of these teams.

By addressing these key ideas, you can build a risk appetite statement that communicates your view on risk-taking and helps you manage to that view throughout the year. The most important thing is to arrive at statements, thresholds, and numbers that *feel* right. Your risk appetite must align with the persona of the company. This includes corporate values and operating style and behavior. Align it to the company's values and the people driving those values.

Ultimately, your risk appetite statement drives the message to the rest of the organization. Make it reflect the way you want to operate your business. If it doesn't feel right, it probably isn't.

The Risk Appetite Statement

The risk appetite statement is both a physical document and a process. The main goal is to write down your business's disposition toward risk relative to return.

The risk appetite statement has three goals:

- To set the risk tolerance for the company (appetite and measures)

- To provide the basis for a risk limit structure consistent with this tolerance and strategy

- To provide management guidance for annual business and the strategic planning process

Risk Factors
The risk appetite is *the* key mechanism for setting the tone from the top. It embodies all of the key directions that the organization requires at a high level and provides the key pieces of information required to manage risk. Risk management teams use thresholds and the confidence interval established by the risk appetite to measure and set limits and other mitigation devices. Also, the risk versus return expectations inform line managers about the type of balance required on their parts.

Once you have determined your risk parameters, elaborate on the ways you see risk playing out. Use the preceding goals to help communicate your willingness and ability to take risk to the organization, board, investors, and any relevant external groups. Answer these questions:

> How would you describe your relative willingness to take risk?
>
> What is the total amount of risk that you can stand?
>
> How does that risk break down among your departments and specific risk classes?
>
> What are your perceived limits?

How Hungry Are You for Risk?

The answer to this question is the name of the game. Think very carefully before you decide how much risk is the right amount for the company.

Very few companies, if any, can succeed without taking any risks. The results of well-chosen risks often separate highly successful from mediocre companies. At some point, you will want to take some risk—even if you are risk-averse. Define, describe, and articulate the amount of risk with your risk appetite statement.

Chances are that most company leaders already have a feel for their risk appetites, but they may not have articulated their feelings—certainly not formally. Have you ever tried to write down your personal feelings about risk?

Pinning down and committing your risk appetite to a formal document is difficult but necessary. Think about how you would describe your risk appetite. Are there examples in your industry that invite comparison? Are there sectors of customers, products, or other elements that allow you to create a clear risk message? Can you think of the types of risks to take—or not take? Some companies clearly state that they will not involve themselves with certain types of risk.

Best Bets _____

Establish a position for your risk-taking relative to competitors and other companies in your industry. Are there companies that you admire whose approaches you can model? Are there direct competitors? How do you compete? Where are you better? What is the key to that success? Is it because you are aggressive? Careful? Because you make more informed decisions? Do you excel in one area, your core competency? Are there aspects of your industry that might prompt you to change your past strategies and forms of risk-taking? Any new competition breathing down your neck or new regulations forcing you to be more careful? How about changes in the supply chain? Use these questions to gain perspective on your overall conduct in the marketplace and what you believe your company requires to successfully meet its goals and objectives.

The next step is to broadly size your risk appetite. Are you aggressive, risk-seeking? Or are you careful, risk-averse? How do you see your company as a whole?

If you are considering strategic planning, then build these questions about risk directly into the process. Every new strategy comes with an objective—and a set of risks, whether small or large. Consider your outlook on those risks as you work through the process.

What Is the Right Amount of Risk?

This is a tough question, possibly the toughest for any company to answer. It haunts senior executives everywhere. The answer offers little comfort: the right amount differs for each company.

Nevertheless, someone must guide the company through the myriad decisions that create a sum total of risk. The idea is to shift the focus from risk appetite as a general concept to establishing specific quantitative anchors. These are described either in economic capital or the confidence interval. As you may recall from Chapter 10, the confidence interval is a set of numbers that reflects the overall riskiness of the company. It is often derived from its target debt rating. To arrive at these numbers, spell out the total risk-taking behavior of the company. After that, understand each of the company's core risks and their relative values. How much of each would you carry?

Risk management experts have identified two ways in which companies can think about their risk appetite quantitatively. These are best described using the following questions:

What is the maximum loss you could sustain and still survive? The answer will certainly establish one clear boundary. It shouldn't reflect a comfortable pull-through, but a situation in which the company *barely survives*. If you need to hold additional capital for investment or dividends, consider those in your final number. That will leave you with an established maximum economic capital figure for your risks.

What is your own company's default probability? Instead of considering your customers' likelihood of defaulting on their loans, think about your own likelihood of default. In other words, if someone were to lend you money, how would they perceive you? Could you pay them back? Or would you become the bad debtor we've been talking about?

More on Credit Ratings

When you determine your company's default probability, you also reveal its likely credit rating. If you have a credit rating for your company already, perfect!

To assess risk appetite, seek the relationship between credit ratings and confidence intervals. If you don't have a credit rating, try a couple of other approaches. First, identify a competitor and check out its credit rating (if it has one). Chances are that your rating will be similar, particularly if your businesses include similar products, similar strengths and weaknesses, and so on. You can also look at companies you admire, particularly within the industry. Check their credit ratings. That may be a starting point for you.

When using this approach, remember that the concluding number is the *target* credit rating. It's where you want to be someday; it could differ from your current position. Of course, you can always evaluate the definitions for each credit rating and go from there. Since you're shooting for a target rating, your final figure will not necessarily be the rating an agency would give you. The important thing is to identify how you want to run your company and be perceived.

Remember that most companies would like to be rated more highly than junk bond status (99.9 percent safety rate). However, those same companies recognize that the AAA rating (99.99 percent) may be too squeaky clean of risks to achieve the growth and profitability they seek. An AAA rating also implies large amounts of capital to be held as buffer, which may be beyond your means and intentions as a firm.

At this point, your risk appetite numbers should correlate directly to the confidence interval. Your risk management people, or outside consultants, will build the measures and buffers to meet the target you set. In so doing, you provide consistency across the organization and through the risk process.

Target Risk and Return

Part of the risk appetite must also consider the reward side. After all, you are in business to make money for the products or services you provide. And your ability to make money depends on how well the risk versus reward relationship runs in your company.

Start by considering how your return target aligns with your capital target. If you merely align these targets, will you be satisfied? Some industries set benchmark returns that need to be topped. Often investors expect some sort of return for their capital investment. How well do these expectations line up with the risk-adjusted return (implied by the economic capital threshold described in the previous section)?

def•i•ni•tion

A **hurdle rate** is the rate of return the company will try to meet or exceed. It is especially handy if you have a company with multiple departments or sales people. It allows you to set a rate in line with the risk-adjusted return implied by your risk appetite.

Use budget and forecasts to set up risk-return expectations. How much revenue do you expect to achieve this year? This should be based on your forecasts. Will there be any reserves required? Work this out to achieve a risk-adjusted return number. Next, divide by the economic capital implied by these activities. At this time, set the *hurdle rate* for the company.

How Do I Take Control?

Once you have quantified key aspects of your risk appetite, take control. Begin to adjust your company to meet your risk appetite. Set thresholds that can be monitored. Establish a target view of economic capital (and possibly reserves, in line with risk appetite expectations) for the year. Then, monitor the risks as they accumulate through the year. You can monitor qualitative statements of risk as well, if you use that approach.

When establishing risk appetite, view the company as a whole. Determine your steps to monitor individual departments or risk classes. These often set the starting point for additional risk limits and controls you may enact for more specific aspects of your business. Companies can monitor risk groups or departments at a high level through the reporting process to make sure that the broad standards set up by the risk appetite are continually being met. You can even set up a formalized limit structure on these high-level targets and build it into your regular reporting, particularly at the board level.

If you take this path, be sure to set up a buffer or trigger point *before* the limit or target is reached. This will give you time to react and respond to risks. This is important for most limits, but especially true of anything that touches or involves the absolute company limit. If it nudges the absolute limit, it might signal or precipitate a serious issue that could threaten the company's survival.

Key Questions to Ask

This section consolidates the list of questions to ask when thinking about a risk appetite. Answer each one, then head to the next section:

How would you characterize your overall willingness to take risk? Is this a strategic choice or a necessity born of the nature of the business/industry?

How do you compare with your competitors when it comes to risk-taking? Do you see yourself as more or less aggressive?

Where have you found your successes—and met your failures?

Are there specific types of risks that you won't take? Things that you won't do?

Are there areas on which you will focus your risk-taking? Where would you allow greater latitude?

Are there any regulatory or compliance expectations that would establish maximum risk-taking or no-go zones?

How will you be viewed by external parties and investors? Do they hold expectations regarding the broad risk-taking of the firm?

Do you have a target credit rating? Do you have a credit rating today—and are you satisfied with it? Is it too high, or too low, to be a long-term target?

Do you have peers or competitors with credit ratings that could serve as benchmarks?

Have you established a maximum sustainable loss? Do you understand what that implies regarding your current operating environment and strategic expectations?

Have you calculated economic capital for each of your risks? The company as a whole? How does this stack up against your current available capital? Your strategic initiatives? What sort of capital consumption do they imply? Have you considered the variance in those expectations and how this would impact your capital levels?

Have you considered each of your core risks quantitatively? Do you hold an economic capital view of them? Can you make a strong qualitative statement about how far you will stretch your core risks?

Have you set up limits for each risk and across each department?

Have you analyzed your yearly forecast to consider expected return for the risks you have identified? How does this stack up against your expectations? Your investors' expectations? Do you have a target in mind? Can you apply that target as a hurdle rate?

Building Your Risk Appetite Statement

The risk appetite statement may take on a variety of forms. However, it always makes a broad statement about the relative riskiness of the company and how that aligns with the way business is conducted. The risk appetite statement could be a one-line declarative comment that is part of a broader mission statement or overarching company policy. Recently, however, companies have branched from the one-liner to compose short documents that elaborate on the one-line statement. Many times the statement is qualitative, but just as often it may include quantitative information.

Navigating Through Risk Appetite

When working out a risk appetite statement, five key steps will enable you to truly reflect on the company's areas of risk hunger, risk aversion, and overall tendency to push the envelope—or not:

Make the high-level risk statement. Build the risk appetite statement as part of the strategic planning and budgeting process. Think about the direction the company is heading and the strategic initiatives that will get you there. Consider how this will impact growth expectations and the budget over the next year, then start with a few qualifying and focusing questions. What sort of growth and activities will happen? Where? How do these factors affect your idea of risk-taking and the types of risks you see playing out in the near and longer term? It's important to arrive at a common idea of these considerations with your board and senior management. Do the hard work; boil down your responses to a few key, overarching statements.

Get specific. Make specific statements about your total risk tolerance. It is best to do this, if possible, in the context of the total amount of capital at stake (economic capital or maximum loss threshold) and for each area of risk. Figure out your target solvency standard—the target debt rating. How will you use this within existing models and measures? What does this imply for current company activities? Conduct these measures in a two-step process. First, identify the key areas to call out. Then, using the plan for the year, forecast the impact on each risk area. If possible, do this quantitatively as well as qualitatively.

> **Best Bets**
>
> When specifying your risk tolerance, also examine how liquidity, economic capital and equity, regulatory capital, earnings, and your image come into play. How much available liquidity, distributable surplus, or free cash flow will you risk? How much economic capital or shareholder equity are you willing to lay out? How much regulatory capital "surplus" will be put at risk? What about projected earnings? Finally, how much of the company brand value could be affected as a result of adverse press, poor products, poor advice to clients, or other reputation issues?

Target risk versus return. Use the specific measures you just set to project the risk-adjusted return on economic capital, RAROC, or economic profit implied by this plan. Test to ensure that it aligns with expectations.

Set thresholds. Establish the key thresholds. Identify the core risks that you monitor, and whether thresholds will be defined for specific departments, products, or portfolios within the company, rather than generally. What is the maximum risk allowable in each area? How do these contribute to your total risk? Build triggers, and a process to identify and address the situation if a trigger is hit.

Socialize and communicate the process. Besides setting the overall appetite itself, this may be the most important step. Your risk appetite statement must be ratified by both management and the board. In doing so, everyone agrees to the framework and the boundaries it establishes. Also ensure that the risk appetite statement is well communicated to all key employees, particularly those involved with risk management and mitigation and those in key risk-taking positions. Make sure everyone understands the direction.

Setting Boundaries

Your risk appetite statement will only serve the company effectively if you establish realistic boundaries and thresholds. Without them, the statement becomes like a fenceless yard: the shape seems obvious, but individual shoots or entire sections will overtake the boundary before trouble is noticed.

Red Flags

When setting boundaries for your risk appetite statement, avoid the temptation to create precise thresholds that can hamper daily operations. Instead, focus on the overarching thresholds into which all risks should fit. Don't scrutinize the level at which each customer is considered or the controls set for the production line; doing so will make the exercise too complex and unrealistic.

It is vital for you to remember that these are high-level thresholds. They create the starting point for other limits—hard and soft, quantitative and qualitative—to set in the future. They are not intended to be day-to-day limits—at least not on most days.

Now for a few pointers. Once you've set the thresholds, monitor and manage them like any other limit, but on a less frequent basis (normally, anyway). Make your boundaries actionable and able to be checked. Include a trigger or buffer so you have time to react in case of a risk event or potential disruption.

Finally, build the process to monitor and report on the status of thresholds while also addressing any breaches of triggers that might occur.

Determining the Framework

The actual structure of the risk appetite statement can vary from one company to another. Some companies use a highly quantitative format; others use a more qualitative approach. This decision generally stems from resources available to the company with respect to its risk measurement and forecasting capabilities.

Risk Appetite Statement XYZ Inc.

Part I. Summary Risk Appetite Statement:

XYZ Inc. will operate within a _____ (e.g., low, medium, high) tolerance for risk. As such, we will utilize a target credit rating of _____(e.g., AAA, AA, A, BBB) as our benchmark solvency standard, and in line with that a confidence interval of _____(e.g., 99.9%, 99.95%, 99.97%) as our target threshold applied to our risk models. Commensurate to these levels, we will not risk more than _____% of economic capital/equity and _____% of earnings.

This will be reflected in our willingness to focus on the following core activities and risks: _____.

Further, we will specifically refrain from pursuing the following activities and risks: _____.

Part II: Statement of Key Risk Taking:

XYZ Inc. will operate under the following considerations for our key risks and other factors:

Financial Risks: Our core financial risks are _____ (liquidity, interest rate, credit, market). We will operate within the following expectations for each:

  • e.g., Liquidity Risk: XYZ Inc expects an aggressive posture on liquidity risk over the next year and plans to consider _____% of free cash flow at risk.

Operational Risks: Our core operational risks are _____ (people, systems, process, etc.). We will operate within the following expectations for each:

Strategic Risks: Our core strategic risks are _____. We will operate within the following expectations for each:

  • e.g., Reputation Risk: We consider our reputation to be our greatest strength and commercial asset. We will take a conservative position regarding the protection of our reputation. All new undertakings must be reviewed at senior management committee. Any emerging issues with customers or the community must be escalated immediately.

Part III: Risk vs. Return:

We will target _____% risk adjusted return on capital (RAROC) and apply that as our minimum hurdle rate for new projects and other transactions. We expect that each department will generate a return that meets or exceeds that level. A forecast for the company return and risk composition is attached as an appendix.

Part IV: Thresholds:

Each risk will be monitored in line with the operating policies in place and a quarterly report will be provided monitoring the level of risk taking against thresholds as set out below in total and for each of our departments. A buffer of 15% will be set for each risk. A trigger monitoring framework will be used in order to signal activities in advance of a limit breach.

Example:

Risk	Department A		Department B		Total Company	
Credit Risk	$	Exposure	$	Exposure	$	Exposure
Market Risk	$	Economic Capital	$	Economic Capital	$	Economic Capital
Operational Risk	$	Economic Capital	$	Economic Capital	$	Economic Capital

A risk appetite statement enables companies to determine their willingness to take risks.

Nevertheless, the framework of the statement is usually similar. An effective two-page (or shorter) summary can be broken down into four distinct sections:

◆ **Summary statement/objectives.** Clearly state the overall view of risk-taking within the firm, and list any key "do's" and "don'ts."

◆ **Breakdown of risks.** List your core risks and the key levels expected or allowed for each. Make this a quantitative breakdown, if possible. Another alternative is a combination of qualitative and quantitative statements. This section may also include the summary of risks and how it adds up to present the total view.

◆ **Risk-return view.** Consider the implications of risk-taking on your return. The projected RAROC or economic profit can be developed here. The hurdle rate may be stated. This section may also describe how the key business lines or products are likely to stack up from a risk versus return perspective.

◆ **Threshold management.** Indicate how risks break down by department, product, or business function, and how the thresholds will be managed across the company. State or summarize the total threshold for both the company and each risk. Also describe the monitoring breakdown across businesses or departments. The management of triggers and buffers may also be included.

Putting It to Work

The risk appetite effectively begins a process. The process starts with board and senior management strategy and risk appetite discussions. These talks result in the setting of the risk appetite statement, followed by establishing allocations and limits.

A risk appetite process chart tracks the information flow as companies determine their risk appetites.

Risk Appetite Process

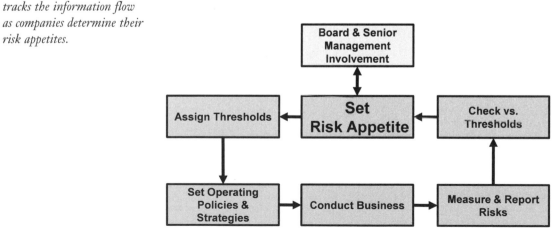

Once this is complete, the organization can take off running, with knowledge of the boundaries for lower-level limits and policies intact. From there, measure your risks, check them against your limits and thresholds, and then manage the process.

The risk appetite should be managed on a yearly cycle, as part of the business rhythm. This enables you to adapt it to new strategies and to consider improvements. In fact, it can serve as the impetus for improvement.

The Least You Need to Know

- A risk appetite statement describes the types and degrees of risk a company is willing to take.

- Set a hurdle rate to establish a minimum expectation for risk versus return outcomes.

- You can guide a company through the year according to the parameters set in the risk appetite statement.

- Set up risk thresholds with triggers to warn you before your company runs into trouble.

- Share your risk appetite statement with all of your key personnel.

Chapter 22

Profiting from Risk

In This Chapter

- ◆ Finding profitable risk opportunities
- ◆ Targeting specific products and services
- ◆ Managing the customer life cycle
- ◆ Pricing for risk
- ◆ Creating better, faster processes

When organizations hear the words "risk management," they often seize up with fear that arises from a single question: "How can we possibly make any money at this?" They also struggle with how to justify risk management investment when things seem to be going "well enough" on the loss front. After all, don't they have more burning issues, such as growing and maximizing profits, reducing costs, and improving revenues?

Now for the good news: with risk, you can have your cake and eat it, too. At least to a degree. Risk management may not be a silver bullet, but you can use it to improve profitability and growth. Information developed in risk measures can be used to optimize processes, which reduces decision time and accelerates execution of transactions or production while improving quality. That same information can help you manage customers better, using targets and guidelines to match customers with the right products at the right price. And finally, you can use your risk information to improve risk-adjusted profitability by offering optimized pricing to better support the risks and costs associated with each customer and product.

For many companies, this is *the* way to justify risk management capabilities and risk-adjusted profitability measures. It certainly presents a better investment case if you regard risk management as more than a way to prevent losses and manage the aftermath. What if you also view it as a means of improving profitability—regardless of potential events?

Risk and Reward Day to Day

It is difficult to convince some management and boards that they need to invest to prevent losses that haven't happened yet. They sometimes think that they can slide by; remember the "It can't happen to me" excuse? Often, good risk management serves as its own worst enemy. If you manage risk well, then often the events don't happen or are minimized, and people start to grow complacent. Maybe, they think, they can ride with less risk management. Maybe they can even ride with none at all. Both trains of thought eventually prove detrimental.

Circumvent this mentality by pursuing all of the returns you can, whether or not the risk actually materializes. Use risk to improve processes, reduce costs, and make money on a daily basis. Begin by moving as much as possible toward specific, quantitative risk measures. Is it possible to get the benefits without this strategy? Yes, but they will be smaller and more limited.

Since it's usually difficult to measure risk and return every day, build the philosophy into the core of your day-to-day operations. Each key decision on operation and process set-up should consider risk and return, either implicitly or explicitly. Using some of the starting measures that follow, establish a relative view about which risks are better and more profitable in each activity. If you've been identifying risks, building tools, and taking the measures described so far in this book, then you may have everything you need to get started.

Where to Look

Roll up your sleeves and prepare to make some money! First, identify your risks and their root causes. This should give you a pretty good idea of what processes, products, or transactions generate your risks. Also determine which risks generate the most variation.

For most companies, the greatest opportunities tend to appear in sales processes or points of contact with customers. This grows both from day-to-day decision-making and from a company's realization that the road to profits travels directly through the customers. This is generally the place that holds the most opportunity for variances (unexpected loss or earnings volatility), as well as different operating models for the process of targeting, selling to, and servicing customers.

Best Bets _____

The object of the game when seeking profit-making opportunities from risk is variation (or unexpected loss). The greater the variation in return generated by your risks, the greater your opportunity to manage your processes and decisions with the intent to profit.

There may be other potentially profitable locations specific to your company and industry, so don't limit your thinking to the customer base. For example, companies that produce physical products are rife with opportunity in their production lines. Many project-oriented companies find opportunities through the way they construct contracts and execute projects. The principles are generally the same.

Three Opportunity Areas

Focus on the following three broad areas when building a risk-and-return approach.

Customer management. Customer management is the process of identifying, targeting, managing, servicing, and addressing customer issues, including collections. This lasts from the time the customer knocks on your door (or you knock on his) until the day he walks away, hopefully satisfied. Each stage of the customer life cycle is an opportunity to use risk information to improve processes and decisions. Which customers generate the best and worst returns? Conduct the same exercise for risk. What are your best and worst risks? Are there stages of the life cycle where this matters more? Look for how (or if) the process changes over time.

Pricing. Arguably a step in the customer life cycle, pricing assumes some unique characteristics. After all, this is the money-making measure. By understanding the nuances of customers and products, you can generate new opportunities to build risk-adjusted profitability directly into your pricing equation. This holds true even if you are in a fairly commoditized industry. Think about how you might adjust your pricing to account for the risk presented by each product and each customer. Would some be higher or lower than the average?

Processes. Does it seem attractive to make faster decisions? Can you reduce costs or catch opportunities by doing so? Does it make sense to identify a "go/no-go" point earlier in the process? If any of your answers are "yes," then it's likely an opportunity exists to use risk information to benefit financially. Focus on streamlining processes and identifying early "go/no-go" points. Consider which processes possess these characteristics and where decision points exist within them. Would certain checks or information at these points change your decisions?

Developing and Targeting Products

Do you know which products are your riskiest? Are there products that are particularly labor-intensive, much harder to make? Or services that seem trickier to execute? Does it matter what sort of customer chooses a particular product?

Risk information can be very useful in the ultimate development of products. You can apply risk information to product development and targeting activities by developing products that are easier to manage and deliver, using risk information to identify broad pricing parameters for products in development, and obtaining new products to help manage already existing risks.

Developing products. You can use existing information from products to work through the development and delivery of a new product. Understand what has gone wrong in the past. Also review the general risk profile on other products to inform your future development. In addition, you can use many techniques, particularly root cause analysis, to test the potential weaknesses in your new products. Once armed with this information, you can avoid pitfalls, build more efficient mitigation and control capabilities, or even choose not to launch a product. This information can also help you price products or target them toward specific customer segments.

Managing risks. Sometimes companies develop new products to help diversify or mitigate risks they already hold. Consider new products that may be targeted toward certain types of customers. This can create diversification in your customer base and better insulate the company against economic downturns or other risks. Depending on your industry and offerings, you may also be able to provide products and services to mitigate your risks. Consider offering installation services with the equipment that you sell. That can often reduce customer complaints and callbacks. Limited warranties are also nice. Some companies offer credit insurance when they extend terms, a direct mitigation to credit losses. Some companies include service contracts. Others provide training and education services associated with other services and equipment already provided.

Pricing products. By better understanding your product profile before you launch a new product, you can price more efficiently. You can better project the cost of the product, as well as what sort of risk mitigation might be required. This helps to determine the type of economic capital associated with these products. From there, evaluate what sort of pricing is required to achieve the returns you seek. You can even consider different pricing for products that provide company-wide risk mitigation or diversification benefits. This approach can also work for products that may attract customers with a better risk versus return profile.

Using Risk Information to Target Customers

Who are your favorite customers? Chances are that your favorite customers personify your "target customer." They are best suited to your products and services, they pay well and on time, and they keep coming back for more. They don't present many customer service problems, nor cost you much time and effort to manage. These are the customers about which you say, "If only they were all like that!"

Try to understand more about which customers are your best, and why. Start by using existing customer information to seek out target customers and those who are almost ideal. There are three broad steps to take in this regard: analyze your current customer base for their risk and return profiles, group the customers into categories or segments, and develop "treatment strategies" for each group.

Best Bets _____

Treatment strategies provide ways to target and deal with each customer group. For some, the treatment strategy might be as simple as saying "avoid." For others, use normal information and marketing processes. Some customers will prove most valuable; you will want to treat them better or lure them in with special offers. Make sure that the special offer's discounts or incentives don't erode the financial benefits of having preferred customers (this sounds obvious, but it happens more than you think). There are more treatment strategies, but this is the way to start thinking about customers.

Targeting customers with risk information generally focuses on prospective customers, not existing buyers (though it works for them, too). You're using information on past customers to help identify new customers. Look for characteristics in old customers to help spot behavior patterns or mannerisms in new customers as they walk in the door.

Categorizing Customers

There is a simple, effective four-part approach to categorizing customers:

Understand the return. Which customers are the most profitable? Amazingly, few companies ask this question. Consider the revenue each customer generates, as well as the total cost (including soft costs) to the company to produce and provide each product. Consider which customers call most often to complain or report problems and which seem to find your processes more difficult. Build this in as a cost. Next, try to rank your customers using the profitability you have just determined. Are there particular characteristics you've spotted? Do some customers provide great revenues but also prove costly? Are there low-cost customers? You can establish some early segment information just by looking at the simple components of profit, even before throwing in risk.

Best Bets _____

Always consider your customer when determining profitability from risk. Do you have repeat customers? Customers that order often? One-time customers? Chances are, you possess all three. Some repeat customers are slow and steady; they seem to fly under the revenue radar. They tend to buy small but continuous amounts, and this often adds up to better business than the "big deal" customer.

Understand the risk. Repeat the previous exercise, only with risk. Can you rank your customers based on their relative riskiness? Better yet, if you have scorecards, can you generate an expected loss and unexpected loss for each? Use specific measures, if available.

Build your segments. Try to plot risk on one axis and profitability or a profitability ranking on another. Often, groupings or clusters of customers will appear. You can even try to get fancy and look at a three-way view of revenue, costs, and risk.

Identify drivers. Drivers are the core characteristics that "drive" whatever outcome you are observing. In this case, the goal is to figure out which customer characteristics you can identify within moments of the customer's walking in the door. These might include features like industry, geography, occupation, age/phase of life, life situation, and so on. If you have public risk information, you may be able to include that information in your set of drivers. Do you have a *FICO* score or credit rating for that customer? Customers with whom you have already done business should be an open and shut case, or nearly so. If you work with drivers, collect information on your customers at every juncture. Save this to apply later to risk versus reward and other risk-as-profit exercises. It will not only help you learn more about your current customers, but also to learn about the segments they may represent.

def•i•ni•tion

FICO is the most widely known type of consumer credit score, representing the credit-worthiness of a person. FICO scores are used in risk-based systems by mortgage lenders to determine the possibility that a borrower may default on financial obligations to the mortgage lender. Every adult in the United States that has ever bought something on credit has a FICO score. FICO specifically stands for Fair Isaac Corporation.

If you own or manage a small company, you may already have a good idea about each customer. Reconsider the characteristics just mentioned. You probably won't require sophisticated analysis, but it doesn't hurt to keep track of customer information or to write down observations on your customers and their transactions.

Customer Scorecards and Risk Profiles

Customer scorecards (introduced in Chapter 16) can be used very efficiently as part of this process. Develop a scorecard or risk profile on your customer or the segment that the customer represents. Use the scorecard to achieve a specific risk score or set of scores (likelihood and severity) for each customer. This allows you to understand your customer base in a more specific, individual way. Also use these scorecards with your normal customer management process.

Risk Factors

Scorecards can help with critical up-front decisions concerning customers. Scorecard information can help you spot ideal or preferred customers as they walk in the door (or before) by identifying the key characteristics that create their strong risk-and-return profiles. Scorecards can also help you decide whether or not to do business with a customer—to cut your losses before they occur. Finally, they help you set the business terms or, oppositely, help you determine what you would be willing to do to retain a particular customer.

When a customer walks in the door (or even before, if possible), identify his or her risk. Fill in the scorecard. Involve the customer by asking key questions or developing an application or customer information form. (Banks do this with loan applications. They collect much of the required information to fill in a scorecard and determine the risk of doing business with you.) This information can help you make quick decisions about your customer. What kind of risk is presented? Do you want to do business at all? Maybe you are diverse and can offer different products, services, or prices to the customer based on his risk profile.

Another angle to consider is how you can change the risk level of the customer. For example, if a riskier customer asks for credit, you might want to reduce her exposure. Don't let her charge as much as a more creditworthy customer. Manage the risk before you've even taken it.

Considering Risk in Pricing

Regardless of the type of business you own or manage, there are particularly risky customers and products (and combinations of the two). Virtually everyone in business can tell stories about his or her most challenging customer. In retrospect, would you have priced the customer differently if you knew the risks he presented in advance? Would you have guided him toward a different product offering? Would you have been willing to let him walk away?

There are always customers who take more time and effort than they are worth. Perhaps they are contentious or financially volatile; some even may be litigious. Perhaps they don't pay well—or at all. How do you capture these potential problems and offset the risks in your pricing?

Fortunately, pricing for risk is one of the cleanest, clearest ways to yield big returns through the direct use of risk information in the business process. You can start with a measure that, by now, should be somewhat familiar—RAROC.

A Risk Pricing Equation

Use your RAROC or economic profit calculation (or even a general view of the same information, if you don't have specific details). Have you set a hurdle rate, an average price or minimum return goal you would like to achieve for every customer? That answer becomes your minimum target price. Apply the same information from the equations that we used before. The equation often used is as follows:

$$\text{Price} = \text{Hurdle Rate} \times \text{Economic Capital} - \text{Costs} - \text{Expected Loss} - \text{Taxes}$$

If you have developed real data and measures, this approach works swimmingly. If you don't have all of this data, then consider it in relative terms. Rank your customers and break them into at least three groups—those to whom you would charge the highest prices, average prices, and preferred prices (based on your good relationship with them or other characteristics, such as diversification, that they bring to your "portfolio").

Customer Considerations

When pricing risk, you must decide whether you're going to provide separate packages for customers based on their risk profiles. If you do, several considerations then enter the picture.

One is the preferred customer, the individual whose standing is so good and risk so low that you want to keep doing business. So you offer discounts. Often a discount returns its weight in gold, but sometimes companies go too far. Many make the mistake of pricing too low or providing preferred relationship pricing in advance of the customer's prospective business (which doesn't materialize). In their efforts to sustain good relationships, these companies price themselves beneath profitability. The irony is that the most solid customer often, though not always, enjoys the discretionary income that makes her the most likely to be able to afford your higher prices. Don't discount so steeply that you erode the benefits of the good customer relationship.

Now for the flip side. You may discover that your risk-based pricing assessments yield very high suggested prices for your worst customers. Are these customers you might be willing to forgo? Some companies use scorecards to determine that they don't want these customers. If a customer scores higher than a threshold number on the scorecard, then sensible companies won't do business with him. Other companies may be more willing; if you're one of them, charge the customer for it. If you price correctly, it may be worth the risk. However (out comes the red flag!), remember that you encounter all of the risks attached to that customer. Be prepared. Don't assume you can reap the reward without putting in the work.

Another benefit of risk-based pricing is reducing *adverse selection*. Data and experience show that customers often possess an intuitive feel for their own riskiness. These customers will often seek out appropriate prices for their relative risks. If you price too low, you will attract many moderate- to high-risk customers. If you price too high, you will shoo away good customers. This is particularly true with competitors using risk-based techniques for their pricing or where prices are heavily negotiated. Customers are especially aware of where they stand, particularly since credit scores are as easy to obtain as a single mouse click on a computer.

def•i•ni•tion

Adverse selection occurs when you misprice products or services and consequently attract risky customers or lose good customers. This often happens when risk is not factored into pricing or different risk levels among customers are not considered.

Some companies may be concerned that they don't have a way to reflect risk in their pricing. Maybe they work in a fixed-price market or sell a commodity. The risk level might not be directly reflected in the price, but adjustments in other aspects of the deal, such as services, terms of payment, volume arrangements, etc., can produce the end effect that you seek.

For example, take the difference between up-front payment and payment in arrears. Discounts are often given to those who pay up front, especially in tough economic times. Those who pay late face late fees and additional finance charges—not to mention dragging out their principal balance. When looking at payment-based consumer services, such as satellite TV, companies might extend free installation or delivery to acquire the customer, then offer an additional premium movie channel for three or six months to a well-paying customer.

Managing Customers

Risk-based approaches also work well in managing customers through other aspects of their life cycles. In addition to their natural inclinations, customers develop varied characteristics and buying patterns over time. Some are overly demanding, while others always lose the invoice. Some pay promptly, while others are notoriously lax. A few might even be litigious.

Monitor these characteristics in your short- and long-term customers. Build them into your risk-based pricing. Do you have customers who return routinely or who have contracts or products with long lives? Service contracts, supply contracts, credit, and even repeat purchase relationships can fall into this category.

When managing customers over time, there are a few key issues to not only address, but solve. Is the customer's risk status changing? Is he or she becoming riskier than before? Or riskier than first anticipated? How profitable (on a risk-adjusted basis) does the customer look overall? Are there opportunities to do more business—assuming he's a good customer?

Customer Profitability

It is vital to monitor the profitability of the customer in two ways: through the products he or she purchases and through the overall relationship.

The first step is to try to identify the RAROC (or economic profit) of each customer. If you don't have these measures, can you find a relative risk ranking to compare against simple profitability? Even a profitability ranking can work (on a 1-to-10 scale, as an example).

Best Bets

To properly study customer profitability, review several key points in your relationship. How does the profitability compare to the customer's risk? Are there opportunities to improve the profitability relative to risk? Are there opportunities to do more business? What is the relationship's overall quality? Do you need to consider the value of the relationship in the price? Or is the customer content? Try to determine the elasticity of demand—the customer's willingness to settle for a certain price. Consider how the customer stacks up on both profitability and risk. Can you reduce his risk in any way? Improve profitability? Seek opportunities to reprice or reduce costs? Are there other items or services to sell?

Any customer who shows a reasonable risk profile is a candidate for well-priced sales opportunities. Consider other offerings that fit within the customer's needs. Over time, those needs are likely to change. Retail customers literally "grow up." At each stage of a customer's life, customers have new needs. They get married, have families, and grow old. Be aware of that.

Business customers are similar. Their companies mature, too. Consider what you offer your customers, and how you stack up against your competitors. Do your competitors hold some of the customer's *share of wallet?* If so, how can you capture a bigger portion of it—or all of it?

Of course, some customers are more sensitive than others to price. The degree of this price-sensitivity is known as the customer's elasticity of demand. At what (high) price will the customer walk away? How low do you have to go before attracting customers? The prices in between are the "zone of indifference." Some companies try to use models (including risk information)

def•i•ni•tion

Share of wallet is the total percentage a customer spends with your company on goods and services compared to what that customer spends with competitors.

to understand these patterns more precisely. Even without models, you may have observed this process when you changed or negotiated prices with your customers. Be aware of where you stand.

Managing the Downside

Not all customers present opportunities for grabbing "share of wallet." In fact, some customers may turn out to be bad news. They seem like good prospects, but for many reasons, their benefit to your business heads south.

How can you tell bad customers from good? Use your risk information to help recognize their behavior, and run through a few revealing questions:

Have you noticed change in your customers?

Are they letting payments slide?

Have they increased the number of times they call for service support?

If the answer to any of these questions is "yes," then your customer is saddling you with increasing risk. Poor payment behavior is a clear sign of a deteriorating customer. If the customer has always paid invoices on time and then starts to slip a bit—or even misses a payment or two—address the matter *pronto*.

> **Risk Factors**
>
> Companies that have many retail customers often use collection scorecards. They work on the same principles as credit scoring but are concerned with identifying the probability of a customer repaying. This allows owners to prioritize the customers on which they will focus and target different strategies to different customers.

Install preemptive practices. Build the responses to the above questions into your scorecards or monitoring approaches. Check your scorecards—and your customers—frequently enough to spot behavioral changes early. Make sure to refresh your scorecards when each payment is due. For some companies, this may require a monthly refresh. Try to recapture those missed payments. If necessary, try another tracking mechanism. Be sure to automate the process if you have a large number of customers.

Collecting from Customers

Few words bring more frustration and anxiety to a business owner than "*collections*." No one wants to take a customer to collections or retain a collection agency to gather the money—at a potential large double loss to the business (loss of money from negotiated settlement and contingency paid to the collection agency). However, collecting something, even 25 percent of the original amount, is better than writing off a complete default. It is vital to learn collections and how to build them into your risk planning and pricing.

Collections are tricky and time-sensitive. A few rules of thumb:

Address a problem as soon as you recognize it. The earlier you start working with your customer on resolution, the better. Chances are, if a customer is having problems paying you, he is also having problems paying others—and those others will pursue payment as well. In this case, be like the aggressive runner who elbows his way to the front of the pack in a crowded race. Work yourself to the head of the line; be the first creditor on the customer's payback list.

Consider the actions you may need to take. Should you look at an immediate contact strategy? Can you discern the customer's situation? Is this issue temporary (a specific event causing the problem) or typical? Look for ways to cut your losses, along with ways to remediate the customer.

When tracking the customer, don't spend more time and effort than the amount owed. This may sound obvious, but it's a trap into which many stumble. Business owners rarely account for time spent on "negative tasks" such as tracking delinquent customers; it's easy to get caught up in the chase.

If you have more than one customer in this position, try to prioritize them. Look at those who owe you the most and have most recently shown payment problems. The longer the time that has passed since payment, the less likely recovery will be. Seek them out early; focus your efforts on those who owe the most.

Creating Better Processes

Risk data can also be used to improve processes and create better ones. Transition points from one process to another provide opportunities to make a measurement of some sort. At each juncture, you can assess the wisdom of moving along with the process or stopping. Many of these pause points require major decisions. They may also provide opportunities to assess your future path. All of this can result in improved decisions, minimized losses, increased profits, or reduced costs within your process.

There are two key approaches to improving business processes as they relate to risk and profitability: staging process decisions and process streamlining.

Staging Process Decisions

With this approach, you intentionally break a process into a series of smaller steps. After each step, evaluate the situation and make a decision: "go" or "no-go." This is formally called *stage-gating*. Stage the process and create "gates" to pass through.

def•i•ni•tion

Stage-gating is a process evaluation method used primarily in project management. The process is broken down and each step assigned criteria to meet before proceeding. These criteria are called "gates." The resulting decision at each gate is black-and-white: "go" or "no-go."

Stage-gating also allows you to build in natural checks. You can easily supply a review forum with hard facts that support transparent decision-making. Stage-gating also lends itself well to documenting results, comparisons, and decisions. You've already tried a form of stage-gating by using scorecards to determine if you want to do business with a customer—or under what circumstances or conditions.

Stage-gating works particularly well in extreme situations. When do you know that things aren't working? If you can spot it, then you can halt the process and stop the bleeding. Even in continuous production line processes, there are times when you might spot that things have moved out of control. Sometimes it's prudent to stop the line and clean or refurbish the machinery. This may be expensive, but it is often even more costly to ignore the problem and churn out bad product, wasting raw materials in the mistaken hope that matters will rectify themselves.

It is more important to stop a process early than to move forward when you know something is awry. Stage the process. That allows for an early end or remediation. Don't continue to spend money that will turn out to be wasted later.

Process Streamlining

Process streamlining works on a philosophy similar to that of stage-gating, but it incorporates other factors, such as multiple decision paths and the need for speed in decision-making. Process streamlining makes an overall business or manufacturing process more efficient. This usually occurs by rearranging process steps or eliminating unnecessary steps. Sometimes, it involves creating new approaches to address exceptions or to expedite specific activities. Often it results in moving decision points earlier in the process. This helps separate treatment approaches that need to be made, which helps eliminate unnecessary additional investment in activities that will ultimately prove fruitless. It also provides critical information earlier in the process, where it can be used to greatest market advantage.

Credit is a good example. When extending credit, it is best to know early in the process if a customer can meet the requirements. If not, then no additional effort is wasted in the sales process. If the customer meets the criteria, then it's important to inform that person so he or she doesn't go to your competitor for the same product that you are providing.

Process streamlining produces two big benefits. First, it reduces repetitive work steps, work-arounds, and time-consuming decision points that are built into the process and may be unnecessary in some cases. Second, it allows you to use existing information to arrive at a decision faster, remove waiting periods, or provide authority to someone or something. This can happen when you use a scorecard threshold to decide "go" or "no-go" or to separate groups or segments into different treatments.

Here's an example. A company wanted to streamline and accelerate its process by quickly determining which customers were most creditworthy and creating a preferred environment for them. The first step was to separate all customers into categories and to determine who could be processed "quickly," with little or no documentation. These customers didn't need a protracted credit history review; they hit the key marks on the scorecard. Other customers required more documentation; still others needed special documentation and treatment.

Through this process, the business weeded out customers who wouldn't survive the checking process. They did so at the start of the process, which saved valuable time and money. Next, the company examined its workforce and matched employee skills and communication styles to each type of task. They assigned more experienced or specialized people to areas that required their skills. Consequently, the company reduced process steps for some customers, sped up actual approvals, and obtained higher-quality results.

The company also enjoyed additional marketplace benefits. By providing a clearer, faster response to its customers and detailing the specifics of the next steps, it was able to jump ahead of its competitors.

Risk management information can often help you decide whether or not it's advisable to move forward or under what conditions to proceed. It allows you to separate product or customer groups rapidly and determine the ways to treat each.

The Least You Need to Know

◆ Each stage of the customer life cycle is an opportunity to use risk information to improve processes and decisions.

◆ Use risk measures to determine potential profitability in a new product before rolling it out.

◆ Vary prices in line with customer risk to manage the downside and provide new profit opportunities.

◆ Stage processes in order to limit risks early.

◆ Use risk information to streamline processes. This will allow you to make decisions faster and reduce unnecessary work steps.

Chapter 23

Lessons Learned

In This Chapter

- ◆ Seeing risk management in action
- ◆ Knowing your business
- ◆ Keeping it simple
- ◆ Finding the right measures

Now comes the culmination of everything for which you've worked on risk management. It's time to see how these models, measures, and mitigating or preventative actions work in actual risk-event situations.

Several cases have already been cited in previous chapters, but it's very instructive to see start-to-finish scenarios of a few situations that are business and risk classics. It's worth spending some time reviewing these sorts of cases. By doing so, you will get a sense of what to avoid and how to develop the right sort of risk responses.

Who knows? If your company is unfortunate enough to run into such a situation, studies such as these might help you catch the warning signs before a risk event occurs.

Case Study: Know Your Business

A company does not have to be too big before a layer or two of management forms. Management can consist of people responsible for sectors of the business or particular geographical locations. It could be as simple as supervising a different shift or running the shop in the next town.

It's perfectly acceptable to delegate management tasks to employees. As a matter of fact, it's often necessary. It's much easier to allow a self-sufficient manager who knows his job to do it than to micromanage every detail. Most of the time, this type of employee empowerment is considered good management.

However, empowerment can sometimes work against you. There are times when it can morph into lax or nonexistent oversight—and that's when things can get out of hand. Companies often start to put so much faith in a good off-site manager that they reduce or eliminate oversight.

Red Flags

Even though media is rife with accounts of business fraud and malicious intent, there are far more incidents of poor judgment causing spectacular business blow-ups and failures. Even some of the situations reported as "fraudulent" were not intended to end that way, though technically, fraud was involved.

Sometimes those good managers overstep their authority and take on new initiatives or make bad decisions. Most of the time, their intent is not malicious (although there are occasional cases of fraud or misappropriation of funds). More often, the problem is a bad or uninformed decision, born out of lack of knowledge of the big picture. Without anyone overseeing the manager's actions, nobody from the top notices at first.

What happens when you lose sight of a person with decision-making ability—and that person makes bad decisions?

Introducing Extensive Enterprise, Inc.

Extensive Enterprise (EE) is an assumed name for a company that consists of a few departments and branches. This company, an old regional magazine publisher trying to branch into new media (Internet publishing, online stores, pop-up advertising, etc.), grew quickly in the past year, thanks to a recent surge in online advertising sales. There are new operational sectors, new locations, new managers, and recently promoted employees. However, EE has been around for a while—since the "good old days" when you could smell the ink from the in-house magazine presses. Often, older companies that experience a growth spurt rely on old approaches and norms. They forget to rethink their view of the world and their operating models.

What's the Case?

When old print media models fell apart from the onslaught of new media in the late 1990s and early 2000s, EE's older management didn't know how to respond to competitors that were shifting to online publishing. EE turned to its younger employees, who knew exactly what to do. They migrated EE's three regional magazines online, set up an online store to sell archival copies of the magazines, created a pool of content that they sold to dozens of other publications, and developed the most dynamic advertising packages of any regional publisher.

As a result, EE started growing—fast. The company promoted a few of its young and upcoming managers, the masterminds of the online migration, to run some of their branch advertising offices. These guys had grown up with the company, so they knew both the old and new practices very well. They were good employees and masterful at their craft; they were hungry for new responsibility.

As they embarked on their responsibilities, the upstart managers' old friend and mentor, the CEO, was completely socked. He had to shoulder the dual responsibilities of managing the core business as well as the exciting new growth. He had new financing and a range of other new issues and activities to address, including finding people to assume the bigger roles and new responsibilities coming their way. The company was outgrowing some of its old employees. They couldn't keep up. The CEO was relieved to know that his young squad could manage the new offices. They would not have to be so closely managed as his older, less-knowledgeable employees.

The young managers in the new branch offices soon realized that their relationships with the CEO had to change. He had always provided guidance before, but now he was too busy. They didn't want to add to his workload. Besides, wasn't this their golden opportunity? They started to test the waters at making their own decisions. At first, they decided what content to package and resell. Soon, though, they were creating and implementing advertising initiatives without first running them by the home base. Some of these initiatives were truly risky, overstepping the company's risk appetite.

Nothing bad happened at first, and the CEO was thrilled. He was clearly relieved that the new managers were handling things. He felt vindicated; they were not only confirming his trust and faith in them, but driving profits as well. After years of being at the company, he had given the young charges their big breaks. His decision to promote and reassign them was proving to be a smart idea on all counts. They could handle it; everyone seemed happy. It would work out well.

It didn't take long before the new branches started to struggle. After a few weeks, business hadn't kept pace with EE's huge profitability the previous two years. No one seemed to be aware of the new locations. One of the managers decided to run a promotion. He found an advertiser of MP3 players who provided a great premium deal. Each time a new client advertised, the client received five MP3 players for his staff. This seemed to boost sales well, so the satellite manager decided to try another promotion—and involve the other managers. This time, a beauty products advertiser with plenty of investment capital and marketing dollars supplied ingredients for facials. After the success of the last promotion, the managers decided to "double down" and buy enough product to reward all of the other advertisers for their commitments.

Unfortunately, two things happened: the beauty products were of lousy quality and the company was forced to change materials suppliers, increasing costs. Not knowing this, the manager mispriced the promotion so that EE spent much more money on premium product than it received in new accounts. It didn't take long before people started to complain.

The promotion backfired. The manager was stuck with a huge lot of lousy beauty products, he lost money on the promotion, and EE's reputation suffered.

The branch that launched the promotion grew so unprofitable that it couldn't recover. To make matters worse, it kept trying to right the ship. It sought new beauty products. It tried to massage its disappointed clients. The young manager was so worried about disappointing his boss that he even hid the results of the promotion! Everyone in the office was so busy trying to rescue the promotion that no one reported the financials or conducted any sort of routine reporting. It was easy to avoid discussion for a long time before the CEO really noticed. By the time he realized what was happening, the problematic promotion and office had drawn down considerable company resources.

In the end, EE was forced to close the satellite office and curtail growth in order to stabilize the company.

What Went Wrong?

A number of risks emerged rapidly with EE. This is very common in companies that are growing, particularly when they have been around for a while and have done well. Not to mention when a company is developing a new core competency—new media publishing—that feeds on the skills of young upstarts while leaving the old crew in the dark. They often lose sight of what is required to thrive in a new environment. They believe they can rely on old capabilities and approaches to survive. As well, the home office was too busy to keep tabs on the satellite office's highly risky association with the beauty products advertiser.

The following risk areas went awry with EE.

Know your business. Even though he trusted his young employees, the CEO lost sight of what they were doing. This was compounded by the fact that the CEO himself was less familiar with the new lines of business.

Lack of internal checks and balances. EE had no internal checks or balances. It relied on haphazard verbal reporting. As well, whatever auditing they had in place was insufficient.

Honesty is the best policy. The satellite office manager began to cover up the failure of the beauty products promotion and its associated costs.

Never ignore stakeholder management. Customers are stakeholders, too. By upsetting its customers, EE assumed a reputation risk that cost the company dearly.

Failure to set limits and boundaries. The manager did not have a clear view of where his authority stopped and started. No one from senior management provided him with clear budget limitations or loss limits.

Mopping It Up

EE eventually closed the troubled satellite office to salvage the rest of the company. The CEO also reassigned the young manager to a role more reflective of his core ability: creating unique opportunities for advertisers in the new media world. The loss was severe, but fortunately not enough to take EE down completely.

During his evaluation, the CEO realized that he hadn't paid enough attention to his new managers and departments, particularly those not under his roof. Thus, he began the mop-up of the operation by setting up several checks:

❑ Have routine phone contact with each key manager to discuss day-to-day operations.

❑ Require each manager to issue a monthly progress report comparing his or her progress against key objectives.

❑ Set clear budget limits.

❑ Establish basic policies detailing items or services people could purchase without approval.

❑ Schedule formal quarterly management team catch-ups that preceded major board and investor meetings.

❑ Issue new instructions to external auditors regarding additional review of checks and controls.

Case Study: Keep It Simple

Frequently, companies will move down the path of risk management and like it. This, of course, isn't a bad thing. Companies become proficient at risk management, find the right uses for it, and begin to embrace its many business advantages. They want to do more and more. This holds particularly true for companies that have the resources or skills to adopt some of the more technical aspects of risk management, especially measurement.

Companies are often tentative when they adopt their first risk measures. Then they see how the measures provide insight and real value, offering improvements in pricing, customer management, and other functions. They begin to adopt risk measures aggressively.

The decision to ramp up risk management measures can be spurred by company senior management staffs and boards enamored of the technical aspects of risk measurement. To them, it is a bit sexy. It provides seemingly accurate assessments of the specific behavior of risks and their value.

With more measures in place, skilled risk management specialists can assess, with great precision, how much economic capital is required, what sorts of hedges are most effective, and how much return they are generating relative to the capital.

Usually, all of this is a good thing. There can, however, be too much of a good thing.

Introducing HiTechUS

HiTechUS is a fast-paced company. It grew up out of the dot-com era and established itself rapidly, and it was one of the few companies to survive the dot-com crash. It managed to sustain itself through difficult times by hiring the best and the brightest, folks with advanced degrees from the best universities. These included engineers, mathematicians, and physics majors. The company placed a lot of value on employees who were accomplished in technical pursuits. The entire senior management held technical degrees, as did all of the board.

The company decided to adopt risk management capabilities in keeping with good corporate governance. They learned the concepts and approaches rapidly. They quickly worked out the benefits of risk management and found that it helped control losses and manage quality much better than they had been. They also realized that they could improve profitability more directly. They loved it!

The board and senior management became fascinated with the idea of building a great risk measurement engine. The engine could make sophisticated measures of VAR for the key risks. Senior management put a small team of PhDs on the case, and soon they watched the engine suck in data from a variety of sources throughout the firm. To measure their work, they used scorecards to develop PE and severity measures. They developed correlations among all of their major product, industry, and geographical segments.

Everything was locked in place … or was it?

What's the Case?

HiTechUS made a fair investment in risk management. The company was gaining strong returns, which it believed to be at least partially attributable to its risk prowess.

Over time, upper management used the information it collected to develop more and more sophisticated activities. In the case of HiTechUS, that meant a financial component. The company expanded quite a bit and found it useful to develop hedging strategies. It began to manage customers and portfolios of risks with greater and greater sophistication. In fact, although the company developed software and related products, it began to grow internationally and created a finance function to manage international credit and hedging activities. The company started offering credit to its larger customers and hedging much of its international exposure. The board and senior management were comforted by the fact that all their models were telling them everything was well managed and working within the bounds of their capital and reserves.

As a result, senior management became more and more risk-seeking. They managed their cash flow closely so that they could use extra capital for new investment. They pushed out a few new products faster and into a wider span of the market. If they continued to move at this pace, they would be able to list the company on the designated stock exchange ahead of schedule. An accelerated listing became one of the many goals and objectives that emerged from their risk success. Since the company had such strong risk and financial management capabilities, management thought it would be a very straightforward process.

The financial strategy of HiTechUS was clearly becoming aggressive. The company used more and more credit to create leverage for new investment. It also took advantage of hedges and even made a few opportunistic investment trades that looked attractive.

As the company's models improved, however, they became more complex. It became challenging to interpret the output, requiring a PhD just to read the results. When a report on the meaning of the output was written, it bordered on thesis length.

The people who operated the models kept building on them to pick up the new financial risks. That made them even more sophisticated. They had to create new assumptions and new components of the models. They didn't have time to revamp or check the models they had already built, so they added on to them. They were hoping that, within a year or two, the company would stabilize and they could finally get around to documenting their models and findings and backtesting to make sure everything was working as planned. For the moment, though, everything seemed to work well enough. The model picked up changes in both the market and the company, so there wasn't a great deal of urgency around documentation and backtesting.

Oversight became correspondingly lax. The board and senior management started to ignore the details of the models. They lost track of the assumptions being made, the risks covered, and the core issues within the framework. They didn't have time to read report details. They couldn't interpret the results easily. Thus, they worked on the assumption that the model was okay and operations were running well within the company.

Eventually, the credit and trading sources of HiTechUS became constrained. Due to a tight credit market, the company could no longer support its growth. Liquidity dried up; the company couldn't support its obligations. It took large losses and defaulted on several payments, which destroyed the company's credit rating. When an onslaught of creditors called, the company was forced to liquidate some of its holdings to support the rest of its obligations.

As it turned out, the high-powered HiTechUS model had missed a critical component: liquidity risk. This is a fairly common omission of even the best models, since it is difficult to model well. It is often managed as a separate endeavor.

What Went Wrong?

A number of key factors cost HiTechUS a once-vibrant operation.

Keep it simple. The models became so complex that the board and senior management couldn't interpret them. They didn't know what information the models contained and what risks and assumptions were really covered.

Models cannot replace common sense. The board and senior management became overly reliant on their models, even as their understanding of the model's findings decreased. The models lacked transparency because they became so complex—dreaded "black boxes"! However, management knew from the models when they began running close to the wire on cash flow. They should have been at least broadly aware of their liquidity risk. By abdicating responsibility to the models, they ignored the warning signals.

Test and review assumptions. The board and senior management lost sight of the assumptions baked into their models. They didn't even know what they were, let alone how to test and review them. It's important to understand the broad framework of risk management, the measures being used, and the basic assumptions and premises on which your risk capabilities are built. This helps you determine the weaknesses in your approaches as well as the opportunities for continuous improvement.

Best Bets

Fancy models are nice to have, but not always necessary. You can often do just as much, if not more, with good common-sense approaches. In fact, models should never be used alone. They need to be backed by common sense in order to truly manage risks.

Validate and backtest regularly. The models were never tested or checked. Senior management should know if models are performing as expected. Without third-party validation, no one noticed that the models were missing at least one key risk.

Stress-test regularly. If the company had conducted stress tests, it is likely it would have learned its cash flow management was insufficient to support even the slightest hiccup in its financial strategy.

Make sure all key risks are covered. HiTechUS had clearly missed a big problem: liquidity risk. The company didn't necessarily need to feed this into its models, but they did need to include it in their review and analysis.

Mopping It Up

HiTechUS experienced a long period of disruption. The company almost went under as a result of its behavior. When the company finally emerged from near-disaster, management promptly dismantled the monster model. The model itself wasn't so bad, but it was far too complex to manage and understand. The risk management team separated the model into modules that were easier to manage and understand, both in isolation and as part of the combined result. Now they could test their assumptions much more efficiently and with greater transparency.

As they did this, the risk managers made sure to document the framework and structure of the model, along with its assumptions and gaps.

HiTechUS also went out of house. The company hired a third-party consultant to review its models and the assumptions built into them. Both company staffers and the consultant monitored the process by routinely reporting to the board. The board took a strong interest in the approach and assumptions being used and the issues being addressed. The board established a routine review approach that included stress testing, backtesting, and validation. The consultant was involved with the final check.

Finally, HighTechUS developed simpler, more direct reports. The reports broke down the key components of risk and model outputs in pieces, as well as in aggregate. The company also reviewed a checklist of types of risks routinely and used scenario exercises to help spot new and growing risks as they appeared on the horizon.

Case Study: Using the Right Yardstick

Elsewhere in this book we've talked about the importance of setting up performance measures and tying incentives to those measures.

Putting performance measures in place is like removing a blindfold. Suddenly you can see what is transpiring in the different areas of the business. You can figure out which products and locations are doing well and which are struggling. You can track down the reasons for this more easily and make better management decisions.

Once risk information becomes a part of those metrics, you can make even more informed decisions. You can better understand mitigation choices, identify origination points for the true value of different business aspects, and see the different products, services, and sectors of the business in a new light.

As with all of these situations, though, there can be a flip side. Sometimes you can become overzealous or implement measures too quickly. When this happens, you can miss some of the subtle aspects of measures, as well as human nature.

Introducing the GoGrow Company

The GoGrow Company found itself in the doldrums. For many years, it had produced fertilizer and seed products for both retail and business uses.

But GoGrow needed to be revitalized—and senior management knew it. They decided to revamp the company through a number of new management techniques. Recently, they implemented a number of new risk management capabilities throughout their production areas. They streamlined processes and improved the quality and control of their manufacturing procedure. Things were going very well.

The next step: building in greater capabilities as part of their sales and customer management processes. Enthusiastic with their results, GoGrow moved on to performance measures and incentives for its sales force.

What's the Case?

GoGrow was beginning to turn itself around; already, it had taken numerous correct steps. Choosing to add risk-adjusted performance measures and align those with their incentives and salary discussion was a good idea.

The company completed the process of building performance measures. Management decided on an approach in which they applied a variant of RAROC and made a number of accounting adjustments to the core equation. That way, they could benchmark the company's performance against competitors. They were thrilled with the prospect of finally being able to get a clear, apples-to-apples comparison against the competition. The measure was so attractive that they decided to use it internally as well.

Before the first quarter had passed, GoGrow's board had become so enthusiastic about the measure that they decided to start using it to remunerate performance. That way, they could align their sales force with internal company objectives. It made sense to use the same metrics!

They rolled out the plan with only the most cursory planning. There was no discussion or education of the sales force or direct management. After all, they were broadly familiar with the risk measures; what discussion was required? In the first quarter, the company ran into some general timing issues with completing the measurement, but management attributed that to first-time set-up issues.

As time went on, though, the sales managers became confused. They weren't sure they understood the measures and how they were generated. Much of the information consisted of items they couldn't track; numerous accounting adjustments further confused them. In addition, they found that the earlier timing problem didn't end with the first quarter. It was too hard to prepare the numbers; they didn't finish until many weeks after the reporting period ended. This interminable lag time without information further infuriated the sales managers.

Eventually, a few of the sales managers started to understand the basics by trial and error. They found that it wasn't too difficult to hit their targets. They just needed to sell some of their mainstream products to easier repeat customers and the problems took care of themselves. They found that they didn't need to sell many specialty products. The sales managers had always found those products a bit challenging anyway, since they were designed for specific customer needs, and the particular customer set who bought them was the most challenging. Additionally, the sales managers no longer felt the need to seek out new customers. The model seemed to be fairly insensitive to how much they sold. All that mattered was that they made good deals. The better the deal, the better their bonuses.

After a while, the sales teams focused on selling fewer and fewer items, cherry-picking deals on a risk-adjusted return basis and weeding out the less attractive prospects. There was no point in working hard on difficult deals when they didn't get paid for it, and management didn't fully understand how the numbers broke down, anyway. Besides, most of the sales force and their immediate management were too frustrated with the measures to care.

In time, the company faced a real shocker. Even though the quality of its deals increased, the volume decreased dramatically. Rather than growing, the company was shrinking. By the time management finally recognized this sharp downturn, GoGrow had severely damaged its market position. This, in turn, increased its unit costs, and the company fell into a downward spiral.

What Went Wrong?

A review of risk management principles as they pertain to GoGrow's situation reveals a series of missteps that coalesced into a major downturn.

Establish simple and transparent measures. GoGrow implemented hard-to-understand measures that were also hard to generate regularly. These measures frustrated the sales force by making it difficult to meaningfully track activities.

Align incentives properly. The measures only captured part of the company's objectives and did not address the need to manage and improve sales volume and growth.

Validate the approach. GoGrow failed to fully plan out the process and its potential consequences. The company didn't realize that its complex measure would be hard to generate and slow to provide feedback.

Communicate and socialize with stakeholders. The new approach was not properly communicated with the sales force. They rapidly lost interest and faith in the approach and opted for the easy route, even though they likely knew it would yield undesirable outcomes.

Mopping It Up

GoGrow eliminated the performance and incentives approach and moved back to the old *modus operandi* of rewarding sales volume. Market share slowly returned. However, it took a while before the company could bring back either the risk-adjusted performance measures or the incentives tied to them. The whole concept of complex performance metrics had so annoyed the workforce that no one wanted to hear any more about them.

Eventually, GoGrow relaunched the program. The company built a simpler measure of RAROC for routine reporting and performance tracking. Then GoGrow waited nearly two years to ensure that the front line would accept the approach again. Finally, management initiated a very clear RAROC program accompanied by growth incentives.

As part of rolling out the new incentives, GoGrow made sure to engage key salespeople and key management in both the process and design of the new metrics. The company ensured that everyone understood the measures and also delivered timely monthly reports that were easy to understand.

It's a Wrap

There it is—risk management in action. Each of these case studies demonstrates that specific risk combinations are unique to each business and its objectives. So are the specific combinations of risk management measures and solutions that are deployed. However, as these case studies also make clear, you can use a particular combination of the same tried-and-true rules and guidelines to effect good results—no matter what type of company you run. That is the beauty of risk management and why it is vital to your company. Especially in these uncertain times.

The Least You Need to Know

◆ Good risk management involves balancing the types of measurement and management approaches against the types and materiality of risks and the level and capability of your workforce.

◆ Seek out tools and measures that work simply and efficiently for your business—no more, no less.

◆ Always use common sense, and don't become overly reliant on even the best models and measures.

◆ Check measurements and monitor potential risks regularly and routinely.

◆ Develop checks and balances within your organization; keep your finger on the pulse.

◆ Use the tried-and-true approaches in this book to build a strong, stable risk management program. Good luck!

Glossary

4ME   A shorthand way of referring to the key root cause characterizations. It stands for Man, Machine, Materials, Method, and Environment.

actuarial theory   The "science" used by actuaries—the people who develop and manage insurance pricing and predictions—that considers risk as the possibility of loss.

adverse selection   When bad results occur because buyers and sellers have different information. This happens when risky buyers show unique tendencies or practices of which the sellers are unaware. These buyers are attracted to certain products which make the cost of supplying the product to them more than original expectations held by the seller when the product was manufactured and the price point established.

backtesting   Checking the effectiveness of risk measurement predictions by verifying how predictions compare to actual results.

basis point   Unit of measure used to describe the percentage change in the rate of a financial instrument. One basis point is equivalent to 0.01 percent.

benchmarks   Data or individual measures drawn from other company examples or calculated from other sources.

black box   A risk model that lacks transparency of its specific risk assumptions, measures, and findings. These models sometimes create as many risks for the organization as they are meant to manage.

blow-up   A sudden major disruption or failing of a known successful business, due to some sort of breakdown. These often entail policy, values, measures, and/or governance issues.

bottom-up approach   A method that takes individual risks and looks at how they behave together in an additive fashion.

business continuity plan (BCP)   An emergency contingency plan that spells out how to recover and restore functions that have been partially or completely interrupted.

business rhythm   The cycle of activities that revolves around financial management and monitoring.

capital allocation   Attribution of economic capital, or other forms of capital, to each core business, product, and/or location.

capital at risk   The amount of available cash that could diminish or be wiped out in the event of an unexpected loss.

capital buffers   Money put aside from the capital base to support unexpected losses. Also sometimes synonymous with *economic capital* and *capital at risk*.

capital multiplier   A number multiplied by the standard deviation (unexpected loss) in order to yield economic capital or capital at risk.

cash crisis liquidity plan   A contingency plan, used in the event of a liquidity crisis, that shows potential sources of rapid cash, sources to call, and parts of the operation to shut down (or initiate).

compliance   The successful fulfillment of regulations, usually set by a financial institution (for borrowing purposes) or industry standards.

concentrated risks   A number of small risks that collect or merge into one big potential risk.

confidence interval   The relationship of economic capital to unexpected loss, reflecting what amount of economic capital will cover all likely losses within a specific risk appetite.

contagion   A chain of events, triggered by one incident, that affects other departments or aspects of a company.

contingency plans   Specific planning designed to create a quick response after the occurrence of a risk event.

continuous improvement   Managing the process of continuous change, upgrades, and advancements in risk skills, measures, uses, and other capabilities.

contribution method   An approach to performance measurement that yields a specific dollar amount rather than a percentage. Economic profit is a contribution method.

correlation   The degree of relationship between two variables; in risk management, specifically the degree of relationship between potential risks.

correlation coefficient   A figure quantifying the correlation between risk events. This number is between negative one and positive one.

correlation matrix   A table that describes the correlations between one factor and every other factor.

cost-benefit analysis   An evaluation that determines the value of an approach relative to its costs and benefits; used in risk management to evaluate mitigation strategies.

covariance   A statistical measure of how much two variables change together

criticality   The level of seriousness of a risk.

customer management   In risk management, the process of identifying, targeting, managing, servicing, and addressing customer issues, including collections.

derivatives   Financial instruments whose values are derived from the underlying value of other assets.

disaster recovery plan   A contingency plan that goes into effect after a full disaster occurs, used to reestablish basic capabilities and resources.

distribution   A common mechanism for portraying and measuring uncertainty in risk. It reflects the range of events that may occur, their frequency or likelihood, and impact.

distribution curve   A graph that shows the way in which risk disperses by potential likelihood and impact, where likelihood is plotted on the y-axis and impact is plotted on the x-axis.

distribution tail   The long end of the distribution curve; the fatter the tail, the greater the risk estimates.

diversification   The branching out of products, assets, or services into several different types and lines or different markets or customer bases.

drivers   Core characteristics that "drive" an outcome.

earnings volatility   The variance of earnings. The lower the figure, the more stable the business.

earnings volatility analysis   Measuring the volatility (standard deviation or unexpected loss) of a company's earnings over time.

economic capital   The amount of capital that could be placed at risk in the event of an unexpected loss. These are the real risks of the business activity. Synonymous with *capital at risk* and frequently with *capital buffers*.

economic profit   A performance measure used to understand real profit contribution when analyzing risk-adjusted returns.

expected loss   The mean loss rate generated by multiplying probability of default, exposure at default, and loss given default.

exposure   The amount of money one could lose in a risk event.

exposure at default   The projected potential total dollar and asset exposure at the time of default.

exposure limits   The total allowable exposure to any particular risk factor.

external event information   Data gathered by studying outside businesses or industries to see how risk events occur and their impacts.

financial risk   The threat of any outside or inside issue or event to the monetary strength, profit margin, or capital investment of a business. This category includes cash flow, liquidity, budgetary requirements, tax obligations, creditor and debtor management, direct capital markets effects, remuneration, and other general account management concerns.

force majeure   The "God forbid" risk of disaster—tornadoes, hurricanes, floods, and fires. War is also considered a *force majeure*.

forward   An over-the-counter contract between parties that determines the rate of interest, or the currency exchange rate, to be paid or received on an obligation beginning at a future date.

four lines of defense   A common organizational model of in-house risk management that includes business management, risk and compliance, auditing, and senior management and the board.

front-page test   A test of reputation risk: What would a newspaper's banner headline say about your worst-case loss scenario?

futures   A standard contract to buy or sell a standard amount and quality of a specified commodity at a certain date, at a market-determined price.

"go/no-go"   A decision to proceed or stop, built into various risk management strategies.

governance   The "checks-and-balances" method that keeps risks in check; a review of measurements, mitigation methods, and risk monitoring results over a period of time.

growing the upside   The process of expanding a business and increasing its potential.

hard risk limits   Setting an absolute numerical limit or threshold of acceptable risk for a particular project or business.

hedging   Offsetting the effect of risks by receiving cash flows when risks are high or the business climate unfavorable.

hierarchy of assurance   A means of monitoring risk relative to seniority of personnel and roles in the company.

historical simulation   The process of running historical financial parameters through one's current portfolio of financial instruments to gauge how that portfolio would have behaved under past circumstances.

horizon time   The target timeline for fulfilling a project or measuring a risk; for risk measures, usually one year.

hurdle rate   The rate of return a company will try to meet or exceed.

idiosyncratic risk   The portion of risk unique to specific factors (the customer, project, industry, operation, etc.).

incentives   Bonuses and other rewards given for meeting or exceeding performance targets.

iterative process   Arriving at a better decision or desired result by repeating rounds of analysis or operation cycles.

key man risk   Risk surrounding the departure or leakage of information from the most vital employee in a department or company.

know your customer   A concept tied to the risk behaviors and needs of the individual customer. In risk management, closely tied to regulation regarding anti–money laundering, external fraud, and antiterrorism measures.

lagging indicators   Data that reflects a slower reaction to economic or market changes; useful to describe trends.

leading indicators   Information that helps to forecast an increase in risk likelihood or severity before it appears in actual risk measures.

leakage   The amount of financial or other resources that fall through the cracks.

life cycle   The life span of a particular business rhythm or activity. There are business life cycles, customer life cycles, and even risk event life cycles.

limit trees   Risk limits that start at a central top limit and break down as "branches" across a company's departments, divisions, portfolios, or product lines.

loss event capture   Recording all losses that have occurred in the organization.

loss given default   Same as *severity*. A measure of losses, net of recovery, all costs, and including the time value of money. Used in financial risk measurement, particularly credit risk.

materiality   The importance or significance of an amount; used in risk management to assess the most important risks.

material risks   Risks that have grown to a size that must be addressed.

metrics   Groupings of data, or numbers, that reflect specific measures or subjects.

mitigation   The reduction or confinement of risk events once they have occurred.

models   Equations or measures developed to evaluate specific types of risk. There are countless risk models.

modern portfolio theory   A popular theory, defining risk as earnings volatility and taking into consideration the concepts of correlation and diversification: the more a company diversifies its holdings, products, and marketplace, the more risk can be reduced—to a point.

monitoring   Systematic tracking of specific risk issues.

Monte Carlo analysis   A method using a random number generator to create a set of market rates and apply them to a specified equation or algorithm; most commonly used in models to generate a distribution of potential outcomes.

Mutually Exclusive, Collectively Exhaustive (MECE)   An ideal way to categorize risk, because it involves every company risk while addressing the issues posed by each.

natural hedge   An investment that reduces undesired risk, often by matching revenues and expenses.

odds   In risk management, the likelihood of an event occurring versus the likelihood of an event not occurring.

operational risk   The risk of loss resulting from inadequate or failed internal processes, people or systems, or from external events. This includes fraud events, security issues, and external events, including natural disasters and political events.

opportunity cost   Loss of money, reputation, or positioning from the inability to seize an opportunity or complete a major task or project.

options   A contract between a buyer and a seller that gives the buyer the right to purchase or sell a particular asset on a future date at an agreed-upon price.

outsourcing   Transfer of a segment of business to another company or specialist.

parametric VAR   A value-at-risk measure that assumes that future behavior will replicate past behavior, applying a normal distribution to mean and standard deviations.

partnership model   A business model that improves understanding of risks and joins together planning and management.

pilot program   A test or experiment that usually takes place in the course of business operations, over a sufficient period of time.

Porter's Five Forces   An economic standard process for identifying the strengths and weaknesses of a company's present competitive position.

portfolio risk   The risk of particular investments and their effects on the overall portfolio.

predictive model   A model that tries to predict future behavior using past behavior.

probability of default   Likelihood that a debtor will default within a one-year horizon time.

probability of event   Likelihood of an actual risk event occurring within a one-year horizon time.

probability of loss   Estimated likelihood of financial and material losses due to a risk event.

project risk   Threats to the management of equipment, finances, resources, technology, time frames, and people associated with specific projects.

rank ordering   An analysis method that evaluates risks from highest to lowest.

recovery data   Information that helps to recover defaulted payments from customers.

replacement probability   Likelihood of risk recurrence following a risk event.

reporting cycle   The frequency of filing risk management and other reports; varies from daily to annually.

reputation risk   The damage to a company's image and standing resulting from outside events or shoddy practices.

reserves   Money set aside to offset expected losses.

risk   A predictable or unpredictable event that has an uncertain outcome.

risk appetite   The amount of risk that a company is willing to absorb and sustain.

risk appetite statement   A working document that spells out the risk parameters of a company, as well as its preferences for taking or not taking specific risks.

risk assumptions   Evaluations of existing risk, completed before and after a risk assessment.

risk classes   Categories and subcategories of risk, stemming from financial, operational, and strategic risk.

risk culture   The corporate policy, philosophy, and attitude that determine how a company approaches risk.

risk dashboard   A summary of risk and related reporting information, generally displayed in a web-based format.

risk event   An event leading to the disruption of operations, caused by factors (risks) either known or unknown.

risk management theory   A theory that uses volatility, risk probability, and severity of loss to determine the level of risk.

risk manager   A company official or outside expert who oversees all risk operations for a department or the entire enterprise.

risk matrix   A graph that compares the likelihood and severity of risks from highest to lowest.

risk profile   The overall sum and degree of risks a company possesses.

risk rating   An assessment measure used to rate a customer's risk (usually risk of default on a financial obligation). This approach may be applied widely to many types of risks and specific applications.

risk register   A record of a company's risks.

risk table   A tool used to better understand and predict the likelihood and/or severity of risks.

risk transfer   Shifting currently or potentially risky activities to another company.

risk versus return   Comparison of projected profits of business endeavors with their associated risk.

risk versus reward   The bedrock comparison when evaluating the profitability of risk-taking: How much reward will come from the risk?

risk-adjusted return on capital (RAROC)   A key measure in risk management. A simple return (earnings) is adjusted for risk losses or costs, then divided by the amount of risk associated with the activity.

risk-weighted outcomes   Strategic projections into which the likelihood of a particular risk, or set of risks, has been factored.

root cause analysis   A procedure that traces through a complete chain of events to find the cause of a risk event.

scenario analysis   The process of identifying and evaluating potential risks to your business, and how they might play out, before they occur.

scorecard   An approach to rating risk used in many areas of risk management. A scorecard is most commonly used for rating customer risk (often individuals) as the probability of default in financial risk management.

securitization   Collecting groups of credit assets (loans) into pools (similar to groups), then reselling them as securities.

severity   The potential impact of a risk event.

share of wallet   The total percentage a customer spends on goods and services with your company compared to what he spends with competitors.

shareholder value   The gauge of a company's value to investors, shareholders, officers, board members, and other interested parties.

soft risk limits   Guidelines for risk thresholds that can be adjusted higher or lower depending upon business activity.

stage-gating   A process evaluation method that assigns criteria, or "gates," that must be met before proceeding to the next step.

stakeholders   People directly affected by a company's status. They include executives, managers, employees, suppliers, distributors, regulatory agencies, service providers, shareholders, media, and more.

standard deviation   The measured range of economic volatility that can occur during the course of doing business.

stop-loss limit   A limit at which operations, typically production, lending, or trading, stop and major remedial action takes place.

strategic risk   The current or prospective risk to earnings and capital arising from the business environment, business decisions, or improper implementation.

stress test   A test of a financial or risk model's ability to sustain extreme amounts of stress to its viability.

swaps   A financial tool in which parties with differing business interests exchange—swap—one cash flow stream with another.

SWOT analysis   A method that enables companies to view strengths, weaknesses, opportunities, and threats together.

systemic risk   The portion of total risk that already exists in the company. Also called nondiversifiable risk.

target credit rating   The goal number companies seek when assessing their credit standing.

thresholds   Risk limits to be approached, but not exceeded.

top-down approach   The method that analyzes overall company health, then breaks down that view into smaller and smaller segments.

total loss exposure   The measure of how much a company would physically lose in a risk event, plus related aftereffects.

traffic lights   Three colored signals used to categorize risk: high (red), medium (yellow), and low (green).

transparency   Identifying, quantifying, and openly reporting on a company's risk and mitigation status.

triggers   Figures, or limits, that alert risk managers of trouble when they are hit or exceeded, usually indicating the start of a predetermined process or action.

unexpected loss (UL)   Losses that happen suddenly or that exceed forecasted amounts. Businesses plan for them by holding aside capital buffers.

value-at-risk (VAR)   A measurement method that yields a standard deviation of return.

volatility   The positive and negative swings in business and risk management. Volatility and risk are directly related and complementary.

war-gaming   An approach to strategic risk scenario analysis that shows the point-of-view of both the competitor and the company.

X-bar/R chart   A pair of deviation charts that reveal abnormal risk behavior.

Risk Categories Cheat Sheet

I. Strategic/Business Risks

Risks associated with changes in the business environment, the effect of poor business decisions, incorrect implementation of decisions, or the inability to respond effectively to changes in the business environment.

Commercial

This category includes the risks associated with market placement, business growth, diversification, and commercial success. This relates to the commercial viability of a product or service and extends through establishment to retention and then growth of a customer base.

Reputation

This encompasses the threat to the reputation of the business due to the conduct of the entity as a whole, the viability of a product or service, or the conduct of employees or other individuals associated with the business.

Stakeholder Management

This category relates to the management of stakeholders, and includes identifying, establishing, and maintaining appropriate relationships. This includes both internal and external stakeholders.

Technology/Obsolescence

This involves the viability of products, production methods, or business management methods. This extends to recognizing the need for and the cost benefit associated with technology as part of a business development strategy.

II. Financial Risks

This category includes cash flow, liquidity, budgetary requirements, tax obligations, creditor and debtor management, direct capital markets effects, remuneration, and other general account management concerns.

Credit Risk

Also known as default risk. In broad terms, the risk that a loss will be incurred if a counterparty does not fulfill its financial obligations in a timely manner.

Market Risk

Exposure to potential loss that results from changes in market prices or rates.

Traded Market Risk

Associated with the potential of loss in the trading portfolio.

Nontraded Market Risk

Associated with the potential of loss due to market forces but associated with the structural financial position of the firm, rather than the trading portfolio.

Liquidity Risk

The risk of loss as a result of a lack of market liquidity, preventing quick or cost-effective liquidation of products, positions, or portfolios. It also is associated with the inability to cover obligations due to the lack of liquidity.

Interest Rate Risk

The potential for loss associated with changes in interest rates. In the case of non-traded interest rate risk, this is associated with changes in assets or payment flows (in or out).

III. Operational Risks

The risk of loss resulting from inadequate or failed internal processes, people, and systems or from external events. This includes fraud events, security issues, and external events, including natural disasters and political events.

People/Organizational

This relates to the internal requirements of a business, extending to the cultural, structural, and people issues associated with the effective operation of the business.

Business Process Management

This relates to a business's ability to consistently manage its day-to-day operations and delivery of services and products. It includes risks related to service delivery (including customer service, product and service delivery, poor response to customer complaints, etc.), clients, products and business practices (documentation, disclosure advisory, product flaws or inadequate specifications, improper business or market practices), and processes and controls (failed transaction processing, vendor and supplier miscommunication or processing, process control failures, inadequate or failed related documentation).

Systems and Equipment

This extends to the equipment utilized for the operations and conduct of the business. It includes the general operations of the equipment, maintenance, appropriateness, depreciation, safety, and upgrade.

Project

This includes the management of equipment, finances, resources, technology, time frames, and people associated with the management projects. It extends to internal operational projects, projects relating to business development, and external projects, such as those undertaken for clients.

Legal and Compliance

This category includes compliance with legal requirements, such as legislation, regulations, standards, codes of practice, and contractual requirements. This category also extends to compliance with additional '"rules,'" such as policies, procedures, or expectations, which may be set by contracts, customers, or the social environment.

Security

This includes the overall security of the business premises, assets, and people, and extends to security of information, intellectual property, and technology.

External Events

This is associated with risks due to external events such as physical damage due to natural disasters and effects of non-natural disasters and events.

Simple Risk Equations

Several simple equations used to measure aspects of risk were introduced throughout this book. To provide you with a quick thumbnail reference, the equations are presented together.

Severity Calculation

Gross Loss = Total Loss Exposure (Immediate plus related additional effects) + Total Clean-Up Costs + Cost of Recovering or Mitigating the Loss.

Next, subtract What Is Recovered (through returning what was lost, insurance settlements, or other restitution). The Sum is your Estimate of Severity.

$$S = E - R + C$$

$$S = E \times \%L$$

$$S = E \times (1 - \%R)$$

E = Total Loss Exposure

R = Recovery

S = Severity

C = Costs of Recovery and Clean-Up

L = All Losses, Net Cost of Recovery

Alternative Severity Estimate

You can also estimate severity by multiplying the Total Loss Exposure (E) by the Percentage of Total Net Loss (L). Or, multiply Total Loss Exposure (E) by Total Recovery (R).

Expected Loss

PE × LGE = EL

PE = Probability of an Event

LGE = Loss Given Event (Severity)

Unexpected Loss

$$\sigma = \frac{\sqrt{(x_1 - \mu)^2 + (x_2 - \mu)^2 + ... + (x_N - \mu)^2}}{N}$$

Where:

σ is standard deviation (or risk)

x is the value of each of the losses that we have observed

μ is the mean

N is the total number of samples

Adding Up Unexpected Loss

This is the equation for adding up the standard deviations (or ULs) from two different risks, X and Y:

(Standard Deviation)^2(X+Y) =
weight$_{X^2}$ (std dev)^2(X) + weight$_{Y^2}$ (std dev)^2(Y) + weight$_X$ weight$_Y$2cov(X,Y)

Where:

Std dev is standard deviation

Weight = the relative amount (%) of any given asset or risk exposure relative to the total portfolio or group of risk exposures

$$cov = covariance = \frac{\Sigma(X - \mu)(Y - \upsilon)}{N}$$

υ is the mean of risk Y

μ is the mean of risk X

N is the total number in the sample

The Correlation Coefficient

$$\rho = \frac{cov(x, y)}{std\ dev_x\ std\ dev}$$

Where cov = covariance

$Std\ dev$ = standard deviation

ρ = correlation coefficient (diversification) between a and b

Economic Profit

Economic Profit = Risk-Adjusted Return – Cost of Capital × Economic Capital

Risk-Adjusted Return on Capital

RAROC = Risk-Adjusted Return ÷ Economic Capital

RAROC = (Revenues – Expenses – Expected Loss – Taxes) ÷ Economic Capital

Risk Management Resources

General Reference

Do a quick scan of your favorite online book retailer and you'll find a plethora of resources on risk management. It can actually be quite overwhelming. I've helped narrow the field by picking resources that are most helpful, particularly when starting out.

Bernstein, Peter L. *Against the Gods: The Remarkable Story of Risk*. New York: John Wiley & Sons, 1998.

Bessis, Joël. *Risk Management in Banking*. 3rd ed. Chichester: John Wiley & Sons, 2009.

Brealey, Richard A., Stewart C. Myers, and Franklin Allen. *Principles of Corporate Finance*. 9th ed. New York: McGraw-Hill, 2007.

Chapman, Chris, and Stephen Ward. *Project Risk Management: Processes, Techniques and Insights*. 2nd ed. Chichester: John Wiley & Sons, 2003.

Cooper, Dale, Stephen Grey, Geoffrey Raymond, and Phil Walker. *Project Risk Management Guidelines: Managing Risk in Large Projects and Complex Procurements*. Chichester: John Wiley & Sons, 2005.

Fabozzi, Frank J. *Duration, Convexity, and Other Bond Risk Measures*. New Hope, PA: FJF Associates, 1999.

Grey, Stephen. *Practical Risk Assessment for Project Management*. Chichester: John Wiley & Sons, 1995.

Hoffman, Douglas G. *Managing Operational Risk: 20 Firmwide Best Practice Strategies*. New York: John Wiley & Sons, 2002.

Hull, John C. *Options, Futures, and Other Derivatives*. 7th ed. New York: Prentice Hall, 2008.

Jorion, Philippe. *Value at Risk: The New Benchmark for Managing Financial Risk*. 3rd ed. New York: McGraw-Hill, 2006.

Koller, Glenn. *Risk Assessment and Decision Making in Business and Industry, A Practical Guide*. 2nd ed. Boca Raton, FL: Chapman & Hall/CRC, 2005.

Lam, James. *Enterprise Risk Management: From Incentives to Controls*. Hoboken, NJ: John Wiley & Sons, 2003.

Martin, Duncan. *Managing Risk in Extreme Environments: Front-Line Business Lessons for Corporates and Financial Institutions*. London: Kogan Page, 2008.

Marrison, Christopher. *The Fundamentals of Risk Measurement*. New York: McGraw-Hill, 2002.

Matten, Chris. *Managing Bank Capital: Capital Allocation and Performance Measurement*. 2nd ed. Chichester: John Wiley & Sons, 2000.

Oakland, John. *Statistical Process Control*. 6th ed. Oxford: Butterworth-Heinemann, 2007.

Oltedal, S., B. Moen, H. Klempe, and T. Rundmo. "Explaining Risk Perception: An Evaluation of Cultural Theory." *Rotunde*, no. 85, 2004.

Tweeddale, Mark. *Managing Risk and Reliability of Process Plants*. Amsterdam: Gulf Professional Publishing, 2003.

Vose, David. *Risk Analysis: A Quantitative Guide*. 3rd ed. Chichester: John Wiley & Sons, 2008.

Trade Periodicals and Official Papers

Canadian Institute of Chartered Accountants. "Learning about Risk: Choices, Connections and Competencies." 1998.

Chapman, Christy. "Tone at the Top." *Internal Auditor*, June 2003.

The Institute of Internal Auditors. "Managing Risk from the Mailroom to the Boardroom," *Tone at the Top*, June 2003.

———. "Putting COSO Theory into Practice." *Tone at the Top*, November 2005.

Financial Executives Research Foundation. "What is COSO? Defining the Alliance that Defined Internal Control." April 2003.

Kaplan, Robert S. and Norton, David P., "Having trouble with strategy? Then map it." *Harvard Business Review* 78, no. 5 (September–October 2000).

The Royal Society of London. "Risk: Analysis, Perception and Management." The Royal Society of London, 1992.

Official Risk Management Guidelines

The following risk management guidelines and resources are very useful but generally hard to find—which is why we're making them known to you. They are among the best references available anywhere for small businesses.

Environmental Protection Agency (1998) "Guidelines for Ecological Risk Assessment," Risk Assessment Forum, US EPA, Washington, DC, EPA/630/R-95/002F. www.epa.gov/ncea/ecorsk.htm

Financial Reporting of Risk—Proposals for a Statement of Business Risk. Institute of Chartered Accountants in England and Wales, 1998. www.icaew.com

IRM/AIRMIC/ALARM (2002). A Risk Management Standard. London: Institute of Risk Management. www.theirm.org/publications/PUstandard.html

Risk Management Guidelines: Standards Australia/Standards New Zealand, Dec. 2005. AS/NZS 4350:2004. www.standards.co.nz

Risk Management Associations and Websites

Business Link
www.businesslink.gov.uk

Committee of Sponsoring Organizations of the Treadway Commission (COSO)
www.coso.org

Global Association of Risk Professionals
www.garp.com

International Organization for Standardization (ISO)
www.iso.org

Professional Risk Manager's International Association
www.prmia.org

Risk Magazine
www.risk.net

Risk Management Association
www.rmahq.org

SME Toolkit
www.smetoolkit.org

US Small Business Administration
www.sba.gov

Regulatory Guidance and Descriptions

The following offer detailed descriptions of how to measure and manage risk. They provide resources for both regulatory guidance of financial services firms as well as further descriptions of how to build the measures and models provided in this book. These are directed at financial services firms, such as banks and insurance companies, but the concepts are easily applied to any company.

Basel II encompasses a broad series of resources and guidance directed specifically toward banks. Solvency II provides similar information for insurance companies.

Basel II:

www.bis.org

www.c-ebs.org

www.federalreserve.gov/GeneralInfo/basel2/

Solvency II:

www.ceiops.org

Index

A

AAA rating, 197, 267
accounting department, 242-243
actuarial theory, 5
adverse selection, 285
advisory group management, 226-227
aftermath of risk analysis, 116-117
allocation of capital, 252-253
America Online (AOL), 2000
  merger with Time Warner, 38
analysis, 112
  aftermath, 116-117
  BCPs (business continuity plans), 206
  cost-benefit, 146-148
  events that lead to losses, 113-114
  exposure to losses, 114
  financial risks, 188
    estimation of credit risk, 188-189
    market risk, 189-191
  groups of risks, 126-129
  operational risks, 200
    loss event capture, 202-203
    root cause analysis, 203-205
    scorecards, 200-201
    teams, 201-202
  recurring events, 115-116
  risk/return, 21-23

risk/reward measurement, 21-23, 134
  applications, 136
  economic profit, 135
  RAROC, 134-135
severity of loss, 114-115
strategic risks
  awareness, 178-179
  residual risk, 180-181
  signals, 178
  stakeholders, 179-180
  stress tests, 130-132
AOL (America Online), 2000
  merger with Time Warner, 38
appetite for risk, 40, 263
  concepts, 264
  control, 268-269
  credit ratings, 267-268
  hunger for risk, 265-266
  initiation of process, 274-275
  key questions to ask, 269-270
  quantitative anchors, 266-267
  statement, 250, 264-265, 270
    communication of process, 271
    framework, 272-274
    high-level, 270
    setting boundaries, 272
    specifics, 271
    thresholds, 271
  target risk and return, 268
applications
  hedges, 170
  indicators, 118-119

risk measurement, 93
risk/reward analysis, 136
stress tests, 131-132
triggers and controls, 154-155
assessment of risks, 52
assets
  protection, 20
  underlying, 194
assumptions (risk), 53
audience, reporting on risks, 259-260
auditors, as line of defense, 238-239
avoiding contact with risk, 141

B

balance, levels of RM implementation, 216-218
Bankers Trust collapse, 231
Barings Bank collapse, 232
basis points, 95
BCPs (business continuity plans), 163
  analysis, 206
  implementation, 207
  organizational rollout, 207
  preparation, 205-207
  solution design, 206
  testing, 207
board management, 226-227
board of directors, 239-240
bottom-up approaches, group analysis of risks, 127-128
boundaries, risk appetite statement, 272
branch limits (limit trees), 152

budget
  blowouts, 19-20
  risk, 250-251
buffers, 166
  financial risks, 192-194
  implementation, 167-168
  operational risks, 207-208
  strategic risks, 183
building RM into business,
  211
  culture, 213-214
  governance, 212-222
    committees, 223
    culture and business
      values, 229-232
    independence, 223-224
    policy framework,
      227-229
    role of management, 222
    stakeholders, 225-227
  levels of implementation,
    216-218
  new projects, 215-216
  organization, 213, 233-234
    framework, 234
    lines of defense, 235-240
    management through
      employee compensa-
      tion, 243-245
    managers, 240-243
    responsibility of all, 234
  processes, 215, 247
    control framework,
      255-258
    development of business
      rhythm, 248-254
    keys to integration, 248
    reporting, 258-261
business continuity plans
  (BCPs), 163
  analysis, 206
  implementation, 207
  organizational rollout, 207
  preparation, 205-207
  solution design, 206
  testing, 207

businesses
  asset protection, 20
  avoidance of surprises,
    18-19
  competitive landscape, 79
  customer risks, 80-81
  efficient issue resolution, 21
  established, risk projec-
    tions, 78-79
  integration of RM, 211
    business processes, 215,
      247-261
    culture, 213-214
    culture and business
      values, 229-232
    governance, 212-224
    levels of implementation,
      216-218
    new projects, 215-216
    organization, 213,
      233-245
    policy framework,
      227-229
    stakeholders, 225-227
  obligation management,
    24-25
  organization evaluation, 81
    governance and
      decision-making, 84
    mission and products, 82
    processes and control, 84
    systems and technology,
      84-85
    workforce, 83
  plans, 249-250
  prevention of emergencies,
    18
  protection for downside,
    17-18
  qualitative assessments, 85
    reports from external
      experts, 87
    scenario analysis, 86-87
    SWOT analysis, 85-86
    war-gaming, 87

  reasons for failure, 16-17
  reduction of budget blow-
    outs, 19-20
  reduction of earnings
    volatility, 19
  risk/return analysis, 21-23
  risks, 64-66
  supplier risks, 80

C

calculation
  expected loss, 122
  unexpected loss, 123-124
call options, 194
capability development, 41-43
capital, 132-133, 166-167
  allocation, 252-253
  implementation, 167-168
  multiplier, 193
  target, 268
capital at risk (CAR), 132-133
case studies
  business blow-ups, 231-232
  Extensive Enterprise (EE),
    294-298
  HiTechUS, 298-302
  keeping it simple, 298
  knowing your business, 294
  performance and
    incentives, 302-305
cash crisis liquidity plans,
  162-163
cash flow predictions, 5
categorizing customers,
  282-283
categorizing risks, 61-64
  financial, 66-68
  operational, 69-71
  reasons for, 62
  rules, 62-63
  strategic/business, 64-66
CEO (chief executive officer)
  responsibilities, 240

CFO (chief financial officer) responsibilities, 242-243

challenges, implementation of risk management, 27
  achieving balance, 34
  fear of transparency, 30-31
  handling opposition, 31
  inadequate data, 31-32
  resistance to change, 28-29
  risk estimates, 32-33
  stalled processes, 34
  system maintenance failure, 29
  tough questions, 33-34
  upper-level support, 35

change, resistance to, 28-29

channel diversification, 171

chief executive officer (CEO) responsibilities, 240

chief financial officer (CFO) responsibilities, 242-243

Chief Financial Officer magazine, 39

chief risk officer (CRO) responsibilities, 236-238

classifications of risk, 6-7

clear direction, 43-44

collections, customer management, 288-289

commercial risks, 64

committees, implementation of risk in governance, 223

communication
  improvement, 23
  stakeholders, 51-55
    forms, 56-57
    process, 56

company pitfalls, 10
  increased potential risks, 11
  invincibility, 11-12
  lack of anticipation, 12
  overdiversification, 10-11
  volatility of risks, 10

comparisons (forecasting risks), 104

competition
  benefits of risk/return analysis, 21-22
  competitive landscape, 79
  Porter's Five Forces, 76

compliance
  costs, 24
  management, 236-238
  risks, 70

concentrated risks, 6

concepts
  risk appetite, 264
  risk measurement, 96
    calculation of risk severity, 96-97
    correlations, 98-99
    estimation of risk severity, 97-98
    financial/time baselines, 99
    likelihood/probability, 96

confidence
  employees, 23
  interval, 132-133

consequence tables, 106

contagious risks, 6

context (RM process), 50

contingency plans, 162
  business continuity plans (BCPs), 163
  cash crisis liquidity plans, 162-163
  disaster recovery plans (DRPs), 163-164
  experiments/controlled tests, 164
  expert advice, 164
  fast action, 164-165
  feedback solicitation, 164
  implementation, 165-166

continuous improvement, 46-47

contribution measure, 135

controlled tests, contingency plans, 164

controls, 153-155
  assessment, 84
  business processes, 255-258
  people-based, 158
  risk appetite, 268-269

correlations
  group risk analysis, 126
  risk measurements, 98-99

cost-benefit analysis, 146-148

costs
  compliance, 24
  insurance, 25

covariance, unexpected loss, 124-126

credit
  payments, 154
  ratings, 267-268, 282
  risk, 66, 188-189

crisis management teams, 165

CRO (chief risk officer) responsibilities, 236-238

culture
  building RM into business, 213-214
  implementation of risk in governance, 229-232
  workplace, 157-158

customer management
  implementation of RM in business governance, 225-226
  profitable risk opportunities, 279-281
    categorizing customers, 282-283
    collections, 288-289
    customer scorecards and profiles, 283-284
    downside management, 288
    monitoring profitability, 286-287

customer risks, 80-81

D

daily rewards of RM, 278
   customer management, 279
   locating opportunities, 278-279
   pricing, 279
   processes, 280
dashboard (risk), 260
decision-making personnel, 84
defenses, 235
   auditors, 238-239
   business management and risk, 235-236
   compliance management, 236-238
   senior management/boards, 239-240
definitions of risk, 4-6
derivatives
   swaps, 194
   transferring risk, 143
development
   business rhythm, 248
     allocation of economic capital, 252-253
     benefits of risks/rewards, 254
     budgeting risk, 250-251
     forecasting risks, 253-254
     incorporation of risk appetite statement, 250
     performance targets, 254
     RAROC, 251-253
     smart business plans, 249-250
   capabilities, 41
   products
     policy framework, 228
     profitable risk opportunities, 280
deviation, 123

direct planning, strategic risks, 181-182
disaster recovery plans (DRPs), 163-164
distribution, 100, 189
diversification, 127
   financial risks, 195-196
   goals, 196
   hedging, 171-172
   overdiversification, 10-11
documentation
   risk measurement, 95
   RM process, 51
downside management, 288
drivers, identification, 282
DRPs (disaster recovery plans), 163-164

E

EAD (exposure at default), 188
earnings
   reduction of volatility, 19
   risk-adjusted returns, 8-9
   volatility analysis, 129
economic capital, 132-133, 252-253
economic profit, 135
economic triggers, 154
economic value analysis (EVA), 135
education
   as form of communication, 56
   employees, 158
EE (Extensive Enterprise) case study, 294-298
efficiency, 21-22
EL (expected loss), 122, 166
elements, reporting on risks, 259
employee
   confidence, 23
   management, 226

RM through compensation, 243
   incentives, 244-245
   linking performance to incentives, 245
employment index, 154
enterprise level stress tests, 130
environments
   root cause analysis, 204
   workplace, 157-158
equipment
   assets, 20
   risks, 70
   root cause analysis, 204
established businesses, identification of risks, 78-79
estimates of risk, 32-33, 97-98, 188-189
EVA (economic value analysis), 135
events (risk), 28
   analysis, 113
     aftermath, 116
     exposure, 114
     recurring events, 115-116
     severity of loss, 114-115
   impact, 121
     expected loss, 121-123
     group analysis, 126-129
     unexpected loss, 123-126
   projection, 45
   reducing likelihood, 149
     limited exposure to risk, 150-153
     outsourcing, 155-157
     people-based techniques, 157-159
     triggers and controls, 153-155
   stress tests
     applications, 131-132
     enterprise level, 130

individual variable
  stresses, 130
  Monte Carlo analysis,
    130
  scenario analysis, 131
  single model level, 130
ever-present risks, 6
expected loss (EL), 121
  calculation, 122
  measurement, 122-123
  reserves, 166
experiments, contingency
  plans, 164
expert advice
  contingency plans, 164
  risk assessment, 87
exposure at default (EAD),
  188
exposure
  limits, 191
  monitoring, 257
  risk
    analysis, 114
    limiting, 150-153
Extensive Enterprise (EE) case
  study, 294-298
external events risks, 71

F

failed businesses, 16-17
fear of transparency, 30-31
feedback solicitation, contingency plans, 164
FICO scores, 282-283
finance
  assets, 20
  baselines, 99
  department, 242-243
  theory, 6
  triggers, 154
financial risks, 66-68, 187
  limits, 151
  management and
    mitigation, 191

buffers, 192-193
  combining buffers and
    reserves, 193-194
  diversification, 195-196
  hedging, 194-195
  reserves, 192
measurement and analysis
  estimation of credit risk,
    188-189
  market risk, 189-191
pitfalls, 196-197
review of risks, 68
fines, 24
fish bone diagrams, 204
forecasting risks, 103
  comparisons, 104, 107-109
  development of business
    rhythm, 253-254
  implementation, 109
  indicators, 117-119
  risk matrix tool, 104-105
  risk tables (tool), 105-107
  scorecards, 109
    likelihood, 110-112
    odds, 111
forms
  communication with
    stakeholders, 56-57
  risk, 6-7
forwards, 194
framework
  building RM into business
    organization, 234
  risk appetite statement,
    272-274
futures, 194

G

geographic diversification, 171
goals
  diversification, 196
  identification, 54-55
  risk appetite statement, 264

GoGrow Company case study,
  303-305
governance (businesses)
  assessment, 84
  building RM into, 212,
    221-222
    committees, 223
    culture and business
      values, 229-232
    independence, 223-224
    policy framework,
      227-229
    role of management, 222
    stakeholders, 225-227
grades, ranking risks, 111-112
groups
  analysis, 126-129
  risks, 257
growth
  objective, 244
  risk projections, 77-78
guidelines, 37
  continuous improvement,
    46-47
  development of
    capabilities, 41
  development of common
    language, 40-41
  expectation of the
    unexpected, 44-46
  identification of risks,
    38-40
  implementation of simple
    measures, 41-43
  provision of clear direction,
    43-44
  understand risk appetite, 40

H

hard risk limits, 151
Heat Map of Industry risks, 72
hedges, 168
  applications, 170
  diversification, 171-172

financial risks, 194-195
insurance, 172-174
natural, 169
transferring risk, 143
hidden risks, 38
hierarchy of assurance,
257-258
high-level risk appetite statement, 270
historical simulation VAR, 190
HiTechUS case study, 298-302
home price depreciation, 154
housing starts, 154
human resources, 241
hunger for risk, 265-266
hurdle rates, 136, 268

I

identification
audience, reporting on
risks, 259-260
drivers, 282
industry-specific risks,
62-63
objectives (RM process),
54-55
risks, 38-40, 51, 75
competitive landscape,
79
customer risks, 80-81
established businesses,
78-79
industry risks, 77
organization evaluation,
81-85
qualitative assessments,
85-87
size and growth projec-
tions, 77-78
supplier risks, 80
idiosyncratic risk, 171
immaterial risks, 92

impact
reduction, 144, 161-162
buffers and reserves,
166-168
contingency plans,
162-166
hedges, 168-174
reporting on risks, 260
risk events, 121
expected loss, 121-123
group analysis, 126-129
unexpected loss, 123-126
implementation
BCPs (business continuity
plans), 207
buffers and reserves,
167-168
building RM into business
processes, 216
balance, 216-218
committees, 223
independence, 223-224
policy framework,
227-229
role of management, 222
stakeholders, 225-227
contingency plans, 165-166
cost-benefit analysis,
147-148
forecasting risk, 109
process, 50
communication with
stakeholders, 55-57
contribution to business
value, 57-58
identification of objec-
tives, 54-55
identification of risks, 51
management of risks,
52-53
measurement and assess-
ment of risks, 52
monitoring risks, 53
stakeholder association,
55

risk management, 27
achieving balance, 34
fear of transparency,
30-31
handling opposition, 31
inadequate data, 31-32
resistance to change,
28-29
risk estimates, 32-33
stalled processes, 34
system maintenance
failure, 29
tough questions, 33-34
upper-level support, 35
simple measures, 41-43
inadequate data, 31-32
incentives
case study, 302-305
employee compensation,
244-245
linking performance to, 245
risk reduction, 158-159
indicators, 117-119
individual variable stresses,
130
industry risks, 62-63, 77
injury, 5
insurance
costs, 25
hedging, 172-174
transferring risk, 142
integration of RM, 211
business processes, 215, 247
control framework,
255-258
development of business
rhythm, 248-254
keys to integration, 248
reporting, 258-261
culture, 213-214
governance, 212
committees, 223
culture and business
values, 229-232
independence, 223-224

policy framework,
227-229
role of management, 222
stakeholders, 225-227
levels of implementation,
216-218
new projects, 215-216
organization, 213, 233
framework, 234
lines of defense, 235-240
management through
employee compensa-
tion, 243-245
managers, 240-243
responsibility of all, 234
interest rate risks, 67
interruptions, business, 25
inviting risk into business,
211, 212
business processes, 215, 247
control framework,
255-258
development of business
rhythm, 248-254
keys to integration, 248
reporting, 258-261
culture, 213-214
governance, 212
committees, 223
culture and business
values, 229-232
independence, 223-224
policy framework,
227-229
role of management, 222
stakeholders, 225-227
levels of implementation,
216-218
new projects, 215-216
organization, 213, 233
framework, 234
lines of defense, 235-240
management through
employee compensa-
tion, 243-245

managers, 240-243
responsibility of all, 234
ISO 9001, 227
issue resolution, 21
iterative process, 53

K-L

key man risks, 69
know your customer (KYC)
concept, 226

lagging indicators, 117-119
leading indicators, 117-119
Leeson, Nick, 232
legal department, 241
legal risks, 70
levels of implementation,
216-218
LGD (loss given default), 188
LIBOR (London Interbank
Offered Rate), 95
likelihood
ranking risks, 110
reducing, 143-144, 149
limited exposure to risk,
150-153
outsourcing, 155-157
people-based techniques,
157-159
triggers and controls,
153-155
risk measurement, 96
scales, 200
tables, 105
limit trees, 152
limited exposure to risk, 150
building exposure limits,
152-153
risk limits, 151-152
lines of defense, 235
auditors, 238-239
business management and
risk, 235-236

compliance management,
236-238
senior management/boards,
239-240
liquidity risks, 67
litigation, 25
London Interbank Offered
Rate (LIBOR), 95
loss
expected loss, 121-123
possibility, 5
predictions, 4
risk analysis, 113
aftermath, 116-117
exposure, 114
recurring events,
115-116
severity of loss, 114-115
unexpected loss
calculation, 123-124
covariance, 124-126
loss event capture, 202-203
loss given default (LGD), 188
Lucas, George, 157

M

machines, root cause analysis,
204
maintenance
policy framework, 229
systems, 29
Major Classes and Subclasses
of Risk chart, 63
management
financial risks, 191
buffers, 192-193
combining buffers and
reserves, 193-194
diversification, 195-196
hedging, 194-195
reserves, 192
obligations, 24-25
operational risks
preparation, 205-207
teams, 207

risks, 140
  avoiding contact with
    risk, 141
  cost-benefit analysis,
    146-148
  impact reduction, 144,
    161-174
  initial considerations,
    140
  reducing likelihood of
    risk, 143-144, 149-159
  technique selection,
    144-145
  transferring risk,
    142-143
  strategic risks
    buffers, 183
    direct planning, 181-182
    range of outcomes,
      182-183
managers, 240
  finance/accounting per-
    sonnel, 242-243
  human resources, 241
  legal department, 241
  strategic planning team,
    241-242
market risk, 67, 189-191
Markowitz, Harry, 8
materiality, 107
materials
  risks, 92
  root cause analysis, 204
McKinsey, 39
measurements
  comparing risk and return,
    8-9
  expected loss, 122-123
  financial risks
    estimation of credit risk,
      188-189
    market risk, 189-191
  operational risks
    loss event capture,
      202-203

root cause analysis,
  203-205
scorecards, 200-201
teams, 201-202
rewards
  economic profit, 135
  RAROC (risk-adjusted
    return on capital),
    134-135
risks, 52, 91
  applications, 93
  concepts, 96-99
  conversion to money,
    132-134
  determination of mitiga-
    tion, 92-93
  distribution, 100
  reasons for, 92
  risk versus return, 101
  rules, 94-95
  simple processes, 95
  what to measure, 99
  strategic risks
    awareness, 178-179
    residual risk, 180-181
    signals, 178
    stakeholders, 179-180
MECE (mutually exclusive,
  collectively exhaustive)
  approach to categorizing
  risk, 62
Metallgesellschaft AG, 38
methods, root cause analysis,
  204
missed credit payments, 154
mission (businesses), 82
mitigation
  financial risks, 191
    buffers, 192-193
    combining buffers and
      reserves, 193-194
    diversification, 195-196
    hedging, 194-195
    reserves, 192
  operational risks, 205-207

risk measurement, 92-93
strategic risks
  buffers, 183
  direct planning, 181-182
  range of outcomes,
    182-183
models
  four lines of defense, 235
    auditors, 238-239
    business management
      and risk, 235-236
    compliance manage-
      ment, 236-238
    senior management/
      boards, 239-240
  measuring risk, 94
  partnership, 237
  stress tests
    applications, 131-132
    enterprise level, 130
    individual variable
      stresses, 130
    Monte Carlo analysis,
      130
    scenario analysis, 131
    single model level, 130
modern portfolio theory
  (MPT), 8
money, converting risk measurements, 132-134
monitoring
  customer profitability,
    286-287
  exposures, 257
  groups of risks, 257-258
  risks, 53
Monte Carlo analysis, 130
Monte Carlo VAR, 190
MPT (modern portfolio
  theory), 8
multiperiod measures, incentives, 244
mutually exclusive, collectively
  exhaustive (MECE) approach
  to categorizing risk, 62

N

natural hedges, 169
net income after cost of capital (NIACC), 135
new projects, 215-216
new risks, 6
NIACC (net income after cost of capital), 135
nondiversifiable risk, 171
nontraded market risks, 67
notices, as form of communication, 56

O

objectives, identification, 54-55
obligation management, 24-25
obsolescence risks, 64
odds, 111
operational risks, 69-70, 199
  buffers, 207-208
  limits, 152
  management and mitigation, 205-20
  measurement and analysis, 200
    loss event capture, 202-203
    root cause analysis, 203-205
    scorecards, 200-201
    teams, 201-202
  predictions, 5
  review of risks, 71
operational triggers, 154
operations diversification, 172
opportunities for profit, 277
  customer management, 279, 286-289
  day-to-day rewards, 278
  locating opportunities, 278-279

pricing, 279, 284-286
  process improvement, 289-291
  processes, 280
  product development, 280-281
  target customers, 281-284
opposition, as challenge of risk management implementation, 31
options, 194
organizations
  building RM into business, 213, 233
    framework, 234
    lines of defense, 235-240
    management through employee compensation, 243-245
    managers, 240-243
    responsibility of all, 234
  risk assessment, 69, 81
    governance and decision-making, 84
    mission and products, 82
    processes and control, 84
    systems and technology, 84-85
    workforce, 83
  rollout of BCPs (business continuity plans), 207
outsourcing, 142, 155-157
overdiversification, 10-11

P

parametric VAR, 190
partnership model, 237
payments, premiums, 194
PD (probability of default), 188
people risks, 69
people-based RM techniques
  checklists, 159

  incentives, 158-159
  people-based controls, 158
  training and education, 158
  workplace environment and culture, 157-158
perfect hedges, 169
performance
  employees, 245
  GoGrow Company case study, 303-305
  targets, 254
personnel assets, 20
personnel risks, 83
pilot programs, 153
pitfalls
  companies, 10-12
  financial risks, 196-197
  strategic risks, 184-185
policies
  buffers and reserves, 168
  framework, 227-229
Porter's Five Forces, 76
possibility of loss/injury, 5
potential risks, 11, 28
precision, hard risk limits, 151
predictions, 4
  forecasting risks, 103
    comparisons, 104-109
    implementation, 109
    indicators, 117-119
    risk matrix tool, 104-105
    risk tables (tool), 105-107
    scorecards, 109-112
  risk events, 45
  stress tests
    applications, 131-132
    enterprise level, 130
    individual variable stresses, 130
    Monte Carlo analysis, 130
    scenario analysis, 131
    single model level, 130
premiums, 194

pricing, profitable risk opportunities, 279
  customer considerations, 285-286
  equation, 284
probability
  ranking risks, 110
  risk measurement, 96
  tables, 105
probability of default (PD), 188
procedural updates (policies), 228
process improvement, 289-291
processes (business)
  building RM into, 215, 247-261
  business assessment, 84
  communication with stakeholders, 55-57
  contribution to business value, 57-58
  identification of objectives, 54-55
  identification of risks, 51
  iterative, 53
  management of risks, 52-53
  measurement and assessment of risks, 52
  monitoring risks, 53
  profitable risk opportunities, 280
  stakeholder association, 55
products
  development
    policy framework, 228
    profitable risk opportunities, 280-281
  diversification, 171
  regulations, 228
  risks, 82
  validations, 228
profiles (risk), 283-284
profitable risk opportunities, 277

customer management, 279, 286-289
day-to-day rewards, 278
locating opportunities, 278-279
pricing, 279, 284-286
process improvement, 289-291
processes, 280
product development, 280-281
target customers, 281-284
program reviews, 56
projection of risk events, 45, 70, 77-78
protection
  assets, 20
  downside of businesses, 17-18
purchasing, policy framework, 228
put options, 194

Q

qualitative assessments
  reports from external experts, 87
  scenario analysis, 86-87
  SWOT analysis, 85-86
  war-gaming, 87
quality improvement, 22, 46-47
quantitative anchors, 266-267
quantitative approach to risk appetite, 266

R

range of outcomes, strategic risks, 182-183
RAROC (risk-adjusted return on capital), 134-135, 251-252

RARORAC (risk-adjusted return on risk-adjusted capital), 135
ratings (risk) scorecard, 109
  grades, 111-112
  likelihood, 110
  odds, 111
reasons for managing risk, 15
  assessment of failed businesses, 16-17
  asset protection, 20
  avoidance of surprises, 18-19
  awareness of obligations, 24-25
  efficient issue resolution, 21
  prevention of emergencies, 18
  protection for downside, 17-18
  reduction of budget blowouts, 19-20
  reduction of earnings volatility, 19
  risk/return analysis, 21-23
recurring events, 115-116
reduction
  likelihood of risk, 143-144, 149
    limited exposure to risk, 150-153
    outsourcing, 155-157
    people-based techniques, 157-159
    triggers and controls, 153-155
  impact of risk, 144, 161
    buffers and reserves, 166-168
    contingency plans, 162-166
    hedges, 168-174
register (risk), 108-109
regulations (products), 228

reports
  as form of communication,
    56
  risks, 258
    elements, 259
    identification of audi-
      ence, 259-260
    impact, 260
    schedule, 261
  RM process, 51
reputation risks, 64
reserves, 166
  financial risks, 192-194
  implementation, 167-168
residual risk, 145, 180-181
resistance to change, 28-29
resolution of issues, 21
responsibilities
  CEO (chief executive
    officer), 240
  CFO (chief financial
    officer), 242-243
  CRO (chief risk officer),
    236-238
  managers, 240
    finance/accounting
      personnel, 242-243
    human resources, 241
    legal department, 241
    strategic planning team,
      241-242
returns
  measurement, 134-135
  performance targets, 244,
    268
  risk-adjusted, 8-9
rewards
  day-to-day, 278
    customer management,
      279
    locating opportunities,
      278-279
    pricing, 279
    processes, 280

risks, 7, 134
  applications of analysis,
    136
  economic profit, 135
  measurements, 8-9
  MPT (modern portfolio
    theory), 8
  RAROC, 134-135
  risk/return analysis,
    21-23
  target, 268
rhythm (business), 248
  allocation of economic
    capital, 252-253
  benefits of risks/rewards,
    254
  budgeting risk, 250-251
  forecasting risks, 253-254
  incorporation of risk appe-
    tite statement, 250
  performance targets, 254
  RAROC, 251-253
  smart business plans,
    249-250
risk
  analysis, 112
    aftermath, 116-117
    events that lead to loss,
      113-114
    exposure to loss, 114
    recurring events, 115-116
    severity of loss, 114-115
  assumptions, 53
  categorizing, 61
    financial risks, 66-68
    operational risks, 69-71
    reasons for, 62
    rules, 62-63
    strategic/business risks,
      64-66
  classifications, 6-7
  company pitfalls, 10-12
  dashboard, 260
  defined, 4-6
  events, 28, 45

financial, 187
  limits, 151
  management and mitiga-
    tion, 191-196
  measurement and
    analysis, 188-191
  pitfalls, 196-197
forecasting, 103
  comparisons, 104-109
  development of business
    rhythm, 253-254
  implementation, 109
  indicators, 117-119
  risk matrix tool, 104-105
  risk tables (tool),
    105-107
  scorecards, 109-112
risk appetite, 40, 263
  concepts, 264
  control, 268-269
  credit ratings, 267-268
  hunger for risk, 265-266
  initiation of process,
    274-275
  key questions to ask,
    269-270
  quantitative anchors,
    266-267
  statement, 264-265
    communication of
      process, 271
    framework, 272-274
    high-level, 270
    setting boundaries, 272
    specifics, 271
    thresholds, 271
  target risk and return, 268
risk matrix tool, 104-105
risk register, 108-109
  hidden, 38
  identification, 38-40, 51,
    75-76
    competitive landscape,
      79
    customer risks, 80-81

established businesses, 78-79
industry risks, 77
organization evaluation, 81-85
qualitative assessments, 85-87
size and growth projections, 77-78
supplier risks, 80
idiosyncratic, 171
immaterial, 92
management
as step in process, 52-53
avoiding contact with risk, 141
cost-benefit analysis, 146-148
impact reduction, 144, 161-174
initial considerations, 140
reducing likelihood of risk, 143-144, 149-159
technique selection, 144-145
transferring risk, 142-143
material, 92
measurement, 91
applications, 93
concepts, 96-99
conversion to money, 132-134
determination of mitigation, 92-93
distribution, 100
reasons for, 92
risk versus return, 101
rules, 94-95
simple processes, 95
what to measure, 99
monitoring, 53
nondiversifiable, 171
operational, 199

buffers, 207-208
limits, 152
management and mitigation, 205-207
measurement and analysis, 200-205
rewards, 7
applications of analysis, 136
development of business rhythm, 254
economic profit, 135
measurements, 8-9
MPT (modern portfolio theory), 8
RAROC, 134-135
risk/return analysis, 21-23, 101
specific, 171
strategic, 177
management and mitigation, 181-183
measurement and analysis, 178-181
pitfalls, 184-185
risk tables (tool), 105-107
risk-adjusted return on capital (RAROC), 134-135
risk-adjusted return on risk-adjusted capital (RARORAC), 135
risk-adjusted returns, 8-9
roles
chief executive officer (CEO), 240
chief financial officer (CFO), 242-243
chief risk officer (CRO), 236-238
managers, 240
finance/accounting personnel, 242-243
human resources, 241
legal department, 241
strategic planning team, 241-242

rollout
BCPs (business continuity plans), 207
contingency plans, 165
root cause analysis, 203-205
rules, 37
categorizing risks, 62-63
continuous improvement, 46-47
development of capabilities, 41
development of common language, 40-41
expectation of the unexpected, 44-46
identification of risks, 38-40
implementation of simple measures, 41-43
provision of clear direction, 43-44
risk measurement, 94-95

S

scales, relative likelihood, 200
scenario analysis, 86-87, 131
schedules, reporting on risks, 261
scorecards
customer management, 283
forecasting risk, 109
grades, 111-112
likelihood, 110
odds, 111
operational risks, 200-201
security risks, 70
senior management, 239-240
services, policy framework, 228
severity (risk events), 188
calculating impact, 96-97
risk analysis, 114-115
tables, 106
share of wallet, 287

shareholder value, 15-16

shareholder value analysis (SVA), 135

signals, strategic risks, 178

single model level stress tests, 130

Skywalker Ranch, 157

soft risk limits, 151

solicitation of feedback, contingency plans, 164

solution design, BCPs (business continuity plans), 206

specific risk, 171

staff risks, 83

stage-gating (process improvement), 289-290

stakeholders, 51
- association with RM process, 55
- communication, 55-57
- implementation of risk in governance
  - board and advisory group management, 226-227
  - customer management, 225-226
  - employee management, 226
- management risks, 64
- responsibilities, 222
- strategic risks, 179-180

stalled processes, 34

standard deviation, 123

statement (risk appetite), 250, 264-265
- communication of process, 271
- framework, 272-274
- high-level, 270
- setting boundaries, 272
- specifics, 271
- thresholds, 271

statistical process control, 154

steps to risk management, 50

communication with stakeholders, 55-57

contribution to business value, 57-58

identification of objectives, 54-55

identification of risks, 51

management of risks, 52-53

measurement and assessment of risks, 52

monitoring risks, 53

stakeholder association, 55

stop-loss limits, 191

strategic planning team, 241-242

strategic risks, 64, 177
- management and mitigation
  - buffers, 183
  - direct planning, 181-182
  - range of outcomes, 182-183
- measurement and analysis
  - awareness, 178-179
  - residual risk, 180-181
  - signals, 178
  - stakeholders, 179-180
- pitfalls, 184-185
- review of risks, 65-66

strategies for risk management, 141
- avoiding contact with risk, 141
- impact reduction, 144, 161-174
- reducing likelihood of risk, 143-144, 149-159
- technique selection, 144-146
- transferring risk, 142-143

streamlining (process improvement), 290-291

strengths, weaknesses, opportunities, and threats (SWOT) analysis, 85-86

stress tests
- applications, 131-132
- enterprise level, 130
- individual variable stresses, 130
- Monte Carlo analysis, 130
- risk measurement models, 94
- scenario analysis, 131
- single model level, 130

subcategories
- financial risks, 66-67
- operational risks, 69-70
- strategic risks, 64-65

subjective view of risk, 4-6

sudden risks, 6

supplier risks, 80

support, upper-level management, 35

SVA (shareholder value analysis), 135

swaps, 194

SWOT (strengths, weaknesses, opportunities, and threats) analysis, 85-86

systems
- business assessment, 84-85
- maintenance failure, 29
- risks, 70

T

tables (risk), 105-107

target customers, 281-284

target performances, 254

target products, 280-281

teams, operational risk management, 201-202, 207

technological risks, 64

technology (businesses), 84-85

terms for risk, 40-41

test plans
- BCPs (business continuity plans), 207
- contingency plans, 165

theories
  actuarial, 5
  finance, 6
  MPT (modern portfolio
    theory), 8
thresholds, risk appetite
  statements, 271
Time Warner, 2000 merger
  with America Online, 38
tools, forecasting risks
  risk matrix, 104-105
  risk tables, 105-107
top-ten risk list, 109
tracking indicators, 117-119
traded market risks, 67
training employees, 158
transferring risk, 142-143
transparency, 43-44
  fear, 30-31
  governance, 212
treatment for risks, 140
  avoiding contact, 141
  derivatives, 143
  hedging, 143
  insurance, 142
  outsourcing, 142
  transferring risk, 142-143
trees (limits), 152
triggers, 153-155

U

UL (unexpected loss)
  buffers, 166
  calculation, 123-126
  covariance, 124-126
uncertain outcomes, 4, 100
underlying assets, 194
unexpected loss (UL)
  buffers, 166
  calculation, 123-126
  covariance, 124-126

updates, as form of communication, 56
upper-level support, 35

V

validation
  products, 228
  risk measurement models,
    94
value-at-risk (VAR), 189-190
values (business), 229-232
VAR (value-at-risk), 189-190
vocabulary (risk terms), 40-41
volatility, 6
  analysis, 129
  as company pitfall, 10
  earnings, 19
  predictions, 5

W-X-Y-Z

war-gaming, 87
workforce (businesses)
  asset protection, 20
  avoidance of surprises,
    18-19
  competitive landscape, 79
  customer risks, 80-81
  efficient issue resolution, 21
  established, risk projec-
    tions, 78-79
  integration of RM, 211
    business processes, 215,
      247-261
    culture, 213-214
    culture and business
      values, 229-232
    governance, 212-224
    levels of implementation,
      216-218
    new projects, 215-216

    organization, 213,
      233-245
    policy framework,
      227-229
    stakeholders, 225-227
  obligation management,
    24-25
  organization evaluation, 81
    governance and
      decision-making, 84
    mission and products, 82
    processes and control, 84
    systems and technology,
      84-85
    workforce, 83
  plans, 249-250
  prevention of emergencies,
    18
  protection for downside,
    17-18
  qualitative assessments, 85
    reports from external
      experts, 87
    scenario analysis, 86-87
    SWOT analysis, 85-86
    war-gaming, 87
  reasons for failure, 16-17
  reduction of budget
    blowouts, 19-20
  reduction of earnings
    volatility, 19
  risk/return analysis, 21-23
  risks, 64-66
  supplier risks, 80
working comparisons, 107-109
workplace, environment and
  culture, 157-158